Thinking about play

Thinking about play

Developing a reflective approach

Edited by Janet Moyles

 Open University Press

Open University Press
McGraw-Hill Education
McGraw-Hill House
Shoppenhangers Road
Maidenhead
Berkshire
England
SL6 2QL

email: enquiries@openup.co.uk
world wide web: www.openup.co.uk

and Two Penn Plaza, New York, NY 10121-2289, USA

First published 2010

A catalogue record of this book is available from the British Library

ISBN-13: 978-0-33-524108-8 (pb) 978-0-33-524109-5(hb)
ISBN-10: 0335241085 (pb) 0335241093 (hb)

Library of Congress Cataloging-in-Publication Data
CIP data applied for

Typeset by RefineCatch Limited, Bungay, Suffolk
Printed in the UK by Bell & Bain Ltd, Glasgow

Mixed Sources
Product group from well-managed
forests and other controlled sources
www.fsc.org Cert no. TT-COC-002769
© 1996 Forest Stewardship Council

FSC

The **McGraw·Hill** Companies

Contents

Figures and tables

Figures

Table

Photographs

Notes on the editor and contributors

Deborah Albon is Senior Lecturer in Early Childhood Studies at London Metropolitan University. She works across a range of programmes including BA and MA courses in Early Childhood Studies and Education and those leading to the award of professional status, such as the National Professional Qualification in Integrated Centre Leadership, Early Years Professional Status. Deborah has worked as both a nursery nurse and teacher in a range of early childhood settings as well as primary schools, including senior management positions. Her current research is focused on young children's experiences of food and eating in early childhood settings, and she has published widely, including *Research Methods in Early Childhood* (with Mukherji, 2009, Sage).

Pat Beckley is the Academic Co-ordinator for the 3–7 age phase on the PGCE Primary course at Bishop Grosseteste University College Lincoln. She has taught children in the 3–11 age range, including organizing an Early Years Unit for a number of years. As an Advanced Skills Teacher, Pat supported colleagues and settings, leading INSET and formulating Action Plans. Her work used research to inform her practice in schools. Her MEd was based on approaches to early years literacy and participation in the *Effective Early Years Project*. Working with the Children's University in Hull, she helped to coordinate community involvement in children's learning. She is currently completing an EdD thesis that concerns a comparison of approaches to early years literacy between Lincolnshire, England and Hedmark, Norway.

Avril Brock is Principal Lecturer in the Carnegie Faculty at Leeds Metropolitan University, leading the MA Childhood Studies and MA Early Years courses. Prior to this she lectured at Bradford College and before that was a deputy head teacher, primary and early years teacher, often working with linguistically diverse children. Avril's books *Into the Enchanted Forest* (Trentham, 1999) and *Communication, Language and Literacy from Birth to Five* (with Rankin, Sage, 2008) reflect this interest. She is the lead editor for *Perspectives on Play: Learning for Life* (Pearson, 2009). Avril's PhD research on early years practitioners' professionalism has resulted in a model of seven dimensions of professionalism that is now being explored across the professions in the early years interdisciplinary team.

Stephanie Collins is an early years practitioner who has worked with young children in a sessional care setting since the early 2000s. Having recently graduated with an Early Years Foundation Degree she is currently working towards Early Years Professional Status. Stephanie is passionate about the role of play in children's learning and believes that they learn best when they are engaged in activities that follow their interests. She also recognizes the important part parents have in children's learning and has worked hard to establish solid partnerships with the parents at her setting.

Jane George has extensive experience in the voluntary sector, in toddler groups and playgroups and managing and teaching for the Pre-School Learning Alliance. She has worked in community education developing and delivering Parent and Toddler at Play classes in areas of social deprivation and to various cultural groups. She has worked in colleges delivering a variety of early years programmes and was awarded an MEd in 2003. In her current role of Curriculum Team Leader for Early Years and Children's Agenda at Bradford College, she teaches and manages the curriculum across the full range of Early Childhood Studies programmes and is an Early Years Professional Status assessor. Her most recent publication is *The Early Years Professional's Complete Companion* (with George and Holland, Pearson, 2010).

Jane Gibbs is a Senior Pre-school Practitioner in Essex, where she has worked for seven years. Jane is fully aware of the importance of starting with the child when planning and developing play ideas, delivering playful pedagogy that keeps children stimulated and enthusiastic with an in-depth understanding for the need to reflect on both the child's experiences and her own. In 1997 she was presented with a Business Excellence Award, achieved by improving business within an aerospace environment from a reflective perspective. Jane has successfully completed a foundation degree in 'early years childcare and education' and is continuing her learning journey on the 'BA Honours early childhood studies route'.

Justine Howard is Senior Lecturer in the School of Human and Health Science at Swansea University and the Programme Director of their Masters in Developmental and Therapeutic Play. She is a Chartered Psychologist and holds a PhD in the psychology of education. Justine has worked as a play specialist alongside children with additional learning needs and retains close links with practice via research and consultancy. Much of her research is concerned with children's perceptions of their play; she has published extensively on the topic of play and is co-author of *Play and Learning in the Early Years: From Research to Practice* (Sage, 2010). She is also the editor of the *Psychology of Education Review*.

Pam Jarvis is a graduate psychologist, social scientist and educational researcher, with many years of experience of creating and teaching development, social science and social policy. She has qualified teacher status and has taught in school within her specialist subject areas of psychology, sociology and history. She is currently working on the Early Years and Children's Agenda team at Bradford College and is an active researcher in child development and education, and has most recently focused on the areas of play-based learning and 'student voice'. Her PhD explored the role of rough and tumble play. Pam's recent publications include *Born to Play* (in Broadhead et al., 2010, Sage) and she was co-editor of *Perspectives on Play* (Pearson, 2009).

Kevin Kelman is Quality Development Officer for Early Years with Stirling Council. He is also a professional expert at the University of Glasgow and an Associate Assessor with HMIe. His previous roles have included programme leader of early years courses and head teacher of two different schools. He has written a number of books and contributed to chapters in edited collections as well as being a regular contributor to *Nursery World* and *Nursery Education* (Scholastic) publications. Kevin has been commissioned to provide consultancy and advice through a variety of CPD and training events in Scotland, England, Wales, Northern Ireland, Dubai and Uganda. He has also been an invited speaker at a range of regional, national and international events.

Linda Lauchlan is a Development Officer for Early Years with Learning and Teaching Scotland. In that role, Linda has been involved in supporting practitioners through workshops and seminars focusing on implementing *Curriculum for Excellence*, Active Learning and Pre-school into Primary Transitions. Linda was a primary teacher in Glasgow and, during this time, was involved in supporting practitioners through a coaching in context role on *Teaching for Effective Learning* strategies and the use of ICT. She has taught in New Zealand and supported Ugandan practitioners with development planning during a recent study visit.

Paulette Luff is a Senior Lecturer in Early Childhood Studies in the Faculty of Education at Anglia Ruskin University, Chelmsford, England. Her main professional interest is early childhood education, with a particular focus on adults' roles in children's care and learning. She is currently completing doctoral research exploring early years practitioners' uses of child observation and has presented and published work on this topic. Paulette has worked in the field of early childhood for more than 20 years, as a teacher, foster carer, school–home liaison worker and as a childcare and education lecturer in further education.

Estelle Martin has been involved as a professional in early years education and care for 30 years across the disciplines including nursery education, further and higher education, teacher education, social services day care, psychology services and postgraduate counselling training. Formerly at Canterbury Christ Church University as Programme Director for the BA in Early Childhood Studies, she is currently an Associate Lecturer and Early Years Professional Status assessor at the University of East Anglia and University Campus Suffolk. Her research interests focus on emotional development, learning and play in early childhood. She is a consultant/trainer for the Thomas Coram *Listening To Young Children* approach and continues to learn and engage with all aspects of teaching and learning with young children and their communities.

Karen McInnes is currently a psychology tutor within the Faculty of Humanities and Social Science at the University of Glamorgan. She is nearing the completion of her PhD, which focuses on children's perceptions of their own play. Previously, Karen was a Senior Researcher with Barnardo's UK Policy and Research team, acting as a research consultant to a local Sure Start. She has also been a Senior Lecturer in Early Years Education at Bath Spa University. Karen has extensive experience of working with young children as a teacher and speech therapist and has published on various aspects of early years education and is co-author of *Planning and Using Time in the Foundation Stage* (David Fulton, 2005) and *Principles and Practice in the Foundation Stage* (Learning Matters, 2003).

Janet Moyles is Professor Emeritus at Anglia Ruskin University and a play/ early years consultant. She has worked as an early years teacher, head and lecturer, and has written and edited widely, including *Just Playing?* (OUP, 1989), *The Excellence of Play* (OUP, 2005) and *Effective Leadership and Management in the Early Years* (OUP, 2007). She has directed several research projects including *Jills of All Trades?* (ATL, 1996), *Too Busy to Play?* (Esmee Fairbairn Trust/University of Leicester 1997–2000), *SPEEL (Study of Pedagogical Effectiveness in Early Learning)* (DfES, 2002) and *Recreating the Reception Year* (ATL, 2004). Her PhD was in the area of play, learning and practitioner roles.

Theodora Papatheodorou is Professor of Early Childhood and Director of Research in the Faculty of Education at Anglia Ruskin University. She joined Higher Education in 1997 and, prior to that, had been a nursery teacher in early years, bilingual and special educational needs settings. Theodora's research is wide-ranging and has an overall interest and focus on pedagogy that is inclusive and offers equality of opportunity to all learners in order to reach their potential. She has published widely in national and international journals and is the author of *Behaviour Problems in the Early Years* (Routledge, 2005) and co-editor (with Janet Moyles) of the book *Learning Together in the Early Years: Exploring Relational Pedagogy* (Routledge, 2008).

Maria Sprawling has worked in the early years childcare field for over 15 years and has gained an immense amount of experience, practical and theoretical knowledge. She has always continued with her studies, gaining a City and Guilds qualification in Family and Community Care, NVQ Level 3 in Early Years Care and Education and has recently gained her Foundation Degree in Early Years Childcare and Education. Maria has worked as a nursery nurse, early years tutor and deputy manager and is now nursery manager of a private day nursery in Chelmsford. She has always enjoyed working within the early years field and finds it a rewarding career to follow.

Lynsey Thomas is co-owner of Cheeky Monkeys Pre-school and works part time as a lecturer at Chelmsford College. She has worked in childcare for 11 years as practitioner, deputy and now manager. Lynsey has had experience in assessing practitioners for their NVQ childcare qualifications and is currently completing Early Years Professional Status.

Pauline Trudell writes and campaigns about issues affecting nursery education. She has been involved with different aspects of early childhood education for over 30 years; as a teacher in Inner London nursery schools and classes, LEA advisory teacher, university lecturer and teacher trainer. She was Head of a Children's Centre in Westminster and the support head teacher to the DfES funded National Forum for Maintained Nursery Schools and Children's Centres from 2004 to 2006. She is a member of the Early Years Curriculum Group and a Vice-President of the National Campaign for Nursery Education.

Rebecca Webster is currently a Senior Lecturer at Anglia Ruskin University where she teaches across a wide range of early years and other modules within the Faculty. Prior to entering higher education, she worked as a teacher across the primary age range. Current research is centred on the influences teachers and practitioners have on the young children with whom they work. Rebecca has previously undertaken research on rewards and sanctions in the classroom environment and the inclusion of traveller culture in schools. Currently, she is working towards a Doctorate exploring what teachers can learn from children as researchers into their own identities and the implications this has for practice.

Bryonie Williams was educated and trained as a teacher in the late 1970s, originally working as an art and craft teacher. While taking her own son to his first school, she began working there as a supply teacher and was offered the position as a reception teacher and later as the nursery teacher. Here her love of the early years developed and she undertook a master's degree in *Early Childhood Studies* at Sheffield University while still teaching full time. At present she is the Foundation Stage Leader in a first school, and teaches the reception class. She is also an external examiner for Leeds Metropolitan University and a *Communication, Language and Literacy Development* leader for Worcestershire.

Maulfry Worthington is currently engaged in doctoral research into the genesis of *children's mathematical graphics* in imaginative play from a semiotic, multi-modal perspective. She has taught in the full 3–8 year age range since the mid-1980s; has worked as an early years consultant and as a National Numeracy Consultant and has lectured in Higher Education on Primary and Early Years Mathematics and on Early Years. Her many publications including *Children's Mathematics: Making Marks, Making Meaning* (with Carruthers, Sage, 2006). The authors' innovative professional development initiative for early years mathematics is featured in the final report of 'Researching Effective CPD in Mathematics Education' (RECME), (NCETM, 2009). Maulfry (together with Elizabeth Carruthers) is a founder of the international *Children's Mathematics Network*: www.childrens-mathematics.net.

Introduction

Janet Moyles

This book intends to promote practitioners to reflect deeply on the play provision they make for children in classrooms and settings and to think through their own values related to play and playful pedagogies. No, don't put the book down: pedagogy is not such a big word! All it means is the way teaching and learning happens. In early years, this could best be described as 'playful pedagogies'; that is, the different ways in which educators engage children in learning through play. This might be through planning, provision of resources, child-initiated activities or adult-inspired interactions. I'm not avoiding the word 'teaching' because we can all benefit by being taught but, unfortunately, teaching has such formal connotations in our education system and there's time enough later for children to receive a more formalized schooling once they are developmentally ready for it.

School is one thing: education quite another! Education starts, we're told, even before birth when the embryo engages with sounds and movement from external stimuli (Hopkins and Johnson, 2005). School is part of education but much learning occurs in other contexts. Babies and infants then learn through their interactions with parents, siblings and other family members and, for those in educare settings, their carers – often without any 'formal' activities. And play in our contemporary society is gradually evolving and becoming more complex, according to Bergen and Fromberg (2006), requiring higher cognitive functioning.

Play is, without a doubt, the most natural way children learn all over the world: this is why it is so important for us, as educators, to ensure that children have every opportunity to engage in play and playful experiences. As I've argued elsewhere, play is powerful (Moyles, 2009: 28): 'Play deepens children's learning and understanding because it enables them to begin learning from first-hand experiences, based on what they already know and can do'. Surely this is one of the basic tenets of early childhood education? But young children are also vulnerable in that they want to please adults so will go along with whatever is asked of them, apparently willingly. However, it is easy to 'fail' when what is expected of the child is more than they are currently able to 'perform'. They need, as Palmer (2007) says, freedom from failure if they are to thrive. Play can relieve that pressure and is also highly effective in generating creative, flexible thinkers (Whitebread, 2007).

Without a doubt, however, young children are capable of more than most people seem to give them credit for – but only on *their* terms! Sir Ranulph Fiennes (the man who has climbed Everest several times) in a profile interview (2010) seems surprised at the knowledge and confidence of his 3½-year-old daughter and appears astonished that she can rule the home, telling him off when she thinks he is not doing the right thing! Why do parents, who are otherwise intelligent, confident and innovative themselves, feel that somehow young children are not capable of these kinds of behaviour? Is it just because they are physically small? Or the different way children think about the world? Or is it because their playful exchanges and interactions are not understood for the strengths they have? We seem to live in a contemporary society where children are treated – and dressed – more like adults and made to bear the burdens of modern life with all its commercialization and media violence (Compass, 2008). It seems to me that we need to stop underestimating children but, at the same time, ensure that the experiences they have are relevant to their age. We wouldn't expect a 3½-year-old to climb Everest but we would expect her to know something of her own mind, have self-reliance and a suitable vocabulary to be able to copy the actions of her parents (along with many, many other skills and knowledge!).

Play is perceived by all educators in settings and schools to capitalize on children's natural inclination and confidence and build upon it, meaningfully and playfully. That's the key role of early years practitioners. As Elkonin in his classical 1978 essay asserts, play prepares the child's mind for the learning tasks of today. Yet, according to Miller and Almon (2009: 4):

> Too many schools place a double burden on young children. First they heighten their stress by demanding that they master material beyond their development level. Then they deprive children of their chief means of dealing with that stress – creative play.

Play is not the *only* way that children can learn, however, so playful pedagogies will incorporate other 'teaching' strategies; for example, modelling, demonstrating, peer tutoring, questioning, encouraging children's observation and listening skills, talking and listening to others. But play is a principal means of learning and a process through which children acquire knowledge and insights into the self (see Photograph 0.1).

So through the chapters of this book, we will involve you, the reader, in reflecting with us, with each other and individually on play and playful pedagogies within the curriculum. The authors aim to involve readers in

Photograph 0.1 Acquiring knowledge and insights.

acknowledging what is involved in critical reflection as a professional process and, in doing so, we aim to deepen knowledge and understanding
about the levels of learning that can be achieved both for practitioners and
children.

At present – and despite the *Early Years Foundation Stage* (*EYFS*) (DfES, 2007)
and the National Strategies play document (DCSF/QCDA, 2009) emphasis on
play – observers and researchers are still noting a lack of appropriate playful
pedagogies in settings and classrooms particularly for 4-year-olds (see Moyles,
2010). Play is still being marginalized in favour of 'work' and direct teaching
and, particularly in reception classes, children are being given tasks that are
not only meaningless to them but deprive them of their right to play within
the *EYFS* curriculum. Are practitioners fully aware that this happening?

What it seems is that play itself for children's learning is valued but
insufficient thought has been given about how to put this into practice
and still remain compliant with the perceived demands of government and

policy-makers. It would seem that practitioners need to be prompted to stand back and reflect on their provision for play for children, and what makes sense to the children, by analysing and evaluating what makes for quality play experiences. This involves reading, reflecting on and responding in principle and practice to the potential impact of the exciting new research into play and learning that is currently producing such positive findings regarding the benefits of play to children's learning and dispositions (see also Broadhead et al., 2010). It will also involve practitioners in considering and perhaps challenging some current policy initiatives and examining some of the aspects that are causing confusion among practitioners and analysing and evaluating the impact of current pedagogical practices on children.

What we mean by play and how the word is used – and misused – in current English and other government initiatives is a main factor we will consider. Critical reflection on, and analysis and evaluation of, the policies and initiatives that govern how we make curriculum provision for children and in what ways (through our pedagogy) is key to enhancing reflective play practices. But more than that, it's vital that practitioners think carefully about their own thinking and ideologies on the issue of play. For example, are we, as practitioners, just following an impetus created by someone else or are we being true to our own education and training in making high-quality play provision? Are we so focused on 'delivering' what we think is required by those in authority that we fail to see the impact our pedagogy is having on the children – and, indeed, on positive curriculum outcomes for them? By this I mean that, in observing children in Year R classes in particular, it is clear that children are often not engaged with the specific learning that a practitioner-inspired activity is intended to promote. An example is given in Adams et al. (2004: 96) that is worth quoting:

> A child deeply engaged in water play was interrupted whilst he was required to stick the letter 'm' on the (adult's) outline of a monkey. To the monkey outline he had also to draw a face, stick ears and then concertina a piece of paper to make a tail. He did the activity with bad grace and did it poorly. It was clear that he felt his task was to complete the activity (rather than to learn about 'm' or monkeys) and there was no check made about what meaning or learning he had acquired. Once the tail was on the monkey, his completion of the task was checked off on the practitioner's list. The child tried then to resume his water play but found that his previous playmates were now engaged in other activities and he could not get back into the group. In his frustration, he resorted to annoying other children and upsetting their play.

This practitioner is so focused on delivering the planned task she has initiated that it seems not to have occurred to her that the child had other priorities and learned nothing from this task except, perhaps, frustration! Surely, there is a better, more playful way that the learning of the letter 'm' could have occurred if it needed to be taught at all at this age? It is the purpose of this book to question practice such as this and to encourage readers to reflect on how learning is presented to young children.

The structure of this book

This book represents an eclectic collection of chapters with different (sometimes contrasting, sometimes complementary) conceptions of play and reflection but we feel that is all to the good because everyone should find something of interest. Many practitioners seem to like these 'dip-in' books and also enjoy reading about others' pedagogical experiences. With a mixture of experienced and less experienced writers, researchers and practitioners, established ideas and new ideas, we hope the collection will make interesting reading across a range of courses and at different levels.

Each chapter includes links between research and practice and also:

- an abstract of the chapter contents;
- a series of initial questions regarding the key messages of the text;
- examples of specific points to be made within the chapter;
- a section at the end 'What do I, the writer, feel about the contribution of this chapter to supporting critical reflection?' to show, in practice, what we are encouraging readers to do!
- a brief section entitled 'Implications for pedagogy: what might *you*, the reader, reflect on now?' to help support your ongoing thinking about the contents of the chapter and to encourage sharing between professionals and teams;
- references and further reading (the latter given in **bold**).

The book is organized into four parts: (1) Theoretical aspects of play and reflection; (2) Reflecting on children's playful learning; (3) Reflecting on playful learning environments; and (4) Reflecting on playful contexts. The first chapter explores practitioner reflection on play and playful pedagogies. It examines the theories and ideologies behind play and playful pedagogies and how both these concepts 'fit' (or otherwise) with current policy and practice. Why and how practitioners should reflect continuously on their play and playful pedagogies is outlined. In Chapter 2, Justine Howard and Karen McInnes identify some of the challenges faced by practitioners in trying to implement a play-based curriculum. The authors argue that one of the biggest challenges relates to theoretical ambiguity regarding the construct of play and that this permeates all aspects of practice. A new way of conceptualizing play is proposed based on children's own perspectives of play and the authors show how this way of looking at play can be utilized to co-construct a play-based curriculum that enables greater playfulness in children and practitioners. Avril Brock in Chapter 3, picks up on the issue of reflecting on reflections on play exploring more about the nature of reflection, its purposes and the different strategies that can be used to elicit reflection-*on*-reflection on play. Avril examines how and why practitioners need to reflect on their provision for play and stresses that the process of reflection-*on*-reflection will continue to enhance provision of play as well as promote feelings of personal and professional accomplishment and enhance job satisfaction. Pat Beckley explores reflections of practice concerning approaches to play, focused on early years literacy in settings in Norway and England (Chapter 4). She describes the issues that led to reflective practice, followed by discussions of international recommendations and theoretical perspectives. The subsequent research and initial findings from the case studies are given and differing strategies are described.

Bryonie Williams' Chapter 5, illustrating child-initiated play in the school context, is the first contribution in Part 2. She explores how child-initiated play can be used to inform planning, observations and the collection and analysis of data. Reflecting on child-initiated play within a setting provides the practitioner with an understanding of how the needs and interests of the children can lead to learning. This is followed by Estelle Martin's Chapter 6, which encourages readers to consider how vital it is that early years educators reflect on the emotional dimensions of play and children's learning and development. The development of a pedagogy of play is explored as is the essential quality of relationships. The contribution of observation, research and reflective dialogues with practitioners is considered. Rebecca Webster's Chapter 7 examines how children's perspectives can be captured, explored and reflected on through listening to children's voices. She investigates the advantages and challenges of using video cameras as a tool to facilitate this process. She shows that opportunities for children to explore and share their own perceptions with adults can offer insight into the views of children as individuals and collectively. By drawing on examples from a research project, Rebecca explores some of the practical, theoretical and ethical considerations of using a visual and auditory approach to elicit children's views and perspectives. Chapter 8, by Debbie Albon, concludes this section. Debbie's research into food issues and young children is somewhat unique: she draws upon her own research for observations in or near role play areas, which offer the opportunity to observe young children's food-related play. Debbie's findings suggest that there are two categories of play: 'playing for real' and 'really playing'. Both categories of play, on reflection, are valuable and generate their own challenges for early years' practitioners.

In Part 3, we move from food to a consideration of learning environments and what children need for their development and learning. In Chapter 9, Theodora Papatheodou stresses that environments are neither neutral nor innocent; they shape and condition how we feel, think and behave. The experiences they offer and the way they respond to individual and collective needs render meaning to our being, belonging and becoming and to our identity and freedom. Pam Jarvis and Jane George's following Chapter (10) then defines the structure, qualities and consequences of 'rough and tumble' play, moving on to advocate its vital importance for healthy human development. In doing so, they introduce a new model of the developing human being, drawn from the 'biocultural' perspective described in the philosophical literature. Moving on, Maulfry Worthington in Chapter 11 interrogates data from her research into children's imaginative (symbolic) play as they explore, make and communicate personal meanings. Maulfry focuses on case studies exploring children's play and interest in popular culture, new media and technologies through their representations or 'signs', evident in their 'superhero' play and in their models and drawings. She raises questions about early childhood cultures and practices, emphasizing the importance of reflective teaching to help understand and support children's play and cultural interests at a deep level.

Physical space, time, resources, routines, relationships and interactions between adults and children feature in Pauline Trudell's Chapter 12. Extended observations in a nursery school are used as a practical illustration of the points raised. The links between imaginative play and other forms of symbolic representation such as language and literacy are explored. Pauline offers insights into the nature of play and early learning in order to encourage a reflective approach to practice.

The final section Part 4 begins with Chapter 13 written by Kevin Kelman and Linda Laughlan focusing on transition, pedagogy and play from early childhood education to primary. They emphasize that children will be expected to cope with many new demands – they may meet new academic challenges; have to adapt to new school and teacher expectations and, perhaps, gain acceptance into a new peer group. Transitions between educational settings can often mean a change in location, educators, curriculum and philosophy – the authors explore the impact and opportunities these changes can have on children.

The final Chapter 14, by Stephanie Collins, Jane Gibbs, Paulette Luff, Maria Sprawling and Lynsey Thomas, covers children's playful learning and adults' observation and documentation as parallel processes. At every age, initial impressions and interests have to be combined with systematic, thoughtful investigation in order to create a pedagogy that provides for education and growth. Four experienced practitioners share and discuss case studies from their current practice, which demonstrate ways in which they are using observation and documentation as a means of thinking through play.

Finalé

> If we are to best serve children and to foster the full professional development of early childhood educators, we must . . . consider all the evidence of decades of research and experience . . . and begin a thorough assessment of our kindergarten policies and practices (Miller and Almon, 2009: 5).

The authors in this book hope that our contributions will support practitioners in understanding and extending how they can best serve children through the powerful processes of play and reflection.

References

Adams, S., Alexander, E., Drummond, M.J. and Moyles, J. (2004) *Inside the Foundation Stage: Recreating the Reception Year*. London: Association of Teachers and Lecturers.

Bergen, D. and Fromberg, D. (2006) Epilogue, in D. Fromberg and D. Bergen (eds) *Play from Birth to Twelve: Contexts, Perspectives and Meanings*, 2nd edn. New York: Routledge.

Broadhead, P., Howard, J. and Wood, E. (eds) (2010) *Play and Learning in Educational Settings*. London: Sage Publications.

Compass (2008) *Commercialisation of Childhood*. London: Compass. Available online at www.compassonline.org.uk (accessed 12 January 2010).

Department for Education and School (DfES) (2007) *Early Years Foundation Stage*. London: DfES.

Department for Children, Schools and Families (DCSF)/Qualications and Curriculum Development Agency (QCDA) (2009) *Learning Playing and Interacting: Good Practice in the Early Years Foundation Stage*. London: DCSF/QCDA.

Elkonin, D. (1978) *The Psychology of Play*. Moscow: Pedagogika.

Fiennes, Sir R. (2010) Interview. Classic FM/Sunday Times, 10 January. Podcast available online at www.classicfm.co.uk/on-air/podcasts/sunday-times-podcast/ (accessed 11 January 2010).

Hopkins, B. and Johnson, S.P. (eds) (2005) *Prenatal Development of Postnatal Functions*. Santa Barbara, CA: Praeger Publishing.

Miller, E. and Almon, J. (2009) *Crisis in the Kindergarten: Summary and Recommendations*. College Park, MD: Alliance for Childhood.

Moyles, J. (2009) Play: the powerful means of learning, in S. Smidt (ed.) *The Early Years: A Reader*. London: Routledge.

Moyles, J. (2010) Introduction, in J. Moyles (ed.) *The Excellence of Play*, 3rd edn. Maidenhead: Open University Press.

Palmer, S. (2007) *Detoxing Childhood: What Parents Need to Know to Raise Happy, Successful Children*. London: Orion.

Whitebread, D. (2007) Developing independence in learning, in J. Moyles (ed.) *Early Years Foundations: Meeting the Challenge*. Maidenhead: Open University Press.

PART 1
Theoretical aspects of play and reflection

1 Practitioner reflection on play and playful pedagogies

Janet Moyles

Summary

This chapter explores the theoretical and practical aspects of reflection, its history and contemporary interpretations. The writer also examines the theories and ideologies behind play and playful pedagogies and how both these concepts 'fit' (or otherwise) with current policy and practice and the extended focus on play as a learning process. It explores why and how practitioners should reflect continuously on their play and playful pedagogies through thorough analysis of the impact of these on children's learning and development. The chapter raises a new issue of 'reflecting-on-reflection', a metacognitive process intended to sustain and extend enhanced play practices.

Key questions as you read . . .

1 Can you honestly say that your values and beliefs about play are actually put into practice in your setting or classroom?
2 What would *you* achieve by undertaking a critical reflection on your current play principles and practices?
3 Do you understand what is meant by 'playful pedagogies'?
4 How would *children* benefit by you undertaking a critical reflection on play and playful pedagogies?

. . . and points to consider

- 'Of-the-moment' reflections and retrospective and prospective reflections, as well as reflection on these reflections, will each provide a different level of analysis, evaluation and interpretation of practice.

- There are challenges, political and policy-wise, to planning and making provision for children's learning through play but these are worthwhile reflecting on for the sake of children's well-being, meaningful learning and understanding.
- In educational contexts we need to understand play, playful learning and playful teaching and to develop our own constructs.

Introduction

Play seems to 'suffer' by everyone apparently knowing what it is in terms of children's activities but no one being absolutely convinced how much children learn from their play experiences. Most early years practitioners, if challenged, will be adamant that children learn through play but how many can articulate that principle with in-depth knowledge, sufficient to convince, for example, other more sceptical colleagues or parents? How many (honestly!) base the majority of the children's learning experiences on play and child-initiated activities?

My own research over the years has shown that practitioners almost always *state* the value of play for children and hold it dear in their repertoire of skills (e.g. Moyles and Suschitzky, 1997; Moyles and Adams, 2001; Moyles et al., 2002; Adams et al., 2004) but observations in their settings and classrooms reveals that play is more often than not subordinate to adult-led activities. Sometimes the 'play' is only available when children have finished their 'work' (which, of course, some children never do!). Often the play happens for some children when the practitioners are tied up with doing 'work' with others in groups and, therefore, it goes unheeded and unobserved by practitioners (see Adams et al., 2004). This gives a clear message to children that their play is not valuable: only the 'work' done with the practitioners is important and valued (see Chapter 2). If we think about it, this actually shows disrespect for children whose innate abilities and understanding are more often than not reflected in play and child-initiated activities which, unwittingly, we are suggesting have less value than what we do.

There are a range of reasons given by practitioners for not including play – my brief responses are given in parenthesis:

1 pressure from 'above'; for example, heads, local authority personnel, colleagues teaching older children. (So why aren't you showing and explaining to them why play is so important?);
2 fear of not being seen to 'teach'. (Remember that playful pedagogies

are teaching: just teaching in a different and more appropriate way for young children.);

3 no time because of pressure from policy implementation, e.g. OfSTED compliance, National Strategies in England. (It is easy to misinterpret and go overboard about what you feel are policy requirements; learning through play is sanctioned and deemed essential for all young children and can provide much of what they – and you – need to fulfil perceived requirements.);

4 confusion in England over where *Early Years Foundation Stage* (*EYFS*) starts and finishes. (Children do not start statutory schooling until the term after they are 5 years of age. Until that time, they are subject to *EYFS* curriculum requirements and its focus on play.);

5 the need for early years practitioners to feel they have status and to actually *have* status. (Ask how many of those perceived as being 'in authority' have the fortitude, insight and knowledge to teach young children.);

6 the feeling that 'play is a child's work'. (No, it is a child's *learning*, which is quite different. Play = learning and learning dispositions and this must be paramount in thinking.);

7 a strange, historically based work ethic that predominates in Western societies – if it doesn't hurt then it can't be doing any good. (Rubbish! Children can only learn when they are allowed to make mistakes without feeling failures. They do not need pressure and stress – it is counterproductive in learning.);

8 lack of play content in initial and continuing professional development courses. (Do you really need to go to all those 'how to deliver the curriculum' sessions? Demand some quality play and child-initiated learning sessions; for example, Inspire, 2009.);

9 a covert lack of appreciation/understanding of play on the part of policy-makers. (Become more political, join a lobbying group and make more noise about quality practice.);

10 practitioners themselves not appreciating the power/excellence of play. (Observe, analyse and reflect on children's play then you won't be able to deny it.);

11 parents and other politicians/some heads often feeling 'the sooner the better' in relation to skills; for example, writing. (Use your child development knowledge and show them that children are often not developmentally ready to, for example, hold pencils or sit still for long periods.);

12 the lack of definitive research showing the value of play to children's learning and development. (There is mountains of it out there and growing by the minute – just look at books such as Broadhead et al., 2010 and Moyles, 2010a.).

How many of these apply to *you*? While being very sympathetic to the pressures on practitioners, the results of *not* ensuring that children play can mean practitioners working in ways that are both alien and uncomfortable to them and inappropriate for the children. Play for children – like teaching for adults – is purposeful: it can be 'fun' but it can also be extremely serious; for example, when children are playing out traumas and challenges in their lives or struggling to solve a problem. We need to understand not only *that* children play but *why* children play and what the process provides for them if we are to truly serve their developing needs. The only way that will happen is if we stand back and reflect on what is, what has been and what might be in relation to making high-quality provision for children's play and learning and our role in it.

Why should we reflect?

> Critically reflective practice is about moving away from uncritical, routinized or standardized forms of practice towards more informed, imaginative and value-driven approaches.
>
> (Thompson and Thompson, 2008: 107)

Photograph 1.1 Play can be purposeful and serious.

Professionals will always want to improve their practice to the benefit of the children, families and communities within whose learning environment they work. As Thompson and Thompson (2008: 162) insist, 'Being professional involves drawing on professional knowledge and values bases and having professional accountability'. We can be asked to account for our own actions at anytime (not just during an OfSTED inspection!) and reflection helps us be prepared to do so. There is a danger in the early years that practitioners are very 'busy' but that 'busyness' may not always be productive in terms of analysing and evaluating children's learning and their role in it. Working with young children can be exhausting, both physically and mentally: reflection on practice – and play practices especially – can help us to better understand because the process:

- surfaces practitioners' personal knowledge and professional thinking/ values about play and learning;
- enables deeper understanding of one's own and others' practices;
- puts us in touch with our emotional responses and feelings towards our role and children's play;
- promotes greater understanding of how playful pedagogies affect the children;
- supports greater links between play theories, research and practice;
- highlights the assumptions we may make in thinking and practice;
- helps us critique and review our own thinking and practice;
- enables us to make decisions and solve problems;
- empowers us to be ambassadors for children, play and early childhood;
- encourages us to analyse, evaluate and critique our own play practices;
- provides the evidence needed for planning for children's (and our own) playful learning and development;
- gives us confidence in our own playful pedagogies;
- keeps us up to date and aware of new play research and thinking;
- expands our repertoires of strategies for our own and children's play and learning;
- leads to some form of action (mental or physical).

. . . all of which go to make for better pedagogical practices especially when these are playful pedagogies for young children as we see later.

Perhaps I have still got a long way to go to convince readers of the merits of reflective practice. To support that thinking, the rest of this chapter focuses first, on what is reflection, second, on thinking more about what we mean by play and playful pedagogies and, third, on bringing reflection and play practices together and explaining a little of how reflection might be accomplished.

Reflection = thinking, learning and understanding

Reflection is thinking deeply about what we do – when working (and playing) as a practitioner – why we behave in the way we do, what values we bring to a situation, how we feel about our role, whether what we do 'works' (for us and the children), how an activity might have been different, what we might do on another occasion and critiquing this thinking and reflection. It requires a questioning approach to personal and professional values and pedagogical practices and is related to deep learning. Deep learners are characterized, according to Marton and Saljo (1984), as those who aim not just at learning but at *understanding*. This is often accomplished more readily in dialogue with others. Just as children thrive in 'shared sustained thinking' contexts (Siraj-Blatchford et al., 2002), reflection often involves interaction with others as well as with self, particularly in early years multi-professional contexts.

Reflection as a concept has been around for a long time but most people are aware of its basis in works by Dewey and, later, Schön. Dewey (1933) coined the term 'experiential learning', which has always been at the heart of early years practice. He also believed that experience without reflection was unlikely to produce real learning. Dewey suggested five phases of reflective thinking: recognizing problems, intellectualization of the problems; hypothesizing on solutions; reasoning and elaboration; and testing out ideas.

Schön's (1983, 1987) interest was in reflection and he developed a theory of reflection-in-action and reflection-on-action; the former being immediate, day-to-day thinking in the setting or classroom, and the latter being undertaken at a later stage, perhaps after the children have gone. Schön also theorized about what he calls 'knowledge-in-action' (tacit knowledge accumulated by practitioners through experience) and knowledge-on-action (thoughtful contemplation afterwards). Let me explain: we know that practitioners make minute-by-minute, even second-by-second, decisions about pedagogical events (Eraut, 1994) and this is vital to survive in the classroom or setting – it is this instantaneous, intuitive responding to children and situations that makes the job so exhausting but stimulating! But this can mean practice becoming dominated by only immediate thoughts and actions. An example might be useful here (Cameo 1).

Cameo 1

A practitioner reading a story to the children seated on the carpet was continually having to reprimand two children (and interrupt the story) because they kept crawling under a table situated immediately beside the carpet. Her knowing-in-action response is to tell the two children to be good and stop spoiling the story for others. Her reflecting-in-action, her tacit knowledge, tells her to move the children to sit on either side of her as an immediate solution. But, in reflecting-on-action afterwards, she knows that this problem will continue every story time unless something is done (knowledge-on-action). What can she do? Who or what is to blame for this situation?

In reflection-on-action later in the day, she might consider some possible reasons and solutions:

- These two children find concentrating in a large group difficult: could they sit at a table and draw, for example, during the story?
- Was the story sufficiently engaging for these and other children?
- Was there another member of staff available to read a different story to these two children?
- Would it be beneficial to move either the table or the reading area to allay future problems?
- Could story time be implemented in a different way for some children?
- How do other practitioners in other settings resolve this kind of problem?

Many other issues will, no doubt, spring to mind from this simple scenario but we can see immediately that just these six points show different levels and types of reflection.

Reflecting on critical incidents like this is often about questioning things that we take for granted. It is so easy in classrooms and settings to ignore things that are really quite irritating or, worse still, to blame the children when more reflection on the environmental circumstances would show other aspects requiring attention. Moss (2008: xiii) suggests that '. . . reflective practice is about a rigorous process of meaning-making, a continuing process of constructing theories . . . testing them . . . then reconstructing those theories'. In other words, reflective practitioners are likely to be those who see themselves as learners as well as the children in their care. As people who reflect and learn we are, essentially, turning ourselves into researchers. Continually questioning what one sees is at the heart of research into classroom and settings and those who work and play in them. While we should always endeavour to be objective, there is also a strong emotional component of reflection: connecting with our feelings about a situation is extremely important and part of who we are. Yet developing a disciplined mind is also vital to undertaking successful reflections.

To my mind, reflection occurs on at least four different levels: (1) there is the '*of-the-moment*' reflection; (2) *retrospective* reflection on what has been; (3) *prospective* reflection on what might be; and (4) reflection-on-reflection, which is a metacognitive process; reflecting on our own knowledge through the reflective process usually with another. Of-the-moment reflection is very much related to Schön's reflection-in-action; retrospection (reflection-on-action) allows us to look back at events and consider what might have happened differently, whereas reflecting prospectively enables us to think about how things might be in the future. As McAlpine and Weston (2002: 69) suggest:

> . . . intentional reflection [is] for the purpose of making sense of and learning from experiences for the purpose of improvement . . . reflection requires linking existing knowledge to an analysis of the relationship between current experience and future action.

Moon (2004: 82) asserts reflection is '. . . often a process of re-organizing knowledge and emotional orientations in order to achieve further insights'.

How should we reflect?

Of-the-moment reflection draws on practitioners' tacit knowledge and intuition, but both retrospective and prospective reflection can be supported by thinking about some useful self-evaluative questions such as those used by Moyles et al. (2003) (see Figure 1.1).

Play and playful pedagogies

Play and pedagogy have much vocabulary associated with them; for example, free play; free-flow play; spontaneous play; directed play, to name but a few. Play is always purposeful to the child even though at times it may seem purposeless to the practitioners (Smidt, 2010). Having explored some aspects of play above and in the Introduction (as well as numerous explanations and terminology appearing elsewhere in this book), in this section, I want to concentrate on what I am calling 'playful pedagogy' and try to simplify some of the complications that this terminology above creates for practitioners. To my mind, there are three major concepts of play and playfulness that need to be explored when we are considering our pedagogy:

1 *Play* – this is 'pure' play under the control of the child(ren). It is initiated and led by the child(ren) and sustained and developed by them for their purposes. It represents activities and responses chosen and owned by the child(ren) and used at their own discretion. It is highly creative, open-ended and imaginative. This 'pure' play may only partially be achievable in educational settings but is the type of play that links most closely to children's intuitive ways of learning. The adult's role is to make resources available, to be an interested observer

Retrospective:
- What were your intentions/aims/purposes in this session/activity?
- How far were you successful in this?
- How did you come to this view?
- How did you decide what outcomes were appropriate?
- What evidence/information/values/beliefs did you base this choice on?
- What did you expect the children's experiences to be?
- How/why was it different?
- What does this tell you?
- How might your professional practice be improved?
- How did you feel about the session/activity?
- What are the roots of these feelings?
- How did your actions/thinking/feelings affect the children and the other staff?

Prospective:
- What alternative solutions/actions/views might be appropriate in future sessions/activities?
- Do the values represented in the pedagogy need to be reviewed?
- What other values might be applicable to your pedagogy?
- What source of new knowledge/skills/information might be useful to you now?

Reflection-on-reflection
- What did you learn from reviewing your own actions/thinking/feelings?
- What values are represented in your pedagogy?
- What does this lead you to think now about your pedagogical processes in supporting children's play learning?
- What will you now do in similar situations in the future?
- How will you monitor your own learning in future contexts?

(adapted from Moyles et al., 2003: 144)

Figure 1.1   Reflective/analytic questions for practitioners.

(curriculum and assessment), to interact – if invited – and to understand the children's play from a developmental perspective. This requires a very open-ended planning system by the adults.

2   *Playful Learning* – this relates to learning experiences that are child- or adult-initiated or inspired, which engage the child in playful ways and, as near as possible, reflect the child's instinct to play. It may be 'guided' by playful teaching but, remember, the child may *not* perceive the activity to be (pure) play. Children often learn from one another in this context. The adult's role is to be sensitive to children's playful learning modes, make planned provision, model, participate, interact, enhance vocabulary, to perceive curriculum and learning intentions within the play and to observe and assess children's learning needs linking to planning.

3   *Playful Teaching* – this is teaching that utilizes the child's natural and innate joy in playful learning. It will ensure that 'tasks' presented to children are open-ended as far as possible, imaginative and active.

Such teaching will draw on resources perceived by children as 'playful', but practitioners should not expect the child to see the activities as play. The intention of this teaching must relate to what the child needs to do or find out in the context of what the adult wants the child to learn. The adult's role is to ensure the tasks are planned and presented in an enjoyable and meaningful way to the child(ren) and to make links with the required curriculum and assessment procedures. This will probably involve 'sustained shared thinking' episodes.

These three amount to 'playful pedagogies' as they involve different pedagogical (teaching and learning) strategies from the adults. In practice, they need to be considered both separately and together. When practitioners reflect, they need to consider how many opportunities in a day and week each child has for being engaged with these different pedagogies and plan accordingly. But as the DCSF/NS (2009: 11) play document maintains:

Practitioners cannot plan children's play, because this would work against the choice and control that are central features of play. Practitioners can and should plan for children's play, however, by creating high-quality learning environments, and ensuring uninterrupted periods for children to develop their play.

Perhaps with careful background planning, the children could spend all day in pure play contexts and still cover the planned curriculum (Goouch, 2010). Certainly, Bryonie Williams gives evidence of this in Chapter 5. Perhaps some practitioners will work towards more pure play opportunities simply by having this reminder of the different kinds of playful pedagogies! Playful learning and teaching provides adults with greater opportunities to become involved in the play. Once practitioners reflect on their reflections about why they enjoy teaching more playfully, evidenced by children becoming more engaged, it becomes easier and easier to modify one's pedagogy and planning.

The DCSF/NS (2009: 14) play guidance stresses: '. . . a playful approach supports learning because:

- playful children use and apply their knowledge, skills and understanding in different ways and in different contexts;
- playful practitioners use many different approaches to engaging children in activities that help them to learn and to develop positive dispositions for learning'.

Children equally need time to reflect on what they have learned, what they already knew and what they would like to do and learn. How children feel about the play and playful pedagogies will often provide a good indication of how they perceive the experiences they have (see Chapter 2). In these play experiences, children and practitioners may well move from pure play to playful learning and playful teaching but this should, as far as possible, be a seamless transition (see Cameo 2):

Cameo 2

Three-year-old Gemma was playing outside with Rupal and Donja in a nursery setting. The children were exploring the Garden Centre that they had helped to set up and were examining the plant pots, compost and seeds, tapping the pots, shaking the seeds, commenting on the flowers shown on the packets and letting the compost run through their fingers. They investigated the textures, sounds, colours, shapes and quantity of the materials and helped each other to sort the pots into sizes and the flower seeds into colours – pure play. The practitioner, who had observed this play, gradually moved nearer the children and was 'invited' to help them plant some of the seeds but on their terms: they told her which pots they wanted to use and which seeds they wanted to plant. She guided their learning in a playful way by rattling the seed packets and trying to guess what size the seeds would be inside. Then she asked if they would like to plant some seeds and helped them select appropriate pots for what they had chosen. She then modelled for them what they would need to do including counting out a number of seeds and helping them to get the water they needed – playful teaching.

When practitioners reflect, they need to consider how many opportunities in a day and week each child has for being engaged with the three different pedagogical styles. One reflection question might be 'Could the children spend all day in pure play contexts and still cover the planned curriculum?' Perhaps some practitioners will work towards more pure play opportunities simply by having this reminder of the different kinds of playful pedagogies! Playful learning provides adults with greater opportunities to become involved in the play and it might be that, with retrospective reflection, practitioners will see how pure play experiences might be extended. Playful teaching is fun – much better than having to continually discipline children for not concentrating or fidgeting!

Do we need any more reassurances about play and playful pedagogies? With the *UN Convention on the Rights of the Child* to play (UN, 1989), the *Every Child Matters* agenda (HM Treasury, 2004) and the *EYFS* insistence on play in England as vital to children's learning (DfES, 2007), we have all the justification we need for adopting playful pedagogies. Remember 'Skilful adults understand that children develop as players at different rates, and are able to support patterns of development within play' (DCSF/QCDA, 2009: 15).

Reflection on play and playful pedagogies

We have looked briefly at reflection and at play. Practitioners' reflections on play and playful pedagogies will enable them to feel more professional and confident in their practices and be able to share their thinking and evaluations with other colleagues and parents more knowledgeably.

Asking questions about practice such as those identified In Figure 1.1 (and others you will be able to generate with professionals in your team) will enable practitioners to identify challenges in classrooms and settings. For example, we have all seen young children fidgeting and not concentrating on seat-based, adult-led tasks – particularly boys – so why do we pursue a pedagogy that forces children into situations where there is clearly no meaning for them; where they learn only that they do not enjoy what they are being asked to do and cannot do it? (Clarke and Featherstone, 2008). Just reflect for a moment on Max in the final Cameo (3).

Cameo 3

Max is almost 5-years-old and towards the end of his time in Year R. He's continually told that he must sit down and concentrate on what he's doing before he goes to 'big school' but copying letters and words and trying to write 'simple sentences' defeat him. He fidgets, looks through the window, looks under the table at his feet, pulls faces at the child across the table from him and runs his pencil down the edge of his writing book. He is continually told to pay attention or he won't grow into a big boy.

Contrast this Max with the boy who, when engaged in outdoor play set up as a garage, can organize all the toy cars and bikes in size order, unasked fetch paper and pencil and sit at the 'office desk' writing down all the makes and 'number plates' (in fact he is so motivated that what he can actually see are the serial numbers!), arrange a system whereby the cars and bikes can be 'hired' by the children whose names Max writes down and ticks off as they 'hire' and return vehicles. He concentrates for an hour or more on these activities only getting frustrated when it's time to pack up.

Observation and retrospective reflection will show the practitioner how much Max was learning in the play context and how competent, self-sufficient, sociable, reliable and trustworthy he is. Yet his profile shows him, for example, lacking concentration and motivation and being poor at writing skills! Max appears to know his own play and learning style; that is, the ways in which he learns best. In fact, one could say that he has greater understanding of his own learning needs than the practitioner who insists on him sitting down to write things that make no sense to him. This practitioner could have at least engaged in more playful learning and teaching strategies if only she had focused and reflected more on the child. And that probably also means asking oneself: would *I* enjoy that activity? If the answer is 'No!' why do we expect children to? Mostly, because we have not critically reflected on them from a child's perspective or encouraged the child to reflect on experiences him or herself.

How can reflection (of-the-moment, retrospective and prospective) of the kinds outlined above become second nature to all practitioners? Well, it takes time and commitment to adapt everyday practices to include reflection and practitioners have to develop a questioning approach to their pedagogy and see themselves as 'the learner' as well as children. Being 'satisfied' that Max's problems are related to the child, rather than understanding that the task is the culprit, is an easy habit to get into, especially when one feels under pressure. But if we are genuinely to accept that every child is unique and *Every Child Matters* (HM Treasury, 2004), requiring to be understood and taught as an individual, then there is no approach other than to reflect on how each child 'receives' the curriculum. One crucial reflection question might be 'Are we teaching children to perform or do we want children to internalize their learning?' (see Moyles, 2010b). Jumping through hoops is no substitute for real, in-depth learning – and that applies to children and practitioners! Play provides that basis for deeper learning in all the ways we discuss in the chapters of this book. The DCSF/QCDA (2009: 4) play document uses some of the above thinking and emphasizes that: 'The more we are aware of our practices – what we do, why we do it, its impact on children and their learning – and the more we reflect, learn and develop our practice, the more effective we will be. This is developing our pedagogy'.

Reflection, play and playful pedagogies

No doubt you are now wondering where to begin or extend the process of reflecting on play and playful pedagogies. There are many strategies, most in common use in nurseries for recording children's experiences. Perhaps the time has now come to turn the video or the digital camera on yourself! This has proved to be an extremely useful strategy, particularly to engage in 'video-stimulated-reflective-dialogue' (VSRD) with one or more colleagues (Moyles et al., 2002, 2003; Whitebread, 2007; see also Chapter 3). This simply means sharing your of-the-moment and retrospective reflections on the practice captured on camera in order to think more deeply about its quality and impact on the children and the learning environment. Often it is useful to have looked at the video or photograph yourself to consider: what were you thinking at the time? What did that mean to the way you reacted to the child(ren)? What values were associated with your actions and reactions? With hindsight, would you respond in the same way again? Sharing with a colleague will then offer you perhaps a different insight into your actions and reactions and bring another set of thinking to broaden your perspective. Clearly this is something that will only be done occasionally (perhaps once a week/fortnight) but the time used can more than be made up for in the benefits it provides to pedagogy. Practitioners involved in VSRD report its very positive benefits, with one stating 'It is very useful to see yourself actually teaching . . . it has made me so much more aware of what I am doing, what I could be doing and what I am not doing . . . or could develop further' (Moyles et al., 2003: 150). Another sharing process is to write about your experiences on an early education blog – describe a situation on which you are reflecting and request comments from others. Sometimes this adds yet another dimension to thinking.

Writing down of-the-moment thoughts on sticky notes and then reflecting on them retrospectively later is also a superb means of documenting very quickly your tacit, intuitive knowledge and actions and can provide you with snippets for your own 'Learning Journey Profile' (see Chapter 14) or for the children's developmental profiles. A Learning Journey Profile for practitioners (it can also be called a Reflective Journal or Professional Portfolio – see Goodfellow, 2004) is rather like a diary in which retrospective and prospective reflections on playful pedagogies can be recorded, providing evidence of your in-depth thinking about your own practices. They also provide opportunities for reflection-*on*-reflection as you look back over your entries. Any kind of portfolio is useful for staff evaluation and development purposes as well as thinking about the children's experiences and recording your impact on them.

Do not forget, too, that opportunities for reflection should be provided for the children: even the youngest children will respond well to being asked about their play, what they did, who they played with, what they felt about it, and so on. That way, they learn to articulate their thinking and practitioners learn what they gained from different play experiences.

Conclusion

In this chapter, I have explored a range of issues to do with reflection – of-the-moment, retrospective and prospective – and explained a little of the theories behind reflecting on practice. Reflection is a kind of self-observation, an articulating of conscious inner thoughts, feelings and values. It relies on practitioners thinking, reasoning and examining their own practices, sometimes independently and sometimes with others. It is a huge part of professional practice for early years educators especially in providing for play and using playful pedagogic strategies.

What do I, the writer, feel about the contribution of this chapter to supporting critical reflection?

In all the time I have been writing this chapter and editing this book, I have tried to put myself in the position of the practitioner – what do I need to know, understand? How can I possibly set about explaining clearly what this complex-sounding but worthwhile process involves and why it is so important? My professional life has been tied up very closely with research, theory, practice and constant questioning of the relationships between the three. In that time, I hope I have learned to take nothing for granted and always to dig that little bit deeper in an endeavour to make children's and practitioners' experiences of early childhood education that little bit more satisfying. My intention was to share just a little of this with you, the reader. Only you will be able to analyse, evaluate and reflect on whether I have succeeded.

Implications for pedagogy: what might *you*, the reader, reflect on now?

- The list of questions in Figure 1.1 is only a starting point: each play and playful learning and teaching session will be different and will be unique to you and the children in your care. What questions do you need to ask of your own practice?
- What questions and challenges do you want to share with your team?
- How can you and the team ensure that everyone has time for observation and reflection, perhaps through video or digital photography?
- How will you take your of-the-moment and retrospective reflections forward into the prospective process of reflection and, ultimately, reflection-on-reflection?

References and further reading

Adams, S., Alexander, E., Drummond, M.J. and Moyles, J. (2004) *Inside the Foundation Stage: Recreating the Reception Year*. London: Association of Teachers and Lecturers.

Broadhead, P., Howard, J. and Wood, E. (eds) (2010) *Play and Learning in Educational Settings*. London: Sage Publications.

Clarke, J. and Featherstone, S. (2008) *Young Boys and their Writing*. Market Bosworth: Featherstone Education.

Department for Children, Schools and Families (DCSF)/National Strategies (NS)

(2009) *Learning, Playing and Interacting: Good Practice in the Early Years Foundation Stage*. London: DCSF/QCDA.

Department for Education and Schools (DfES) (2007) *Early Years Foundation Stage*. London: DfES.

Dewey, J. (1933) *How We Think*. Boston, MA: DC Heath.

Eraut, M. (1994) *Developing Professional Knowledge and Competence*. London: Falmer.

Goodfellow, J. (2004) Documenting professional practice through the use of a professional portfolio, *Early Years: An International Journal of Research and Development*, 24(1): 63–74.

Goouch, K. (2010) Permission to play, in J. Moyles (ed.) *The Excellence of Play*, 3rd edn. Maidenhead: Open University Press.

HM Treasury (2004) *Every Child Matters*. London: HM Stationery Office.

Inspire (2009) *Stepping Into Play*. Coventry: Inspire Consultancy Ltd. Available online: (at www.inspire.eu.com).

Marton, F. and Saljo, R. (1984) Approaches to learning, in F. Marton, D. Hounsell and N. Entwistle (eds) *The Experience of Learning*. Edinburgh: Scottish Academic Press.

McAlpine, L. and Weston, C. (2002) Reflection: improving teaching and students' learning, in N. Hativa and P. Goodyear (eds) *Teacher Thinking, Beliefs and Knowledge in Higher Education*. Dordrecht: Kluwer Academic Publishers.

Moon, J. (2004) *A Handbook of Reflective and Experiential Learning: Theory and Practice*. Abingdon: RoutledgeFalmer.

Moss, P. (2008) Foreword, in A. Paige-Smith and A. Craft (eds) *Developing Reflective Practice in the Early Years*. Maidenhead: Open University Press.

Moyles, J. (ed.) (2010a) *The Excellence of Play, 3rd edn*. Maidenhead: Open University Press.

Moyles, J. (2010b) Introduction, in J. Moyles (ed.) *The Excellence of Play, 3rd edn*. Maidenhead: Open University Press.

Moyles, J. and Adams, S. (2001) *StEPs: Statements of Entitlement to Play*. Buckingham: Open University Press.

Moyles, J. and Suschitzky, W. (1997) *The Buck Stops Here! Nursery Nurses and Teachers Working Together*. Leicester: University of Leicester/Esmée Fairbairn Trust.

Moyles, J., Adams, S. and Musgrove, A. (2002) *SPEEL: Study of Pedagogical Effectiveness in Early Learning*. London: DfES Research Report No. 363.

Moyles, J., Hargreaves, L., Merry, R., Patterson, F. and Esarte-Saries, V. (2003) *Interactive Teaching in the Primary School: Digging Deeper into Meanings*. Maidenhead: Open University Press.

Schön, D. (1983) *The Reflective Practitioner: How Professionals Think in Action*. Aldershot: Arena.

Schön, D. (1987) *Educating the Reflective Practitioner*. San Francisco, CA: Jossey-Bass.

Siraj-Blatchford, I., Sylva, K., Muttock, S., Gilden, R. and Bell, D. (2002) *Researching Effective Pedagogy in the Early Years*. London: DfES Research Report No. RR566.

Smidt, S. (2010) *Playing to Learn: The Role of Play in the Early Years*. London: Routledge.

Thompson, S. and Thompson, N. (2008) *The Critically Reflective Practitioner*. Basingstoke: Palgrave MacMillan.

United Nations (UN) (1989) *United Nations Convention on the Rights of the Child*. Available online at: www.everychildmatters.gov.uk (accessed 10 December 2009).

Whitebread, D. (2007) Developing independence in learning, in J. Moyles (ed.) *Early Years Foundations: Meeting the Challenge*. Maidenhead: Open University Press.

2 Thinking through the challenge of a play-based curriculum

Increasing playfulness via co-construction

Justine Howard and Karen McInnes

Summary

This chapter identifies some of the challenges faced by practitioners in trying to implement a play-based curriculum. The authors argue that one of the biggest challenges relates to theoretical ambiguity regarding the construct of play and that this permeates all aspects of practice. In keeping with current ideology regarding listening to children, a new way of conceptualizing play is proposed based on children's own perspectives of play. Drawing on current and ongoing research evidence, the authors discuss how this way of looking at play can be utilized to co-construct a play-based curriculum that enables greater playfulness in children and practitioners.

Key questions as you read . . .

1 How do the traditional definitions of play compare to your own definition of play?
2 What do you understand by play, playfulness and learning?
3 How do you think the children in your setting view play?
4 What aspects of your practice do you think influences their view of play?

. . . and points to consider

- Children make play–work distinctions based on their perceptions of classroom experience.

- Looking at play through children's eyes shows there are differences in perceptions of play between children and adults.
- Understanding play from the children's perspective enables an alternative theoretical conception of play – one based on children's definitions of play, rather than adults.

Introduction

'Thinking through the challenge of a play-based curriculum' may seem quite an unusual statement. Why is implementing a play-based curriculum a challenge and what exactly is there to think through? The value of play for children's learning and development is generally taken as agreed fact (Lindon, 2001) and considering that play is often regarded as children's principal occupation (Piers and Landau, 1980), there would seem little for the early years practitioner to do. In reality, however, the story is far less simple and while the idea of a play-based curriculum might evoke a romantic vision, the play activity that occurs in settings and classrooms must be reconciled with the fundamental notion of education, the need for children to learn.

Historically, a play-based curriculum has its roots in the work of early years pioneers such as Froebel (1782–1852), MacMillan (1860–1931) and Isaacs (1885–1948). Current curriculum initiatives in the UK (DfES, 2007a, 2007b; Welsh Assembly Government, 2008) continue to stress the importance of play in the curriculum for young children: 'all the areas must be delivered through planned, purposeful play, with a balance of adult-led and child-initiated activities' (DfES, 2007a: 11).

However, it may be argued that delivering a play-based curriculum is not a straightforward activity. It is, in fact, challenging and, despite practitioners instinctively understanding the benefits of play and having this practice endorsed by curriculum guidance, many recognize the challenges inherent in doing this and are unsure of the best way to proceed. In a small-scale study, Bennett et al. (1997) discussed some of the difficulties faced by teachers in implementing play in the classroom. Ultimately, it is a way of practice that requires in-depth training and continuous reflection by the practitioner (as discussed in Chapter 1).

This chapter aids reflection by identifying some of the challenges faced by practitioners in trying to implement a play-based curriculum. It is argued that one of the primary challenges is one of theoretical clarity concerning play. A new way of conceptualizing play is provided that enables practitioners to co-construct a play-based curriculum, which is both meaningful to adults and children. It is hoped that empowering practitioners with this new way of looking at play will result in increased confidence in practitioners and perceptions of professionalism.

The biggest challenge – what is play?

Defining a construct is essential for shared understanding (Pellegrini, 2009) and play is no exception. Play is an activity that is shared by humans and animals and something that most people engage in. Within early years education play is viewed as essential for learning and development (Bergen, 1988; Bruner et al., 1976). However, it is an extremely elusive concept to define (Moyles, 1989). As Sutton-Smith (1997) argues almost anything can be described as play.

Traditionally, play has been viewed in relation to work, a highly unhelpful construct as aspects of play may be considered work and work may be playful (Schwartzman, 1978). Within the early years this distinction is decidedly blurred as play is seen as the child's work and it is frequently purported that children are unable to distinguish between play and work (DfEE, 2000; Manning and Sharp, 1977). In attempting to define play three distinct groupings have been proposed: category, criteria and continuum (Howard, 2002).

A categorical definition was first proposed by Piaget (1951) who described a developmental structure of three types of play: practice play, symbolic play and games with rules. Smilansky (1968) added to this proposing a fourth category of constructive play to be inserted between practice and symbolic play. However, this attempt to define play was criticized as children do not progress through all distinct stages in their play and the categories do not account for all types of play. In an attempt to remedy this broader categories have been suggested such as epistemic and ludic play (Hutt et al., 1989) but these have been deemed too broad to be useful.

Criteria definitions focus on dispositions of play – for an activity to be defined as play it must demonstrate certain dispositions including: intrinsic motivation, locus of control, non-literality, freedom from rules and positive affect (Neumann, 1971; Krasnor and Pepler, 1980; Rubin et al., 1983). However, the importance, and even validity, of these different criteria have been criticized. In a small-scale study, Smith and Vollstedt (1985) found that when rating children's play, adults did not use the criterion of intrinsic motivation despite this featuring in most definitions of play. In addition, Sutton-Smith and Kelly-Byrne (1984) suggest that play does not necessarily involve pretence nor does it have to appear enjoyable.

Alternative to the criteria approach is that play can be defined across a continuum (Neumann 1971; Pellegrini 1991). In this way criteria are used to define how play-like an activity is – the more criteria that are present the more like pure play it is. Again, the criticisms levelled at the criteria approach to defining play apply here.

So where does this leave the practitioner other than probably in a muddle?

How can the practitioner decide which is a valid definition to use? Which one makes sense within the parameters of playful behaviour displayed by children in the setting? Some expressions may seem to denote play such as laughing but equally a group of children engaged in a work-like task might also be laughing together – is that play? Are some areas in the setting more likely to promote play than others? Are children engaged in play in the role-play area? What about filling up different size beakers in the sand area or completing a mathematical puzzle at the computer? Should the practitioner label everything that occurs within the setting as play? Or, alternatively, label everything as work? What about typologies of play: free play, directed play, structured and unstructured play? Or the practitioner who says 'We're doing free-flow play today'? These are genuine dilemmas for practitioners and the proposed definitions of play discussed above do not provide an adequate theoretical basis from which practitioners can implement a play-based curriculum. Not only can we question whether the characteristics presented in criteria or continuum models exist, but sometimes these characteristics are extremely difficult to see.

Further challenges – the link with theoretical ambiguity

There are other challenges faced by practitioners in trying to implement a play-based curriculum including: pressure from parents, pressure from other key stages, assessment outcomes and uncertainty concerning the adult role in relation to play (see Chapter 1). These are real pressures for practitioners. However, it may be argued that a secure theoretical basis in relation to play will empower practitioners and enable them to meet the challenges with confidence.

Uncertainty concerning the adult role in children's play is hardly surprising. Originating with the work of Isaacs (1885–1948), practitioners have been advised not to interfere in children's play. This viewpoint changed with studies into play training (Smith and Dutton, 1979) and the work of Vygotsky (1976). Currently, as Johnson et al. (2005) state, teacher involvement has been increasing but the quality of this involvement remains problematic. Indeed, studies into the outcomes of teacher involvement in play report mixed findings. Positive findings have been found such as children play longer and more elaborately when a teacher is involved (Sylva et al., 1980). However, adult intervention has been found to disrupt children's play (Manning and Sharp, 1977). In addition, doubts in relation to the adult role also impact on assessment in terms of when and how to assess, planning and the provision of child- and adult-initiated activities and planning of the environment.

As has been argued elsewhere, teachers are arguably the most important group of play professionals, yet they receive a minimal amount of training in the field by comparison to others such as playworkers and play therapists (Howard, 2009). It is also very difficult for practitioners to defend and feel confident in their play practice when they are generally unaware of the evidence base that underpins their work. We can empower teachers by ensuring they are aware of the theories surrounding play, the relationship between play, learning and development and their role in relation to this.

Play and learning

Children learn effectively by modelling, by rote and via direct teaching, so why bother with play at all? Of course we all instinctively know that play is useful but why? What is it about play that makes it so special? What exactly is it that separates play from other modes of action? Moyles (1989) states that it is the internal, affective quality of play that is important in development: enthusiasm, motivation and willingness to engage. Dewey (1933) made the distinction between this internal, affective quality and play itself by differentiating between playfulness and play 'the former is an attitude of mind; the latter is an outward manifestation of this attitude' (p. 210). Playfulness also implies freedom and flexibility, again important for learning. Viewing playfulness, as an attitude of mind, rather than play, the outward act, may be the most helpful way yet of thinking about this elusive concept and of providing a theoretical basis for implementing a play-based curriculum. So, how do we get to playfulness?

A different conception of play – playfulness

All the definitions of play discussed earlier in this chapter are based on an adult view of the observable act of play; they depend on what play looks like to others. We argue that this does not get to the heart of playfulness or the characteristics of play that separate it from other modes of action. Our proposition is that the important thing about play is not what it looks like, but rather, what it means to approach a task as play. To conceptualize play in this way, it is necessary to obtain a definition of play from the players themselves – the children. This is in opposition to the long-held view that children do not distinguish between play and work but if we do listen to children then hopefully we get to understand not only what play looks like but also what it feels like. We can begin to learn what play means to children, what determines whether an activity is or is not play and as a result we can determine whether different behaviours are associated with play or non-play states. Listening to children is currently the subject of much interest and is embedded within *Every Child Matters* (DfES, 2004). It is an activity that should be at the heart of early years practice: however, there is a paucity of research on gaining the views of young children (Clark and Statham, 2005) and even less on children's definitions of play.

The few studies that have been conducted looking at children's views of play have employed a variety of methodologies: interview, observation and experimental methodology (e.g. Wing, 1995; Keating et al., 2000; Howard, 2002; Howard et al., 2006). All the studies conclude that children do distinguish between play and work and that they do so using cues, both emotional and environmental. Emotional cues include the amount of choice a child has in an activity, whether the activity is voluntary or not and how easy it is. Environmental cues include where the activity takes place, whether or not an adult is involved or evaluates what the child has done and the physical nature of the activity (for an overview of cues used by children see Table 2.1).

Children do view certain activities as play and others as work; for example, activities occurring outside involving construction or role play are generally seen as play while activities involving reading, writing and being taught skills are viewed as work. However, they use the above cues to determine how play-like an activity is and how playfully they approach it. For example, a construction activity may be viewed as work-like if it occurs at a table and play-like if it occurs on the floor. Therefore, children use the cues to break down the play–work divide and define a play–work continuum as evidenced by the authors when asking children to sort photographs into play and not play activities they often ask for a third category to go in the middle – 'a bit play'.

It has also been shown that children make play–work distinctions based

Table 2.1 Cues children use to distinguish between play and work activities

Play		Work	
Emotional cues	*Environmental cues*	*Emotional cues*	*Environmental cues*
Voluntary	On the floor	Compulsory	At a table
Under child's control	Lacks adult involvement	Under adult control	Includes adult involvement
Easy	No adult evaluation	Hard	Includes adult evaluation
Fun	Can be continued – focus on the process	Can be fun	Has to finish – focus on product
	Physical		Not physical

on classroom experience with children in more structured settings making greater play–work distinctions (Howard, 2002). Unsurprisingly perhaps, it seems that the play–work distinction changes with age and becomes more defined as children get older (Parker, 2007).

It can be seen that looking at play through children's eyes there are differences in perceptions of play between children and adults. While there is overlap, for example, in relation to control within an activity and focus on process rather the end product, there are clear differences. Choice is clearly important to children despite the findings from Smith and Vollstedt (1985). Positive affect is clearly ambiguous; play is fun but work can be as well. Children also view the adult role differently with adult involvement and evaluation both rendering an activity as less play-like.

Playfulness and learning

We suggest that it is the affective quality of play, namely playfulness, which supports learning. But is there evidence to support that viewpoint? A small number of studies and current, ongoing research would suggest that there is (Thomas et al., 2006; Radcliffe 2007; McInnes et al., 2009). In these studies some of the cues children use to differentiate between play and not play activities have been manipulated under experimental conditions to create playful (on the floor, adult proximal, voluntary) and formal (at a table, adult present, compulsory) practice conditions. Children have been allocated to one of the practice conditions and then been involved in a familiar problem-solving task in a four-stage procedure: pre-test, practice, post-test and delayed post-test.

Results from these studies show that children in the playful practice condition perform and behave differently to children in the formal practice condition. They exhibit a significantly improved performance in time taken to complete the task. They show greater involvement in the activity as measured by the *Leuven Involvement Scale* (Laevers et al., 1994). They also exhibit greater motivation as shown by behaviours such as leaning towards the puzzle, smiling and greater focus on the activity and employ more purposeful problem solving using less repetitive behaviours and trying out new ways to solve the problem. In addition, asking children to rate the practice condition they experienced shows that they are alert to the cues being manipulated with children in the playful practice condition rating it as far more play-like than those children in the formal practice condition.

Overall, it would seem that listening to children and gaining insight into their conceptualization of play is beneficial. Children appear to use cues to define play and, manipulating these cues impacts on children's performance and behaviour during a task. Understanding this, and working with it, enables practitioners to develop a new pedagogy of play (Rogers and Evans, 2008). This is one that has an alternative theoretical base and is co-constructed with, and for, children. This new conceptualization frees practitioners from the constraints of providing activities that look like play (Wood and Attfield, 2005) and empowers them to inject playfulness into a variety of their classroom practices.

Co-constructing a play-based curriculum

Understanding play from the children's perspective enables an alternative theoretical conception of play – one based on children's definitions of play, rather than adults. Children use cues to define an activity on a play/not play continuum, which then impacts on the attitude and approach taken. Using this research as a guide, practitioners are able to listen to children and understand the cues children are using to define play in their own settings. Practitioners can then work with children to co-construct an environment and atmosphere that reduces the cue distinctions, blurs the boundaries between play and not play and engenders greater playfulness. The way in which children's own perceptions of their classroom activities can feed into the planning process is demonstrated in Figure 2.1.

1 Informed classroom practice
Having a theoretical concept of play based on children's own perceptions of play and knowing that there is increasing empirical evidence supporting a way of working based on this concept should enable a feeling of confidence within

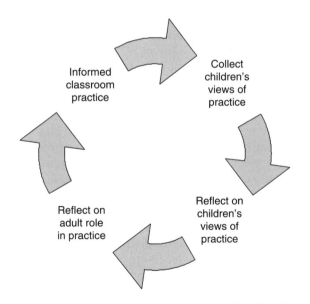

Figure 2.1 Children and practitioners co-constructing a play-based curriculum.

practitioners. They can feel confident that this is a valid conceptual base and that children respond positively according to their own playful cues. It should empower practitioners so that they can argue the merits of playful practice with parents and practitioners in other key stages and that learning skills in a playful way is advantageous to children.

Using these cues should enable practitioners to feel confident in their language when discussing play. Practitioners may feel that they can dispense with some typologies of play; for example, structured and unstructured or free play and directed play. It may be argued that to some extent all play is structured or directed either by the resources available to children or the play frame they create (Moyles, 1989). Using the cues should allow practitioners to discuss playfulness, either in approach or attitude, which can be facilitated in all activities.

2 Investigating children's own views on play practice in the classroom

The cues children use to define play and not play activities are clearly described in the literature. However, practitioners could confirm the cues children are using in the setting as a part of the initial getting-to-know-you process. Practitioners routinely take photographs of the children in their setting. Photographs could be taken of the children at play in different areas of the setting, with the adults, with their peers and at different times of the day. Children could then be asked whether they think these are a lot like play or not much like play.

Practitioners can then talk with children about why they have categorized the photographs in the way they have. This information will enable them to identify how children conceptualize play in their setting. Furthermore, practitioners will then be aware of the cues children are using and will be able to work with these to modify the provision available and their practice.

3 Using children's views to reflect on practice

Utilizing children's cues of playfulness to co-construct a play-based curriculum does not mean that practitioners should move away from traditional good practice. As always, when planning activities, a wide range should be available to children and these can be a mix of both child- and adult-initiated activities. However, careful thought might be merited in relation to adult-initiated activities and choice. Children use the cue of choice in making play and not play distinctions. Choice, or even the illusion of choice, has been found to increase motivation and learning in children (Swann and Pittman, 1977). Therefore, practitioners might want to consider giving children a range of adult-initiated activities from which they can choose, and complete, during a week. They might also want to facilitate choice within an adult-initiated activity so that children feel they have choice and control within the activity (you will see the links between this and playful learning and teaching as discussed in Chapter 1).

One of the cues children use to make play and not play distinctions is where the activity takes place, either on the floor or at a table. Practitioners, therefore, need to consider the physical layout of the room. Making many activities available on the floor or allowing children to stand at tables will blur the distinction between play and not play and ensure that children approach activities with a more playful attitude. In addition, creating a layout with more floor space and fewer tables will allow children to be more physical, another cue children use in making play and not play distinctions.

An example of using the cues to make activities seem more like play to children so that they can approach them more playfully is provided in a reception class engaged in a whole class phonics activity. Children had to write three-letter words using a variety of initial consonants. A large piece of paper was rolled out on the floor and children were allowed to choose where to sit, kneel and in one or two cases lie to write their words. They were allowed to choose a pen from the variety of different coloured pens provided and they were able to choose different initial letters to write their words. All children were deeply involved in the activity, writing a range of letters, carefully listening to the teacher and eagerly making corrections to their work.

4 Using children's views to reflect on the adult's role in practice
The role of the adult during play is probably the most difficult aspect for practitioners. They are often unsure how much and when to get involved and, as previously discussed, quantity of adult involvement comes at the expense of quality of involvement. Research shows that adult presence is an important cue for children when making play and not play distinctions and that adult presence is equated with children talking less and being less focused on the task. However, this may be mediated by adults becoming play partners in a meaningful way. This involves waiting to be invited into play, taking the lead from the child and thinking about one's own playfulness. In settings where adults successfully achieve this, it has been shown that children do not use this cue as a distinguishing feature – activities can be play whether an adult is present or not (see Chapter 4). However, if practitioners only join in at certain times or in particular activities then that distinction is made.

An example whereby children do not use this cue and rate activities as play whether or not an adult is involved comes from a nursery setting. During the course of a morning session children participate in a range of adult- and child-initiated activities. The adult spends time observing a child at the sand tray then moves on to a small group playing on the floor with the train track. She sits on the floor quietly observing the children who gradually include her in their game. One child is the train driver, clearly in control of the activity, and the teacher takes her lead from him playing as a part of the group. Later in the morning she is outside sitting at a table observing and writing notes. Other children come to the table with clipboards and pens watching and writing, playing the role of teacher. At the end of the morning the children are sitting on the floor engaged in a whole class activity guessing what is hidden in the basket hanging from a pulley on the ceiling. Children take turns to ask questions, make guesses and evaluate each others suggestions. The adult also joins in making guesses, asking questions and guiding their problem solving to a successful conclusion. In this setting the adult is valued as a play partner (and this is a wonderful example of playful teaching as described in Chapter 1).

The cue of adult presence is also important in relation to assessment. Assessment in the early years is often based on observation but sometimes practitioners are concerned that they do not have the time or space to stand back. Evidence surrounding the relationship between play and learning indicates that children can be motivated and engaged when involved in activities without adult presence and, as such, practitioners can feel confident about stepping back and observing. Children also indicate that when adults evaluate their activities they consider this to be less play-like. Practitioners might therefore like to consider peer- and self-evaluation in their assessment repertoire.

Conclusion

This chapter has presented practitioners with an alternative view of play – one defined by children. Children use a range of cues to define play and utilizing these cues means that adults can co-construct a play environment in a way that has meaning to children and enables children to adopt a more playful approach to activities. Current, and ongoing, research indicates that when children are engaged in activities that *they* consider to be play, it is beneficial for their learning.

What do we, the writers, feel about the contribution of this chapter to supporting critical reflection?

The way of working described in this chapter necessitates practitioners reflecting on their own beliefs about play, listening to children and understanding how they view play. It requires them to reflect on their practice and make changes that will facilitate play according to children's cues (retrospective reflection, Chapter 1). It also requires practitioners to consider their own role and how they might adopt a more playful approach in order to be regarded as play partners by children (prospective reflection, Chapter 1). Finally, there are overwhelming implications for the training of early years practitioners whereby the complexity of play is acknowledged and addressed and the difficult task of children and practitioners co-constructing a play-based curriculum together is at the fore.

Implications for pedagogy: what might *you*, the reader, reflect on now?

1   What do I understand about play?
2   How does my understanding impact on my practice?
3   What does this say about how I value play?
4   How does this influence the children's understanding of play?
5   What cues do children use to define play?

The authors recognize that in attempting to answer these questions the reader is likely to experience some initial unease. This we believe is a good thing. Only by questioning and challenging previously held assumptions – *and reflecting on them* – can a new perspective emerge. From this new perspective of play, based on children's definitions of play, it is hoped that practitioners can co-construct a play-based curriculum that facilitates playfulness in approach and attitude by both children and adults.

References and further reading

Bennett, N., Wood, L. and Rogers, S. (1997) *Teaching Through Play*. Buckingham: Open University Press.

Bergen, D. (1988) Using a schema for play and learning, in D. Bergen (ed.) *Play as a Medium for Learning and Development*. Portsmouth: Heinemann Educational Books Ltd.

Bruner, J.S., Jolly, A. and Sylva, K. (eds) (1976) *Play: Its Role in Development and Evolution*. New York: Basic Books, Inc.

Clark, A. and Statham, J. (2005) Listening to young children. Experts in their own lives, *Adoption and Fostering*, 29(1): 45–56.

Department for Education and Employment (DfEE) (2000) *Curriculum Guidance for the Foundation Stage*. London: Qualifications and Curriculum Authority.

Department for Education and Skills (DfES) (2004) *Every Child Matters: Change for Children*. London: DfES.

Department for Education and Skills (DfES) (2007a) *The Early Years Foundation Stage*. Nottingham: DfES Publications.

Department for Education and Skills (DfES) (2007b) *The Early Years Foundation Stage. Effective Practice: Play and Exploration*. Available at www.teachernet. gov.uk/_doc/11293/play%20and%20exploration.pdf (accessed 28 November 2009).

Department of Education and Science (DES) (1989) *Aspects of Primary Education: The Education of Children Under Five*. London: DES.

Dewey, J. (1933) *How We Think*. Boston, MA: D.C. Heath and Company.

Howard, J. (2002) Eliciting young children's perceptions of play, work and learning using the activity apperception story procedure, *Early Child Development and Care*, 172: 489–502.

Howard, J. (2009) Play, learning and development in the early years, in T. Maynard and N. Thomas (eds) *An Introduction to Early Childhood Studies*. London: Sage Publications.

Howard, J., Jenvey, V. and Hill, C. (2006) Children's categorisation of play and learning based on social context, *Early Child Development and Care*, 176(3/4): 379–93.

Hutt, S.J., Tyler, S., Hutt, C. and Christopherson, H. (1989) *Play, Exploration and Learning*. London: Routledge.

Johnson, J.E., Christie, J.F. and Wardle, F. (2005) *Play, Development and Early Education*. Boston, MA: Pearson Education, Inc.

Keating, I., Fabian, H., Jordan, P., Mavers, D. and Roberts, J. (2000) 'Well, I've not done any work today. I don't know why I came to school': perceptions of play in the reception class, *Educational Studies*, 26(4): 437–54.

Krasnor, L.R. and Pepler, D.J. (1980) The study of children's play: some suggested future directions, in K.H. Rubin (ed.) *New Directions for Child Development: Children's Play* (pp. 85–95). San Francisco, CA: Jossey-Bass, Inc.

Laevers, F., Vandenbussche, E., Kog, M. and Depondt, L. (1994) *A Process-oriented Child Monitoring System for Young Children*. Flanders: Centre for Experiential Education.

Lindon, J. (2001) *Understanding Children's Play*, 3rd edn. Cheltenham: Nelson Thornes.

Manning, K. and Sharp, A. (1977) *Structuring Play in the Early Years at School*. East Grinstead: Schools Council Publications.

McInnes, K., Howard, J., Miles, G.E. and Crowley, K. (2009) Behavioural differences exhibited by children when practising a task under formal and playful conditions, *Educational and Child Psychology*, 26(2): 31–9.

Moyles, J.R. (1989) *Just Playing?* Buckingham: Open University Press.

Neumann, E.A. (1971) *The Elements of Play*. New York: MSS Information Corporation.

Parker, C.J. (2007) Children's perceptions of a playful environment: contextual, social and environmental differences. Unpublished BSc dissertation, University of Glamorgan.

Pellegrini, A.D. (1991) *Applied Child Study*, 2nd edn. NJ: Lawrence Erlbaum Associates, Inc.

Pellegrini, A.D. (2009) Research and policy on children's play, *Child Development Perspectives*, 3(2): 131–6.

Piaget, J. (1951) *Play, Dreams and Imitation in Childhood*. London: William Heinemann.

Piers, M.W. and Landau, G.M. (1980) *The Gift of Play: And Why Young Children Cannot Thrive Without It*. New York: Walker Publishing.

Radcliffe, E. (2007) Mathematical development and playful practice. Unpublished BSc dissertation, University of Glamorgan.

Rogers, S. and Evans, J. (2008) *Inside Role-play in Early Childhood Education. Researching Young Children's Perspectives*. Abingdon: Routledge.

Rubin, K.H., Fein, G.G. and Vandenberg, B. (1983) Play, in P.H. Mussen (ed.) *Handbook of Child Psychology: Socialization, Personality and Social Development*, 4th edn (Vol. IV). New York: John Wiley and Sons, Inc.

Schwartzman, H.B. (1978) *Transformations: The Anthropology of Children's Play*. New York: Plenum Press.

Smilansky, S. (1968) *The Effects of Sociodramatic Play on Disadvantaged Preschool Children*. New York: John Wiley and Sons, Inc.

Smith, P.K. and Dutton, S. (1979) Play training in direct and innovative problem solving, *Child Development*, 4: 830–6.

Smith, P.K. and Vollstedt, R. (1985) On defining play: an empirical study of the relationship between play and various play criteria, *Child Development*, 56: 1042–50.

Sutton-Smith, B. (1997) *The Ambiguity of Play*. Cambridge, MA: Harvard University Press.

Sutton-Smith, B. and Kelly-Byrne, D. (1984) The idealization of play, in P.K. Smith (ed.) *Play in Animals and Humans*. Oxford: Basil Blackwell.

Swann, J.W.B. and Pittman, T.S. (1977) Initiating play activity of young children: the moderating influence of verbal cues on intrinsic motivation, *Child Development*, 48: 1128–32.

Sylva, K., Roy, C. and Painter, M. (1980) *Child Watching at Playgroup and Nursery School*. London: Grant McIntyre.

Thomas, L., Howard, J. and Miles, G. (2006) The effectiveness of playful practice for learning in the early years, *The Psychology of Education Review*, 30(1): 52–8.

Vygotsky, L.S. (1976) Play and its role in the mental development of the child, in J.S. Bruner, A. Jolly and K. Sylva (eds) *Play: Its Role in Development and Evolution*. New York: Basic Books, Inc.

Welsh Assembly Government (2008) *Framework for Children's Learning for 3–7-year-olds in Wales*. Available at www.chwaraedysgutyfucymru.gov.uk/topics/educationandskills/policy_strategy_and_planning/104009-wag/foundation_phase/foundationphasepractitioners/frameworkchildlearning/;jsessionid=

jJRpK1QVWJc3J6GX262nmCDJBtvQ2XxD3GJ1CG1YwmLnm4GDpGpP!
469745487?cr=5&lang=en (accessed 15 December 2009).

Wing, L. (1995) Play is not the work of the child: young children's perceptions of work and play, *Early Childhood Research Quarterly*, 10: 223–47.

Wood, E. and Attfield, J. (2005) *Play, Learning and the Early Childhood Curriculum*, 2nd edn. London: Paul Chapman.

3   The nature of practitioners' reflection on their reflections about play

Avril Brock

Summary

This chapter explores the nature of reflection, its purposes and the different strat-egies that can be used to elicit reflection-*on*-reflection on play, examining how and why practitioners need to reflect on their provision for play. The field of early years education requires a knowledgeable and articulate workforce able to reflect on and evaluate their professional role. The process of reflection-*on*-reflection can take the form of a continuous learning journey and, in this way, will not only continue to enhance provision of play but also promote feelings of personal and professional accomplishment and enhance job satisfaction as provision and children's achievements grow in quality.

Key questions as you read . . .

1   Why should we reflect on our play pedagogies?
2   What contributions could a reflective portfolio play in encouraging you to enhance your thinking and practice?
3   How might reflecting on your practice through video observations support your play practices?

. . . and points to consider

- Theory is not divorced from practice: there is much evidence to show that reflection on play and playful pedagogies enhances professional practice.
- There are challenges for teachers in allowing the children to sustain

and develop their child-initiated play. Reflection on such play can support increased knowledge about children's learning.

- The field of early years education requires a knowledgeable and articulate workforce able to reflect on and evaluate their professional role and its practical application.
- Reflection can be challenging and disturbing but, in the end, it is always worthwhile.

Introduction

This chapter explores the nature of reflection, its purposes and the different strategies that can be used to elicit reflection-*on*-reflection on play, examining how and why practitioners need to reflect on their provision for play. The emphasis is, therefore, on Schön's (1987) reflection-*on*-action (see also Chapter 1) and this chapter draws on real life examples of practitioners reflecting on their pedagogies of play to an interested party – myself as either researcher or lecturer. Teachers – experienced, newly qualified and student teachers – nursery nurses, managers of Children's Centres and head teachers provide the reflective contributions. Several 'methodologies' have been used to gain these reflections-*on*-pedagogy. In the role of researcher, I used video-stimulated reflective dialogues (see Chapter 1) but, as a lecturer, assessment is the means of elicitation through assignments focused on quality provision and personal professional reflective portfolios with postgraduates on a master's degree in early years. In this way I present how reflection-*on*-reflection can be most useful for further developing practitioners' everyday pedagogy of play, how this is not just an 'academic' exercise but is actually most purposeful, can support accountability of practice and be inspiring and interesting!

What is reflection on practice? Why reflect?

Reflection is promoted in a range of disciplines, particularly in education, health and social care, and is a vital element of professional practice (Moon, 2004). Professional knowledge and reflection on that professional knowledge is a key dimension of professionalism (Brock, 2006). The field of early years education requires a knowledgeable and articulate workforce who are able to reflect on and evaluate the professional role and its practical application, as this must be the key to professionalism (Hughes and Menmuir, 2002). For critical reflection to be effective, it needs to self-emanate from a desire to do it having understood its value and it can be, in Bolton's (2005: 3) view, the 'pearl grit in an oyster of practice and education'.

Professional practice is contextual and complex and reflective thinking can act as a tool for evaluating practice, helping to determine discrepancies between what is implicit and what is explicitly practised – articulating the inarticulable (Fook and Gardner, 2007; see also Chapter 5). Critical reflection can effect change and improve practice and may occur as a subconscious activity, a conversation with a colleague or through reflective writing. Chapter 1 has already aired Schön's (1987) notions of 'knowledge-*in*-action', and 'knowledge-*on*-action', which both indicate the need for theory embedded within practice, with reflexivity being the practical application of reflecting afterwards relating theory to practice. Critical reflection is both a theory and a practice – the reflective thinking processes enable the making and remaking of knowledge. Eraut (1994) believes theoretical professional knowledge and contextual practical knowledge need to be interlinked: theory is not divorced from practice and helps generate deeper understanding.

Contemporary professionals need to continually gain and interrelate different aspects of knowledge and for most it is complex and multidimensional, crossing a range of expertise and skills. Theoretical knowledge is normally acquired through education and study; practical knowledge is gained on the job through training, experience and practice leading to competence; personal knowledge is developed through combinations of personal previous experience, values and beliefs, education, training and practice. When these knowledge bases are reflected on, articulated and understanding enhanced then professional knowledge is generated. It is essential to integrate reflection with personal and contextual understanding in order to identify the way to develop, change and improve practice.

There is now pressure on contemporary professionals to reflect in and on their professional practice through varied continuing professional development activities. For reflection to be purposeful it needs to be meaningful and, for early years educators (EYEs), therefore, needs to relate to their work with young children and their families. They need to be able to articulate not only their educational and pedagogical aims, but also their personal values to reflect on how they form their actions and responses in order to deliver a genuinely inclusive curriculum (Forde et al., 2006).

So what does 'reflection-*on*-reflection' imply and in what ways is it different to Schön's (1987) reflection-in- and reflection-on-action that has been explored in Chapter 1? Reflection-*on*-reflection indicates an extra dimension to a practitioner's reflective process in that it requires dissemination to a critical friend who will actively listen or read the reflections and then respond in ways that further develop the reflective process itself. The person reflecting is aware that there is an interested party who is evaluating the reflections and may comment on insights, observations, knowledge or relationships. The process is not meant to make judgements on the practice but to act like a mirror for the 'reflectée' and so aims to deepen understanding of the practice or the event. Continuing professional development supports this reflection-*on*-reflection activity – it is not just an academic exercise but a part of the reflective journey essential for a deep-thinking professional who is interested in further developing knowledge and competence. This chapter gives examples of how reflection-*on*-reflection was accomplished through interviews, video-reflective dialogues or reflective writing.

Why is it important to engage in reflection-*on*-reflection on play?

Critical reflection can develop knowledge and understanding of play and also how theory and research relate to the provision of play. It can refresh or change practice for practitioners aiming for higher quality provision of play that meets children's needs and interests, scaffolds their learning and promotes children's metacognition within their play experiences. Critical thinking about curriculum and pedagogy can promote analysis and discourse, supporting a search for new understandings and self-awareness, allowing legitimate engagement with different perspectives (Kilderry, 2004). Educators need to engage with their curriculum and pedagogy and reflect on their practice through participating in ongoing professional development (Brock, 2009). Keeping up to date with the developments in knowledge, empirical research, practice and policy is important. It is stimulating for the profession of early years educators that the field is now informed by respected researchers. As Wood (2007: 309) indicates there are 'interesting challenges' from 'new methodological approaches and theoretical frameworks' about the role and value of play (see also Chapter 2).

Sharing practice and thinking with others can contextualize thinking and develop a supportive culture of critical friends. My research was stimulated by the concerns of EYEs attending in-service modules in the late 1990s. They believed that their teaching expertise and professional knowledge about early years education were being confronted and undermined by government policies (Brock, 2006). This caused them disequilibrium because the values and beliefs that informed their practice were being questioned and, as Moyles (2001) indicates, they found it difficult to counter the political demands for achieving targets. The EYEs who joined my continuing professional development programme had done so to reflect on, further develop and articulate their professional knowledge and practice. The climate of the course enabled professional discussions about those educators' (teachers' and nursery nurses') practices and play provision. While these discussions were supportive, they also involved challenges to thinking in order to develop understanding, accountability and articulation of practice to critical audiences of other teachers and head teachers, OfSTED inspectors and parents. As well as reviewing the 'what' and 'how', these professionals also needed to address the 'why'

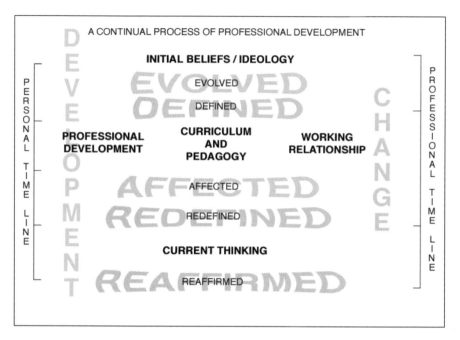

Figure 3.1 Cycle of continuing personal and professional development.

through a continual process of reaffirming and reaccommodating their ideology through reflecting on their values, beliefs and knowledge. This cycle of continuing personal and professional development can be seen in a model derived from research on professionalism with EYEs (Figure 3.1).

Reflection within a climate of policy change

Since the 1970s, EYEs have experienced numerous changes in policy and a range of prescriptive frameworks that have varyingly caused some educators to feel destabilized and have their beliefs and values undermined. Historically, EYEs have not been particularly articulate or assertive enough in justifying and promoting their beliefs and ideologies. According to Anning (2002) the professional knowledge of early years practitioners was often tacit and rarely exposed to public scrutiny. The ongoing changes in educational policy have been effective in improving practice through developments in knowledge and training and through educators, such as my research participants, engaging in Schön's (1987) reflection *in* and *on* practice, as they translated policy into practice.

EYEs broadly welcomed the introduction of the *Curriculum Guidance for the Foundation Stage (CGFS)* (QCA/DfES, 2000) because it acknowledged the importance and value of play. The affirmation of teaching and learning through a play-based pedagogy was seen as reclaiming important principles and practice (Anning et al., 2004; Edgington, 2004). The teachers in Keating et al.'s (2002) study were relieved and felt they could return openly to 'sound' early years practice that some had felt had been undermined by previous curriculum guidance. However, early years pedagogy is a complex phenomenon comprising a wide variety of practices and, while the *CGFS* stated what a practitioner needed to do, most statements referred to the curriculum and a number were actually pedagogically ambiguous (Moyles et al., 2002). The requirements of the *CGFS* were, therefore, over-optimistic for some EYEs, as there were expectations of them having a high level of subject and pedagogic knowledge (Siraj-Blatchford et al., 2002). Tensions about the policy documents continued with the introduction of the *Early Years Foundation Stage (EYFS)* (DfES, 2007). Moss (2006: 5) finds the *EYFS* to be highly prescriptive with 'over 1500 pieces of specific advice', a technical manual with 'no democratic space'.

Moss (2006) suggests practitioners need to be knowledgeable and confident about the provision of play-based pedagogy in order that they do not become technicians. This is why a depth and breadth of understanding of a pedagogy of play is important and why ongoing reflection, debate and research needs to continue in order to promote understanding of the potential of play and how it can be harnessed for young children's learning (Brock, 2009). This is where reflection-*on*-reflection on play makes a difference for educators who desire self-accountability through wanting to develop and move play provision forward. As each major curriculum development has been introduced, educators may have had to radically change practice to work in different ways, and if they have not been trained appropriately, it can be an 'unfamiliar and challenging territory' (Edgington, 2004: 81).

Examples of contemporary research into reflection-*on*-reflection on play

There is doubt as to whether educators and policy-makers sufficiently recognize and include play activities that capitalize on the complexity of learning potential in young children (Broadhead, 2006). This research illustrates the complex learning processes young children are able to engage in through play. Broadhead's (2004) continuum informs adult–child dialogues and supports post-observation practitioner reflection. She established a climate of experimentation, exploration and even risk-taking for the teachers involved in her research. There were challenges for the teachers both in allowing the children to sustain and develop their play but also in observing the play to recognize, qualify and quantify the play themes and the level of sociability and co-operation in the children's relationships. The research team undertook paired post-observation reflections using the social play continuum that promoted critical engagement of play through reflection-*on*-action. The post-project discussions revealed insights and surprises and enabled the sharing of a broader perspective in children's learning with parents. Through these processes of reflection-*on*-reflection on play, the teachers' confidence developed, enabling them to defend and articulate the complexity of play and introduce new approaches and strategies into their teaching repertoires.

Until recently using video cameras for stimulated recall as a research instrument has been limited and underused in professional development (Leat, 2004). Moyles et al. (2003) found the use of video for reflection-*on*-practice to be a successful strategy for eliciting more enhanced thinking and articulation than standard interviewing methods. Each practitioner controlled the focus and pace of the dialogues and identified discrete pedagogical episodes from the video. This meant that the pedagogy became highly contextualized and the reflective dialogue became a useful tool for drawing out practitioners' deeper reflections and perceptions of their pedagogy.

Adams' (2005) research examines whether reflective practitioners think deeply about playful practice at philosophical, ethical or political levels. Her research project comprised five stages – review of past practice; confrontation of issues; conceptualization; deconstruction and reconstruction. The research resulted in an enhanced sense of self-efficacy for the nine participants who began to think differently about themselves and their professional roles. They believed they were becoming more effective practitioners and stated how they were 'discovering knowledge forgotten' and 'able to do things never thought possible about themselves' (Adams, 2005: 226).

Reflection-*on*-reflection on play can occur through introspective thinking, informal chats, conversations with colleagues; online discussions; writing academic essays; digital or paper portfolios; video-reflective dialogues.

What are the most effective ways of eliciting reflection-*on*-reflection?

Strategies for eliciting thinking on play

Reflection can be an exhilarating journey (Bolton, 2005) and this section aims to demonstrate some of the elements of the reflective journeys of some EYEs. Several 'methodologies' have been used to gain these reflections-*on*-pedagogy and so elicit these practitioners' reflective thinking and professional knowledge. In the role of researcher, I use semi-structured interviews and video-reflective dialogues but, as a lecturer, assessment is the means of elicitation through assignments. These are focused on the quality provision of play and personal/professional reflective portfolios with postgraduates.

Video-reflective dialogues

Bennett et al.'s (1997) 'stimulated reflection-*on*-action post-video interviews' and Moyles et al.'s (2003) 'video-stimulated reflective dialogues' proved to be effective ways of eliciting thinking about pedagogy and practice. I simulated practitioners' strategies through effecting 'video-reflective dialogues' with a sample of my respondents to elicit their thinking on an aspect of their practice that held specific interest for them. Several of them used a palm-corder to monitor their provision and practice and to reflect on how it met both individual and groups of children's needs. The following is an extract of a video-reflective dialogue from Najma, a Gujerati-speaking nursery nurse, working in a Foundation Stage setting where 98 per cent of the children speak English as an additional language. Najma and her teacher were making changes to their practice building on knowledge and experience of the children's home backgrounds, previous experiences and language needs. They had decided to provide free play for the children at the beginning of the day and Najma decided to make this the focus of her video-making to determine its effectiveness.

> Using the palm-corder really challenged my thinking. When the children come into school there are a lot of activities set up for them – play dough, sand and the home corner are on-going and we alternate the painting experiences. They choose for 30 minutes . . . but we often pull them to work saying 'Come and do this, come and do that'. We thought some of the children just floated and wandered but actually they are playing purposefully. When I observed through the camera as I was videoing, I realised they are engaging in one activity before they go on to the next; they are making appropriate choices and talking to each other in Punjabi discussing what they were doing . . . That morning there was catalogue pictures to cut and they didn't choose that at all, they obviously didn't find that stimulating enough, they were bored with it . . . Look Fatima's still doing the jigsaw and she's persevered and communicating; she keeps asking for reassurance from the student. The video is very good; it's much easier than just observing. We could use it once a week and then sit back and evaluate it. I've seen so much more of Fatima through the video as it shows that she can concentrate for periods.

Through watching the video Najma determined that (in this video extract) the children's play was focused as they moved around the setting selecting from a range of activities. Najma demonstrates how she is able to challenge her expectations and address her preconceptions about practice and assumptions about individual children. She reflected on issues surrounding bilingualism; use of observations and children's involvement in play and learning. She reflected on her team's pedagogical approaches and pedagogical framing

(Wood and Attfield, 2005). Najma is an experienced observer having participated in the *Effective Early Learning Project* for two years (Pascal and Bertram, 1997) but still found there was much more she could do to develop her reflection-on-practice.

Essays reflecting on the quality of play

For reflective thinking to be effective, we need to immerse ourselves in doing it through writing or talking rather than reading or following instructions (Bolton, 2005). The following examples are extracts from essays written by postgraduate students studying an MA in Early Years Education. The module required them to reflect on their understanding of quality provision in the early years. The students had to select their own focus and these included: effective provision for a child with Chinese as his first language; appropriate resources and activities for an autistic child in after-school provision; and the learning journeys of a group of Year 1 children accessing a new area of play provision. The following examples are from two of these essays.

Example 1: Rachael

The play provision that Rachael felt was least accessed was the small world area, which had recently been moved from a very prominent position to a more enclosed space in her classroom. This concerned her as she believed the children needed space to develop their ideas and work collaboratively. In an assignment for her master's degree she decided to research this area to reflect on quality provision of play. Her observations indicated that the children liked the smaller area, but they used it for relaxing and quiet time rather than for the small world play. Rachael undertook an audit of equipment as she realized that, though it was aesthetically pleasing, there was obviously something that did not attract the children. She decided to track how the children were using the area to determine how she could improve it. During one day only 4 out of 47 children used the area – two within the context of the theme being promoted and two using the equipment for their own agenda. She then decided to introduce a new theme of safari and gave the children the autonomy to prescribe the equipment and resources. Over a three-week period she undertook detailed observations targeting different learning opportunities and challenges. By the end of the third week Rachael found that the children used the new resources within storylines and their role play and that the children's imagination and writing had really developed through playing in the area. This research enabled Rachael to reflect-*on*-action to develop quality play provision and realize that she needed to continue to reflect on learning opportunities that challenged and involved the children.

Example 2: Vikki

Vikki undertook observations focused on her lower ability group and determined that each child tended to play in the same area. She decided that she needed to harness the children's interests to further develop their learning through integrating the resources and through promoting theme-based learning. Researching and writing for an assignment she reflected that she found the balancing of her values and beliefs with statutory demands to be difficult.

> As a newly qualified teacher I am feeling the pressure to achieve academic results in school. I feel torn by this – do I give more support to the lower ability group so that the average result in class will be higher or do I let the children play and develop at their own rate, as I believe they should? Research shows that I am not the only one to feel this 'tension between children having time to play and teachers having time to teach' (Santere et al., 2007). I certainly feel I have the ability and duty to change my own practice but not to influence and change school practice . . . This is where reflective teaching is essential, as I need to review my practice to see if what I am doing now achieves the same aims and outcomes as I originally intended . . . I feel the e-profile does not celebrate achievements, particularly for children who struggle, but rather points out areas for development. Keeping my early years practice play-based is extremely important to me and not something I am willing to negotiate, especially if targets and tick-boxes are the option given to me by the government. What this assignment has taught me is that I have a responsibility to these children to ensure they are unaffected by formal assessment processes and able to have activities that interest them, to encourage and recognise their achievements, allowing them to work independently.

Vikki proved herself to be a very thoughtful practitioner and she raised challenging issues in her assignment writing. They were proving to be valuable vehicles for her reflection-on-action as she met different situations as a newly qualified teacher.

Personal, professional reflective practice portfolios

The construction of professional portfolios has become standard practice in continuous professional development but to be truly worthwhile it needs to be more than just documentation and evidence. The *Personal,*

Professional Reflective Practice module on the MA Early Years requires an assessment of a reflective portfolio, which could include varied writing activities of reflecting on life histories, examining professional experiences, exploring academic thinking and analysing critical incidents. Some of the newly qualified teachers (NQTs) excel in this area. Here are two examples from their reflective portfolios:

Example 1: Liz

> Most teachers reflect without necessarily knowing they are doing it: it can be an unconscious, on-going process . . . As an NQT I have spent a lot of time reflecting-on-action about what has happened in my first term of teaching. I have used diaries to reflect on what has happened and set myself targets for the next week/term. I have also reflected on critical incidents and analysed how I have approached these events and what improvements I could have made. My reflections have developed much more from the first diary entry to my reflection on the second half of the autumn term. I have now started to involve the children in my reflections, asking them what they thought about the activities and also what they would like to do in future sessions. In this way, I aim to develop my belief in promoting an ethos where children are encouraged to take control of their own learning.

Liz acknowledged that reflective writing can be time-consuming if she did it thoroughly, but she believed it to be worthwhile. She found that the work in her reflective portfolio not only gave her success in the module and, ultimately, her Masters degree and contributed to her NQT assessments, but also developed her thinking and practice enabling her to become accountable to colleagues.

Example 2: Aishah

Aishah organized her portfolio into three sections – autobiographical writing, critical incidents and reflective journaling. Within each of these sections she explored a range of different writing techniques. She reflected on her father telling Sudanese stories in Arabic to her and her twin sister and how these stimulated her to use traditional African stories in her teaching to get children to appreciate different characters and events. Later in the portfolio, Aishah used 'critical incidence' theory to reflect on and analyse the following experience that she entitled 'Racism in the classroom':

> I was playing with some small world figures and toys on the floor with a 4-year-old boy in reception class . . . The small world figures were of different races and within the selection there was a

black family. The boy was playing with the dolls and I joined him. I picked up the grandfather figure from the black family. The boy started attacking the grandfather with another figure and nearly broke the figure. I questioned him about this and he said. 'I don't like black people.' I asked him why not and he answered with, 'I don't like them. My mummy says they don't speak English.' I told the boy that this was not true, that people speak different languages and that black people do speak English. He then looked at me because I am of mixed race (black African and white English) and he seemed confused. He was then taken by a teacher to another class and I did not have the chance to say anything else to him.

Aishah wrote at length about the incident. She reflected on her feelings at the time, as she had been shocked, disappointed, sad and frustrated that a 4-year-old had already gained prejudiced and racist ideas. Reflecting on it afterwards, she had been annoyed that she was unable to continue to work with the boy. The interconnection between personal and professional aspects was evidenced, as the incident reminded her of an experience from her own school days as well as others encountered as a student teacher. The experience was critical because she did not feel that she had dealt with the incident effectively and did not inform staff or parents. Aishah stated she has further developed her learning and practice about how young children can acquire racist views, the implications for teachers and the importance of policy and practice. She examined ways of promoting tolerance and respect for racial equality through the provision and use of resources that encourage playful learning and positive imaging of people of different races, engaging in ongoing personal research relevant to her professional practice.

Conclusion

This chapter has advocated engaging in reflection-*on*-reflection – in particular reflection-*on*-reflection on play. The three different methodologies have provided a forum for EYEs to engage in reflecting on their reflections through talking to or writing for an interested external person (myself as researcher or lecturer). These following benefits from the process include:

- developing an understanding of how to critically analyse play;
- deepening thinking through becoming more skilful in reflecting – improve through doing it;

- further developing knowledge of research and theory applied to personal practice;
- promoting change in practice and developing effective play provision that meets children's needs;
- enhancing children's play experiences through understanding how to improve scaffolding of their learning and metacognition within play;
- promoting confidence in teaching, and so increasing job satisfaction, as children learn and achieve;
- endorsing personal success, promoting professional accomplishments through an ongoing personal professional learning journey;
- facilitating articulation and advocacy through sharing knowledge of effective practice.

What do you think about now in relation to your playful pedagogy? You might find yourself experiencing Fook and Gardner's (2007: ix) metaphors of 'exciting walks; dark alleys; bright lights; shadowy mazes; exciting doorways and thorny bushes'.

Be aware of Bolton's (2005) three foundations:

1   certainty uncertainty – acknowledge that you do not know everything;
2   serious playfulness – experiment and perhaps even take risks in provision;
3   unquestioning questioning – that questions give rise to more questions.

There may be tensions arising from your reflection-*on*-reflection with others; whether it is because an academic tutor or an external assessor is assessing your work; whether you are having to justify changes to a line manager or whether you are just finding it hard to articulate your ideas. Remember it will get easier the more you do, as it becomes a natural reflective process. Figure 3.2 gives a diagrammatic view of the process of reflection-*on*-reflection.

Your process of reflection-*on*-reflection can take the form of a continuous learning journey and, in this way, will not only continue to enhance your provision of play but also promote feelings of personal and professional accomplishment and enhance job satisfaction, as your provision and children's achievements grow in quality. Enjoy the process and watch the children (and you) reap the benefits!

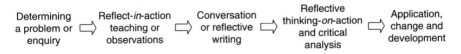

Figure 3.2   The process of reflection-*on*-reflection.

What do I, the writer, feel about the contribution of this chapter to supporting critical reflection?

By giving practitioners the opportunity to reflect through video-stimulated dialogues, I was able to engage with them in deeper levels of thinking, evidenced in their learning portfolios. In turn, their reflections and my subsequent reflections on those reflections helped me better to understand the practitioners and their different, but equally effective, practices. I have learned much through the process of reflecting with these students and on my own contribution to their reflection.

Implications for pedagogy: what might *you*, the reader, reflect on now?

1 When do you undertake reflection on your practice?
2 Do you share your reflections with others? Do you write them down? How does this help?
3 How do you go about 'deep questioning' of your practice in the way described in this chapter?
4 What difference do the outcomes of your reflections make to children's play and curriculum experiences in your setting? What about your pedagogy?

References and further reading

Adams, S. (2005) Practitioners and play: reflecting in a different way, in J. Moyles (ed.) *The Excellence of Play*, 2nd edn. Maidenhead: Open University Press.

Anning, A. (2002) Paper two: Investigating the impact of working in integrated service delivery settings on early years practitioners' professional knowledge and practice: strategies for dealing with controversial issues. Paper presented at the Annual Conference of the British Educational Research Association, University of Exeter, 12–14 September.

Anning, A., Cullen, J. and Fleer, M. (2004) *Early Childhood Education*. London: Sage Publications.

Bennett, N., Wood, L. and Rogers, S. (1997) *Teaching Through Play: Teachers Thinking and Classroom Practice*. Buckingham: Open University Press.

Bolton, G. (2005) *Reflective Practice: Writing and Professional Development*. London: Sage Publications.

Broadhead, P. (2004) *Early Years Play and Learning: Developing Social Skills and Cooperation*. London: RoutledgeFalmer.

Broadhead, P. (2006) Developing an understanding of young children's learning through play: the place of observation, interaction and reflection, *British Educational Research Journal*, 32: 191–207.

Brock, A. (2006) Dimensions of early years professionalism – attitudes versus competences? Reflecting on Early Years Issues – paper on *Training Advancement and Co-operation in the Teaching of Young Children (TACTYC)* website. Available online at www.tactyc.org.uk (accessed 14 July 2009).

Brock, A. (2009) Curriculum and pedagogy of play – a multitude of perspectives?, in A. Brock, S. Dodds, P. Jarvis and Y. Olusoga (2009) *Perspectives on Play: Learning for Life*. London: Pearson Education.

Brock, A., Dodds, S., Jarvis, P. and Olusoga, Y. (2009) *Perspectives on Play: Learning for Life*. London: Pearson Education.

Department for Education and Skills (DfES) (2007) *The Early Years Foundation Stage*. Nottingham: DfES Publications.

Edgington, M. (2004) *The Foundation Stage Teacher in Action: Teaching 3, 4 and 5 Year Olds*. London: Paul Chapman.

Eraut, M. (1994) *Developing Professional Knowledge and Competence*. London: RoutledgeFalmer.

Fook, J. and Gardner, F. (2007) *Practising Critical Reflection: A Resource Handbook*. Maidenhead: Open University Press.

Forde, C., McMahon, M., McPhee, A. and Patrick, F. (2006) *Professional Development, Reflection and Enquiry*. London: Sage Publications.

Hughes, A. and Menmuir, J. (2002) Being a student on a part-time early years degree, *Early Years: Journal of International Research and Development*, 22(1): 147–61.

Keating, I., Basford, J., Hodson, E. and Harnett, A. (2002) Reception teacher responses to the Foundation Stage, *International Journal of Early Years Education*, 10: 193–203.

Kilderry, A. (2004) Critical pedagogy: a useful framework for thinking about early childhood curriculum, *Australian Journal of Early Childhood*, 29: 33–7.

Leat, S.J. (2004) Enhancing spatial information by digital image processing – does it increase visibility for people with vision loss? Paper presented at York University, England.

Moon, J. (2004) *A Handbook of Reflective and Experiential Learning*. London: Routledge.

Moss, P. (2006) Structures, understandings and discourses: possibilities for re-envisioning the early childhood worker, *Contemporary Issues in Early Childhood*, 7: 30–41.

Moyles, J. (2001) Passion, paradox and professionalism in early years education, *Early Years: Journal of International Research and Development*, 21: 81–95.

Moyles, J., Adams, S. and Musgrove, A. (2002) *SPEEL: Study of Pedagogical Effectiveness in Early Learning*. London: DfES Research Report 363.

Moyles, J., Hargreaves, L., Merry, R., Patterson, F. and Esarte-Saries, V. (2003)

Interactive Teaching in the Primary School: Digging Deeper into Meanings. Maidenhead: Open University Press.

Paige Smith, A. and Craft, A. (2008) *Developing Reflective Practice in the Early Years*. Maidenhead: Oxford University Press.

Pascal, C. and Bertram, T. (1997) *Effective Early Learning: Case Studies in Improvement*. London: Hodder & Stoughton.

Qualifications and Curriculum Authority (QCA) and Department for Education and Skills (DfES) (2000) *Curriculum Guidance for the Foundation Stage*. London: DfES.

Schön, D. (1987) *Educating the Reflective Practitioner*. San Francisco, CA: Jossey-Bass, Inc.

Siraj-Blatchford, I., Sylva, K., Muttock, S., Gilden, R. and Bell, D. (2002) *Researching Effective Pedagogy in the Early Years*. London: DfES, Research Report No. 356.

Wood, E. (2004) Developing a pedagogy of play, in A. Anning, J. Cullen and M. Fleer (eds) *Early Childhood Education*. London: Sage Publication.

Wood, E. (2007) New directions in play: consensus or collision? *Education 3–13*, 35(4): 309–20.

Wood, E. and Attfield, J. (2005) *Play, Learning and the Early Years Curriculum*, 2nd edn. London: Paul Chapman.

4 Play and a constructivist approach to literacy learning

Comparing settings in Norway and England

Pat Beckley

Summary

The chapter explores reflections of practice concerning approaches to play, focused on early years literacy in settings in Norway and England. It describes the issues that led to reflective practice, followed by discussions of international recommendations and theoretical perspectives. The subsequent research and initial findings from the case studies are given and differing strategies reflecting the approaches in their environmental context are described. Considerations of challenges faced by practitioners when implementing different approaches are discussed, with questions posed for further reflection.

Key questions as you read . . .

1   How would you define the different approaches to play and literacy learning in England and Norway outlined in this chapter?
2   Are international recommendations in evidence in early years literacy policies and play practices in settings in England and Norway?
3   What challenges are faced by the practitioners in both countries who are trying to implement the policies?

. . . and points to consider

•   How international recommendations may have influenced the formulation of national policies.

- How approaches to play reflect the curriculum and cultural context in which they are placed.
- Interpretation of national policy frameworks has to be of concern to early years practitioners. It is these people, in their complex roles, who will have an impact on the quality of the implementation of the curriculum frameworks.

Introduction

Dahlberg describes change as the 'movement from one epoch to another' (Dahlberg et al., 2006: 176). Issues happening on an international scale impact on the lives of individuals throughout the world, including shared understandings and reflections on the most appropriate ways to facilitate; in my case, play-based literacy learning. Rui claims that:

> An increasing duality has become evident. On the one hand, the way the policy is made is highly contextualized and its implementation even more context-dependent; and on the other hand, policy travels globally and has profound impact in locations far removed from its origins.
>
> (cited in Bray et al., 2007: 241)

This chapter explores and reflects on approaches to early years literacy in settings in Lincolnshire (England) and Hedmark (Norway). It sets these approaches in the context of international policies and different governments' interpretations of them. Findings from observed practice are discussed, which highlight different rationales for incorporating 'playful' literacies and pedagogies into early years practice.

Background

In my earlier teaching career, there was much debate in the setting where I was leader/manager, about the most appropriate ways of supporting young children's literacy learning and development. Along with my immediate colleagues, I was determined to provide the best possible literacy foundations for the children as this was a particular concern for all schools in that locality. But how should we do this? There were national policies and guidelines giving broad indications of what should be covered but how should we most effectively implement these guidelines? Reflecting on these questions led us into various discussions and arguments as there were differing views from colleagues, particularly in other age phases, about what children should be doing.

These views demonstrated a range of perspectives from 'Just leave them to it' to 'Make them work' or 'Don't let them scribble – wait until they're ready, then teach them to write properly'. Conversations with early years colleagues in settings in our area echoed similar dilemmas.

The play-based pedagogy promoted in our setting was based on adult-led activities where an outcome of the learning or activity was apparent; for example, a piece of emergent writing. This formal, instructivist approach contrasted with the approaches used by colleagues visiting the area from Norway, who described how they enabled children to construct their own learning through access to the outdoor natural environment. The approach to early years literacy they described was in stark contrast to our own, yet both groups of professionals felt they were implementing play-based activities for the children.

International policies

It is likely that both groups of early years practitioners were being influenced by international considerations. Contemporary forces in Norway and England have certainly impacted on early years provision and pedagogy. Popkewitz and Block (cited in Kennedy, 2006: 299) suggest that 'the significant driver for early education . . . is a desire to ensure that institutions, like kindergartens and schools, help to produce global citizens or workers through the sanctioning of universalised norms and best practices'.

Colleagues from both countries followed national guidelines influenced by international policy statements promoting universalized best practice ideals. Internationalization appears in literature regarding the early years (Dahlberg and Moss, 2007; Lauder et al., 2008) in relation to the need to prepare children for the future. There is an awareness of the desire to maintain and sustain economic viability, as demonstrated in the G20 meeting in London in April 2009, where leaders of countries met to decide strategies to deal with the current world recession. Political and economic uncertainty helps to drive reflections concerning the purpose of curricula provision for young children, including a spectrum of views ranging from whether young children should be subjected to a narrow curriculum focus as a means to gain specific skills or be subject to a broader curriculum emphasizing childhood as a special period in its own right (Anning, 2010). No doubt we have all reflected on this at various times!

In international policy statements, such as those from the United Nations Educational, Scientific and Cultural Organization (UNESCO), the Organisation for Economic Co-operation and Development (OECD), the World Bank and the European Commission, the promotion of literacy skills as part of children's development is often paramount; for example, the European

Commission include the development of children's linguistic and oral skills in their educational philosophy. A holistic approach is recommended where literacy is developed in all areas of learning through play and playful learning and teaching (see Chapter 1). The approach should also be responsive to the literacy needs of children as individuals and be concerned with other areas of their progress such as physical, emotional (see Estelle Martin, Chapter 6) and intellectual development.

Literacy as a crucial skill

One of the United Nations' (UN's) Millennium Development Goals is to achieve Universal Primary Education for all children by 2015. The UN stresses the need for skills in literacy that will allow individuals to 'function within society' (Lauder et al., 2008: 3). The 'effects of globalization on the world of employment has resulted in new work patterns . . . and has produced a new set of demands on the literacies we need to function adequately in an environment of global connectedness' (Sutherland et al., 2003: 19).

Against a background of global competition for jobs, literacy is a crucial skill where, Johnson claims, 'different countries have responded to the "literary crisis" by adopting strategies to raise attainment' (cited in Sutherland et al., 2003: 19). The desire to ensure children attain high standards of literacy fosters the development of different pedagogical strategies in settings in which children are placed in order to secure this aim, some more playful than others.

Insights into how children become literate has expanded greatly following research on literacy skills 'which draws attention to the ways in which children's later achievement in literacy in school is linked to wider early literacy experiences, such as parents pointing out environmental print and the number of nursery rhymes known' (BERA, 2005: 28; Whitehead, 2010). Research focusing on language learning and development has also been a factor; for example, Trevarthen's (1995) work on early language development. Whatever the research, practitioners tend to adopt their own practices while endeavouring to fulfil national requirements.

A holistic approach to learning and literacy

There are many views regarding the most appropriate ways to ensure literacy learning in young children. International policy statements highlight a broad, holistic approach towards such learning:

> . . . holistic ideology values the whole child and endeavours to understand each young child as an individual within the context of his or

her family, community and culture. With this approach, professionals endeavour to be sensitive and responsive to all of a child's needs and aspects of development – that is, physical, intellectual, social, emotional, cultural, moral and spiritual.

(Woods, 2005: x)

Petrie (2005: 294) suggests 'there is a growing awareness of the "whole" child or young person, rather than the child as the output of the formal curriculum'. To enable individuals to cope with future challenges, skills such as self-reliance and creative thinking are also necessary (Bancroft et al., 2008). This inner resourcefulness enables individuals to access new technologies and innovations, while having the social skills to disseminate them and work with others. Lifelong learning is part of this process.

Holistic approaches represent laudable aims. However, there are different interpretations as to how a holistic approach can be achieved. Vadeboncoeur (cited in Richardson, 1997: 15) states that 'throughout the twentieth century, two competing views of child development have prevailed'. One is the importance of educating 'the individual child in a manner which supports the child's interests and needs', while a second concerns a 'social transformation and the reconstruction of society aligned with democratic ideals'. These differences influence how a holistic approach could be implemented, as does the prevailing view of childhood.

Waller (2005: 59) suggests 'There are multiple and diverse childhoods and in order to study childhood one has to consider a range of perspectives'. Over a number of years, theorists have proffered a range of views on childhood learning and development. *Nativism* stems from the belief that a child has innate capabilities and that children learn from an appropriate environment (see Miller et al., 2009). This emphasizes the need for a stimulating learning environment to encourage the development of children's abilities through their engagement and inquisitiveness in their surroundings. *Empiricism* incorporates the notion of children being rather more passive in their learning with practitioners delivering learning through an appropriately devised curriculum and environment. This includes an instructivist approach with an emphasis 'on preparing for school and focusing on literacy . . . aiming for equality of educational opportunity and the means to improve later education' (McQuail et al., 2003: 14). She continues, this approach is used 'where early childhood services for children 3–6 are seen as the initial stage of schooling'. *Instructivism* implies that children should be instructed in predetermined facts to enable them to progress in their learning. To me, overriding all these is constructivism.

In a *constructivist* approach, early childhood is seen as a stage in its own right, with children viewed as competent learners and co-constructors of their learning: this view is part of the ideology of many early years practitioners (e.g. Bruce, 2005). Constructivism:

acknowledges that children are born with cognitive capabilities and potential, and each child constructs his/her own knowledge and develops through cognitive activity in interaction with the environment. Children create their own meaning and understanding, combining what they already know and believe to be true with new experiences.

(Woods, 2005: 5)

In addition, *social constructivism* highlights the need for children to use social interactions with their peers and adults to formulate constructions of their world and develop concepts (Vygotsky, 1978).

The inclusion in, and pursuit of, one of these learning theories in early years settings has major implications for literacy learning and child development. Through a devised strategy, a child gains an understanding of the world in which he or she is located. Therefore, the strategies used in the setting are crucial to the ways in which children are likely to respond to the world around them (see Chapter 5). I have to agree with Brannen and Moss (2003: 37) who state 'Young children are viewed as active subjects with rights and voice, members of a social group and located both in the family and the wider society'.

Munton argues that 'There can be no general formula for . . . universal best practice. There can only be particular choices situated within particular contexts' (cited in Moss et al., 2003: 7). This suggests international recommendations need to be disseminated and implemented according to the contexts of early years provision. Rui argues 'There is a dialect at work by which these global processes interact with national and local actors and contexts to be modified and transformed' (cited in Bray et al., 2007: 253).

We must, however, recognize that policies from international organizations or different countries' practices cannot be transferred from one culture to another because of varying background conditions. Values and beliefs of local communities will impact on policies and practices that will evolve according to the requirements of the locality. Rui highlighted the research by Bowe et al. (1992) that revealed 'Practitioners interpret policy with their own histories, values, and purposes' (cited in Bray et al., 2007: 250). The context of where the policies are placed will be considered in relation to early years settings in Hedmark (Norway) and Lincolnshire (England).

The Norwegian context

The population of Norway is about 4.5 million, about 500 000 of whom live in the capital, Oslo. Seventy-four per cent of the total population live in towns or built-up areas; the remainder live in areas of scattered populations

(OECD, 2006: 11). According to *Equity in Education* (OECD, 2006: 11) 'Norway is a rich country with one of the highest gross domestic products per capita in the world. The unemployment rate in 2004 was only 4.7%.' However, in the early 1990s neo-liberal deregulation of the credit market resulted in the Norwegian socialist government having to take over or support three of the largest banks in Norway. Broadhead (2001: 21) argues:

> In communities increasingly fearful for their own economic viability, the construct of educational freedom becomes aligned with the need to be economically self-sufficient, rather than with the right to contribute to the design of one's own learning experiences.

Children need to be able to learn to deal with the demands of the future in a challenging environment. By 2003, 48 per cent of children were attending Barnehager (my research kindergarten) full time and a further 21 per cent attended on a part-time basis. The OECD (2006: 12) review for Norway in 2004 highlighted the Norwegian government's assertion that 'everyone in the country should have the opportunity to participate in – and influence – the development of a knowledge economy'. The framework for learning in early years settings moved to a design ensuring children were provided with the skills needed.

Kamerman suggests 'Historically "child care" and "pre-school" have evolved as separate systems' (cited in Neuman, 2005: 132). Norwegian early years settings developed from a basis of care, while English settings have always had a strong educational element where education was seen as serving intellectual needs, and care as serving physical and emotional needs. Recently, this has appeared an unnatural divide and both elements are incorporated into early childhood education and care (ECEC) practices. According to Mooney and Munton (1997) 'it is now widely acknowledged that education begins at birth and separating education and care is no longer sensible' (cited in McQuail et al., 2003: 14).

In a report for the OECD, the key features of Norwegian provision are outlined as:

- the child as a subject of rights: autonomy, well-being. The child is a member of a caring community. An outdoors child of pleasure and freedom. A time for childhood that can never be repeated;
- community and parental interests with no pressure placed on children;
- a broad national guideline;
- focus on working with the whole child;
- confidence is placed in the child's own learning strategies and centres of interest;

- growing confidence in the national language;
- broad orientations rather than prescribed outcomes;
- the environment and its protection is an important theme;
- formal assessment not required;
- quality control based on educator and team responsibility.

(OECD, 2006: 141)

The accepted importance of care has a crucial part in the formulation of early years provision in Norway. Dahlberg et al. (2006: 39) suggest 'care, as an ethic, has an important influence on how the project of education is conceptualised and practised'. It is reflected in the broad, developmental approach used in Norway, where care for the child as a holistic strategy is accepted. 'Norway is the only OECD country where child poverty can be described as very low and continuing to fall' (UNICEF, 2005: 4). Children who live in families below the poverty line account for 3.4 per cent in 2005, the third lowest rate in OECD countries, behind Denmark and Finland. Clarke and Waller (2007: 7) identify key features of the provision including a holistic approach to caring, upbringing and learning; a resistance to sequential discipline-based learning, cognitive skills and school readiness; a disapproval of testing and assessments that rank young children; the primacy of play (see Photograph 4.1).

Norwegian early years provision is based on a social constructivist approach where early childhood is a stage in its own right (Photograph 4.2). Children are seen as competent agents of their own learning, co-constructing knowledge through dialogue with practitioners. This goes alongside an approach integrating age groups of children from birth to 6 years with groupings across ages for at least part of the time. Well-trained adults scaffold children's learning, while 'appropriate interventions are various and require discrimination and professional discretion' (McQuail et al., 2003: 15). Children take risks in their play, learning from their own mistakes and finding out what they are capable of doing and what their next steps might be. Adults in the setting observe and support when invited by the children. Practitioners use their professional judgement to organize and manage the facility, to work as part of a team to devise access to an appropriate environment to promote children's development and construction of learning.

Research into the Norwegian approach to early years literacy learning began in 2004 in Hedmark where I observed daily routines from six settings – the outdoor natural environment was the young children's main learning resource. Children constructed their own meanings through the natural environment while interacting with their peers and adults to construct new meanings about the world around them. They observed the changing seasons, worked with natural materials and found a growing awareness of their place in the natural world, how they could be part of it and use it productively, for

Photograph 4.1   Children practise their communication skills at lunchtime after helping to cook their meal.

example, to make bird boxes and help wild life in the locality. Children developed their language through exploration and interactions with others. This promoted cognitive development and appreciation of the uses of language, supporting their understanding of the patterns, rules and constructs of written forms.

In 2006, Norway introduced a national framework for early years literacy. This incorporated a specific literacy area of learning where practitioners were required to implement strands of guidelines. There was a mixed response from the practitioners in the settings. Most were unsure of the requirements and how the implementation would work in practice, as the previous guidelines were broad and allowed for practitioners to use their own judgement in providing appropriate resources and facilities for the children in their care as shown above. One practitioner interviewed stated that the proposals would not allow practitioners to have the freedom to choose what was best for their children, while another felt the new framework was a positive initiative as all settings would cover similar requirements that would support children moving between settings and help schools to have a better understanding of aspects covered in children's learning. Many practitioners used

Photograph 4.2 A group of children plan and make their den in the forest.

their knowledge of children constructing their own social literacy learning but added more formal activities to this, either as small group activities in the kindergartens or as interactions with adults outdoors. Practice was changed to accommodate the new government requirements.

The English context

Jensen (2009) argues that the Norwegian model is very different from the structured programmes in England. She suggests that '. . . there are huge differences between the Nordic and the Anglo-Saxon models for Early Childhood Education (ECE) in terms of learning, standards and assessments' (p.13). Solberg also highlights the differences stating 'the two countries differ, for example, in the degree of urbanization: compared to central parts of Britain, Norway can be seen as a collection of villages' (cited in James and Prout, 1997: 130). In 2009, Lincolnshire had a population of some 640 000 of whom around 40 000 were children of 5 years of age or under. With a population in excess of 50 million, England is much larger than Norway and has, arguably, more challenges associated with educating its children, particularly in literacy skills, as the English language is known to be more complex than the Norwegian language (Goswami, 2005).

According to Janzen (2008: 290) in Norway the child is viewed 'as co-constructor of knowledge, identity and culture'. Children can interpret the culture in which they engage in their own ways. In England, Janzen suggests:

> the traditional sociological position of the child as cultural reproducer constructs the child as a relatively passive recipient of socialisation in order to transform the child into an adult . . . and reproduce what society has deemed important.

She also states, 'the child is viewed as a reproducer of knowledge, identity and culture' (p. 290). Children are perceived as 'not there yet', with universal goals of development forming the basis of progression for learning, with a consideration of those who do not conform at risk from failing to achieve prescribed goals.

The OECD publication, *Starting Strong* (2006: 141), notes key features of the English early years system and includes the following curricula traditions:

- The child is a person to be formed.
- An early years centre is a place of development, learning and instruction. Children are expected to reach predetermined goals.
- There is a prescribed ministerial curriculum with goals and outcomes.
- There is a focus on learning and skills, especially in areas of school readiness.
- The national curriculum must be 'delivered' correctly.
- A growing focus on individual competence in the national language. There is an emphasis on emergent literacy practices.
- Prescribed targets are set at a national level.
- Indoors is the primary learning space, with resources focused there.
- Learning outcomes and assessment are required.
- Quality control is evident with inspection undertaken by external regulators.

This approach to learning emphasizes and promotes progression in *cognitive* development rather than in the *holistic* development approach in Norway. Gammage argues that the best possible care and education is 'not about "hot-housing" children, or about forcing them into early academic endeavour' (2006: 241), a sentiment with which I very much agree. The English government's *Children's Plan* (DCSF, 2007: 2) builds on the *Every Child Matters* agenda securing commitment for the welfare and development of children as unique individuals. The *Early Years Foundation Stage* (*EYFS*) framework (statutory from 2008) provides six areas of learning guiding practitioners through children's developmental stages from birth to 5 years of age (DfES, 2007). It is underpinned by a broad remit of four strands including a unique child, positive relationships, enabling environments and learning and development. These broad aims encourage, in principle, a play-based early years learning environment but there is much argument (as we have seen in the Introduction to this book) about the interpretation of these aims, particularly in relation to literacy (see Moyles, 2006; Photograph 4.3).

Children's progress is assessed during the year in which the children are 5 years of age through the *EYFS Profiles* (QCA, 2008). The teacher and the age phase team decide when the child has reached the specific targets within these assessments. The introduction of Letters and Sounds (following the Rose Review, DfES, 2006) provides a developmental approach in a pack of information and activities to use while children are in the early years leading through into primary school. However, Urban (2008: 139) states that 'Early childhood practitioners [have a] contradictory professional context [where] they are expected not only to give children a "good start" but to achieve predetermined, assessable outcomes'. In the sessions observed in the English context, children constructed their knowledge and understanding through adult-led activities but also, increasingly, through child-initiated

Photograph 4.3 Meaningful contexts in the UK for playful literacy.

Photograph 4.4   Children use the outdoor environment to extend their learning.

interests, drawing on an indoor learning environment and the natural outdoor space (see Photograph 4.4) showing some evolving relationship to the Norwegian system.

Many practitioners in England have successfully endeavoured to build on practice with strategies focusing on meaningful contexts for children. Children's independent speaking and listening skills are developed alongside more formal sessions such as whole class and small group adult-led tasks (see Photograph 4.5) but questions remain in some practitioners' minds as to how much learning occurs in child-initiated contexts and there is anxiety about meeting required outcomes by child-oriented means.

English early years practitioners are themselves sharing practice in networks at local, national and, in some cases, at international levels. The interconnected networks for sharing pedagogy provide discussion and reflection points for comparisons of practice that could profoundly affect the nature of play-based learning. As James and Prout (1997: 79) argue 'it would be a mistake to over-estimate these trends towards context sensitivity. They are a ripple against the tidal wave of globalisation'.

Photograph 4.5 Exploring imaginative speaking, listening and writing activities.

Conclusion

While in Norway, socially constructed pedagogy is incorporating the use of adult-led activities as a preparation for children to meet the needs of future schooling, it would seem that English early years practitioners are evolving a more child-initiated practice to attempt to meet the needs of a contemporary society as defined in international policy. Children are encouraged to interact with others and develop their thinking skills, using their whole environment both indoors and outdoors as a place to learn.

Practitioners in Hedmark and Lincolnshire work within different frameworks for children's learning, yet they respond to the needs of the children in their setting, the community and the resources and space available (see Chapter 9). A sharing of pedagogical differences encourages reflective, personal practice and broadens understanding of approaches to the provision of playful literacy and child-initiated activities (see Avril Brock, Chapter 3).

Practitioners are faced with complex challenges in implementing changes and working with others to provide a seamless progression of learning and experiences. According to Laurie 'the number and speed with which new initiatives have been introduced over recent years has made significant demands on practitioners' (cited in Beckley et al., 2009: 12). Through initial observations and discussions in the settings, it is evident that practitioners have the best interests of young children at the heart of their practice and strive to give them strong foundations for positive play and literacy learning experiences.

What do I, the writer, feel about the contribution of this chapter to supporting critical reflection?

The chapter supports reflections on the rationale for approaches to play and playful pedagogies, how aspects of early years literacy are influenced and evolved through international recommendations and how they are interpreted and implemented by those responsible for the children and settings. It considers differing perspectives on approaches to learning, while acknowledging the complex role undertaken by early years professionals. Reflection can be developed through a thorough critique of the pressures on personal practice of implementing local, national and international initiatives. Challenges to thinking are raised through an exploration of comparative contexts.

Implications for pedagogy: what might *you*, the reader, reflect on now?

1   What changes are being made in the provision for play and literacy learning in a setting with which you are familiar?
2   How do these changes benefit the children? And how do you know?
3   What rationales do you know of regarding provision in other settings – in the locality, the county, nationally, in a European context or further afield?
4   Are there aspects of that provision you would like to include in your own practice; for example, more outdoor play? Why? What is your rationale for saying this?

References and further reading

Anning, A. (2010) Play and legislated curriculum, in J. Moyles (ed.) *The Excellence of Play*, 3rd edn. Maidenhead: Open University Press.
Bancroft, S., Fawcett, M. and Hay, P. (2008) *Researching Children Researching the World: 5×5×5=Creativity*. Stoke-on-Trent: Trentham Books.

Beckley, P., Elvidge, K. and Hendry, H. (2009) *Implementing the Early Years Foundation Stage: A Handbook*. Maidenhead: Open University Press.

Bowe, R., Ball, S.J. and Gold, A. (1992) *Reforming Education and Changing Schools: Case Studies in Policy Sociology*. London: Routledge.

Brannen, J. and Moss, P. (2003) *Rethinking Children's Care*. Buckingham: Open University Press.

Bray, M., Adamson, B. and Mason, M. (eds) (2007) *Comparative Education Research*. The University of Hong Kong: Springer Publishing.

British Educational Research Association (BERA) (2005) Early Years Special Interest Group *Early Years Research: Pedagogy, Curriculum, and Adult Roles, Training and Professionalism*. Available online at www.bera.ac.uk (accessed 15 December 2009).

Broadhead, P. (2001) *Curriculum Change in Norway: Thematic Approaches, Active Learning and Pupil Cooperation – from Curriculum Design to Classroom Implementation*. York: University of York.

Bruce, T. (2005) *Early Childhood Education*, 2nd edn. London: Hodder.

Clarke, M.M. and Waller, T. (2007) *Early Childhood Education and Care*. London: Sage Publications.

Dahlberg, G. and Moss, P. (2007) *Ethics and Politics in Early Childhood Education*. London: RoutledgeFalmer.

Dahlberg, G., Moss, P. and Pence, A. (2006) *Beyond Quality in Early Childhood Education and Care: Languages of Evaluation*. London: Routledge.

Department for Children, Schools and Families (DCSF) (2007) *The Children's Plan: Building Brighter Futures*. London: DCSF.

Department for Education and Skills (DfES) (2006) *Independent Review of the Teaching of Early Reading: Final Report* – The Rose Review. London: DfES.

Department for Education and Skills (DfES) (2007) *Early Years Foundation Stage*. London: DfES

Gammage, P. (2006) Early childhood education and care: politics, policies and possibilities, *Early Years: An International Journal of Research and Development*, 26(3): 235–48.

Goswami, U. (2005) Synthetic phonics and learning to read: a cross language perspective, *Educational Psychology in Practice*, 21(4): 270–82.

James, A. and Prout, A. (1997) *Constructing and Reconstructing Childhood: Contemporary Issues in the Sociological Study of Childhood*. London: RoutledgeFalmer.

Janzen, M.D. (2008) Where is the (postmodern) child in early childhood education research? *Early Years: An International Journal of Research and Development*, 28(3): 287–98.

Jensen, B. (2009) A Nordic approach to early childhood education (ECE) and socially endangered children, *European Early Childhood Research Journal*, 17(1): 7–21.

Kennedy, A. (2006) Globalisation, global English: 'futures trading' in early childhood education, *Early Years: An International Journal of Research and Development*, 26(3): 295–306.

Lauder, H., Lowe, J. and Chawla-Duggan, R. (2008) *Primary Review Interim Report. Aims for Primary Education: Changing Global Contexts*. Available online at www.primaryreview.org.uk (accessed 15 December 2009).

McQuail, S., Mooney, A., Cameron, C., et al. (2003) *Early Years and Childcare International Evidence Project*. London: Thomas Coram Research Unit, Institute of Education.

Miller, F., Vandome, A. and McBrewster, J. (eds) (2009) *Child Development Stages: Child Development, Nativism, Parenting, Family, Attachment theory, Infant vision, Erikson's Stages of Psychosocial Development, Theory of Cognitive Development*. Beau Bassin, Mauritius: Alphascript Publishing.

Mooney, A. and Munton, T. (1997) *Choosing Childcare*. Farngate: Ashgate Publishing.

Moss, P., Cameron, C., Candappa, M. et al. (2003) *Early Years and Childcare International Evidence Project*. London: OECD Report, Thomas Coram Research Unit, University of London.

Moyles, J. (2006) Is everybody ready, in S. Featherstone (ed.) *L is for Sheep – Getting Ready for Phonics*. Husbands Bosworth: Featherstone Education Ltd.

Neuman, M.J. (2005) Governance of early childhood education and care: recent developments in OECD countries. *Early Years: An International Journal of Research and Development*, 25(2): 129–41.

OECD (2006) *Starting Strong II, Early Childhood Education and Care*. Paris: OECD Publishing.

Petrie, P. (2005) Extending 'pedagogy', *Journal of Education for Teaching*, 31(4): 293–96.

Pugh, G. and Duffy, B. (ed.) (2009) *Contemporary Issues in the Early Years: Working Collaboratively for Children*, 5th edn. London: Paul Chapman.

Qualifications and Curriculum Authority (QCA) (2008) *Early Years Foundation Stage: Profile Handbook*. London: QCA.

Richardson, V. (ed.) (1997) *Constructivist Teacher Education*. London: Falmer Press.

Sutherland, R., Claxton, G. and Pollard, A. (2003) *Learning and Teaching Where World Views Meet*. Stoke-on-Trent: Trentham Books.

Trevarthen, C. (1995) The child's need to learn a culture, *Children and Society*, 9(1): 5–19.

UNICEF (2005) *Child Poverty in Rich Countries*. Florence: UNICEF Research Report No. 6.

Urban, M. (2008) Dealing with uncertainty: challenges and possibilities for the early childhood profession, *European Early Childhood Research*, 16(2): 135–52.

Vygotsky, L.S. (1978) *Mind in Society*. Cambridge, MA: Harvard University Press.

Waller, T. (ed.) (2005) *An Introduction to Early Childhood: A Multidisciplinary Approach*. London: Sage Publications.

Whitehead, M. (2010) *Language and Literacy in the Early Years 0–7*, 2nd edn. London: Sage Publications.

Woods, M. (2005) Preface, in J. Taylor and M. Woods (eds) *Early Childhood Studies* London: Hodder Arnold.

PART 2
Reflecting on children's playful learning

5   Reflecting on child-initiated play

Bryonie Williams

Summary

This chapter represents reflections on child-initiated play in the school context, though ideas are transferable to other early years settings. It explores how it can be used to inform planning, observations and the collection and analysis of data. It suggests that reflecting on child-initiated play within a setting provides the practitioner with an understanding of how the needs and interests of the children can lead to learning. Aspects of the writer's personal practice are outlined and illustrate how the above can be accommodated and achieved.

Key questions as you read . . .

1   What is your understanding of child-initiated play?
2   What do you feel is the adult's role in child-initiated activities?
3   How can practitioners plan for child-initiated activities?
4   How do practitioners know that children are learning?
5   What role does reflection have in daily play-based pedagogies?

. . . and points to consider

- Child-initiated play can and should form the basis of all curriculum experiences for young children.
- Observations of children's play can provide a huge amount of information in completing development profiles and information about children's learning outcomes.

- Each child is unique – no two children have the same interests and learning needs and equally neither do two cohorts of children.
- Some adult interaction with children in play is necessary and useful to learning more about the child's interests.
- It is important to trust the children to know their own needs and trust your own instincts and reflections.

Introduction

> Play is the natural way in which children go about the business of learning. It enables them to integrate and consolidate a wealth of experiences that enhance their cognitive, physical, social and emotional development. It naturally encourages cooperation and collaboration, requires the use of fine and gross motor skills and demands cognitive application. It is pleasurable, but also helps children face pain and sorrow. It is consuming and challenging and motivating.
>
> (Fisher, 2008: 140)

As a practising teacher and Foundation Stage Leader, and having taught both nursery and reception aged children within a maintained school, I have set out in this chapter to share my professional experiences, in particular my own reflections and observations on child-initiated play.

The message I hope to convey is 'It can be done!' Child-initiated play *can* form the majority of a child's day in the early years. Observations of their play *can* be used to inform the *Early Years Foundation Stage Profile* and our planning. Most importantly, readers will see how the children *can* progress and develop within this ethos. Through reflection, answers to some of the play and learning challenges can be found for all settings, ensuring practitioners develop pedagogies most suited to individuals and groups of children.

David (1996) expresses her concern that many early years practitioners have difficulty in expressing or understanding what a child gains from play – I have been shocked and truly saddened when reading contributions to early years forums from reception class teachers (e.g. TES Connect, 2008). They talk of their struggle to understand how to arrange the daily routines and activities. They acknowledge that the children should be spending more time playing but cannot see how they will meet their own professional targets without filling the day with formal teaching. To compound the problem, there are top-down pressures that ensure any willingness to make changes remains just an idea.

In this chapter, I outline:

- what is practitioner reflection;
- why it is important to reflect on child-initiated play;
- what role the reflective practitioner plays in child-initiated play.

First, however, I start with some of my own definitions to clarify terms used in this chapter, as in our daily practice the early years practitioner may be planning an 'adult-focused' activity, preparing the 'learning environment' or 'continuous provision' or observing 'child-initiated play' – and I have found subtle differences in meanings within texts and individual practitioners' understanding of these terms.

- **Practitioner**: all adults who are involved with the care and education of a child.
- **Setting**: any venue where the *Early Years Foundation Stage* is implemented.
- **Child-initiated play/work**: any activities that are started by the child, meeting their needs and interests. Play and work are interchangeable terms here. 'Play will not be effective or of high quality if it is seen as having a different status to work' (Fisher, 2008: 130).
- **Adult-initiated activity**: an activity that is promoted by the adult in response to a child-initiated activity.
- **Adult-focused activity**: a planned learning opportunity with a specific outcome taught by an adult to whole class, groups or individual children.
- **Continuous provision**: 'The core of everyday resources that should always be available to children in early years settings' (O'Connor, 2008: 18). Children initiate their playful activities with these resources and there is *free flow play* between the outside and indoor learning spaces.
- **Learning Journey Diary**: a photographic and written record of observations of child-initiated play.
- **Learning environment**: indoor and outside provision.

What is practitioner reflection?

Chapter 1 has outlined some of the main principles and theories in relation to reflective practice and critical reflection. During the day as practitioners, we take part in reflection many times – we make isolated decisions having observed children at play (reflection-in-action). The result of this process may be to supplement the existing resources with something new to encourage the children to develop their own play or it may be to speak to a child and further discover their needs and interests. We may make a note (mental or otherwise) to include a particular activity in the next plan, as we had observed children working on an idea, which had drawn other children into their play, so becoming an effective learning platform. We often make reflective remarks to one another 'on the hoof'. A decision may be made there and then, or it may require a meeting to discuss with the whole team (reflection-on-action). Reflection is neither onerous nor difficult and often, as practitioners, we may not be aware that we are going through the process. Reflecting in and on our actions is intuitive for many practitioners – it is also vital to reflect on our own reflections so as to ensure that we make the right decisions for children and the team.

Why reflect?

Pound (in Paige-Smith and Craft, 2008: 45) comments that 'The process of reflection is vital to effective curriculum planning, sound assessment of children's development and progress'. As practitioners reflecting on child-initiated play, we quickly become aware that no two children have the same interests and learning needs and equally neither have two cohorts of children. The *Early Years Foundation Stage (EYFS)* (DfES, 2007) refers to the 'unique child' and Dubiel (in Featherstone and Featherstone, 2008: 94), when commenting on factors that affect assessment, is adamant that:

> . . . however convenient it might be to simplify the reality of children's learning, treating everyone the same in order to produce a neat and tidy data set . . . will inevitably result in that most useless of exercises, the collection of data that is unusable and meaningless.

This is also true if we recycle our planning year after year. It displays a lack of reflection and understanding on the part of the practitioner of the current and future learning needs of the children. 'There is never a moment when we can say "I've cracked this now. I can do it like this for ever" ' (Fisher, 2008: 191). It is what is being learned and not what we are teaching that is important. Through observation and reflection practitioners become attuned to the learning needs of the children, guiding their practice and provision. Most importantly we become aware of what a child is doing when they initiate an activity and why they feel the need to initiate it.

Reflecting on child-initiated play

Child-initiated play is described in the *EYFS Practice Guidance* as 'when a child engages in a self chosen pursuit' (DCSF, 2008: 7) and Fisher (2008: 67) describes it as being:

> . . . the cornerstone of good FS practice for it allows the child to try

new skills, to play alongside other children and to develop socially, to use their imagination and creativity and to try out things that are fascinating and preoccupying them at the time.

Child-initiated play may start from an idea from home or be copied or adapted from a previously presented adult-initiated or focused activity – or its origins may have become lost – but what we do know is that it makes explicit the learning needs and interests of that child at that time. It becomes child-initiated because the child has chosen to play that way (see Moyles, 2008). In my own setting child-initiated play makes up the greater part of the day, as the children follow their own ideas and needs, free-flowing between the outside and inside areas, using whatever resources they can find in whatever ways they choose. The only adult restrictions imposed on activities are when there is a danger to themselves or another child or if the playful learning interests of other children are compromised.

Some feel that child-initiated play should have no restrictions placed on it: if it is planned or resourced in any way by adults then it loses its 'child-initiated' tag but my view is that there has to be some adult interaction or intervention at some level (see also Howard and McInnes, Chapter 2). The researchers from the *Effective Provision of Pre-school Education* (*EPPE*: Sylva et al., 2003) project use the term 'freely chosen' to 'underline that good practice requires children to be able to select, without adult direction, from a well resourced learning environment' (Lindon, in Featherstone and Featherstone, 2008: 13). I can understand that many practitioners may interpret this as a recipe for chaos; the learning environment being taken out of their hands completely. In our setting the adults will have provided that 'well resourced learning environment' from their observations of, and reflections on, child-initiated play. However, as often happens, the children will make it their own. They will take a resource and use it in an area or way that was not expected; then it becomes 'freely chosen'.

When talking to colleagues or introducing students to our practice, there is always initial scepticism: how do I know that the children are learning when they spend so much of their day doing what they like? How can I know what a child can do if we do not tick activities, skills or knowledge off on a list?' My immediate answer is that our day is seemingly unstructured for the children but not for the adults. As practitioners we have a daily timetable, which expects us to observe, record, react to learning opportunities and situations initiated by the children, to focus an activity on an agreed outcome and to reflect continuously on our practice, whether indoors or outside.

When observing child-initiated play we will be looking for a range of experiences – is this something completely new for the child; has the child adapted something from another activity; is this a repeat of the previous day's activity; has the child extended the activity; what skills, knowledge and language is the child using? It is also about being a learner and learning how to learn (Moyles, in Featherstone and Featherstone, 2008: 30). I have always found the children very knowledgeable about their own learning needs; they know what interests them, what to repeat, to extend and when to move on. First *trust the children* in your care and second, *trust your instincts* as a practitioner and your capacity to reflect effectively.

Paige-Smith and Craft (2008: 18) suggest that the Reggio Emilia approach of documenting the children's learning is a method of exploring 'what has engaged and focused children: it helps us to make predictions about what they know and are confident with, and what they are grappling with' (see also Chapter 14). In our setting we record our observations of child-initiated play on sticky labels and these are supported by photographs, both of which are placed in the children's individual 'Learning Journey Diaries' (see Figures 5.1–5.4). These books are started in the nursery and contain observations of learning in both the home and setting and are presented to the parents at the end of the reception year. They make a wonderful record for parents of their child's achievements but for us they reveal so much about our practice.

For the Nursery and Reception classes the diaries are divided into the six areas of learning. They are also used by colleagues in our 'Nursery Plus' where they have been found to be most useful kept as a continuous record of development (these children have particular and special learning needs). Each written observation indicates which area(s) of learning are being addressed and, as so often in the early years, the children's activities could be placed in all the six areas, so here we decide which area is being explored or developed, where sustained effort or thinking is taking place or if this is new for an individual focus child. If we note a lack of observations in a particular area of learning, reflection on our practice takes place – we do not see this as a failing on the part of the child. Moyles (2005: 269) suggests practitioners should evaluate the curriculum 'in relation to how children are actually receiving it, not just performing within it: having information in itself is not enough: it has to be used in meaningful ways to become "knowledge", both by children and practitioners'.

We question our own actions and planning: is it because we have not provided the right resources or ideas, or allowed the children to see that we value this area of learning? Or are the children initiating play in that area but we have yet to note it? This is easily done as often an activity that seems to have the same outcome for whoever uses it can be overlooked. An example of this in our setting was the tyre walkway, which requires the children to balance and jump. Every day this is used by many children and, as adults, we may not give it the attention it deserves as the same thing appears to be happening every day. However, on closer observation, two girls who had helped each other as they had learned to balance now used it for creative play. They still moved on it in exactly the same way as every other child but

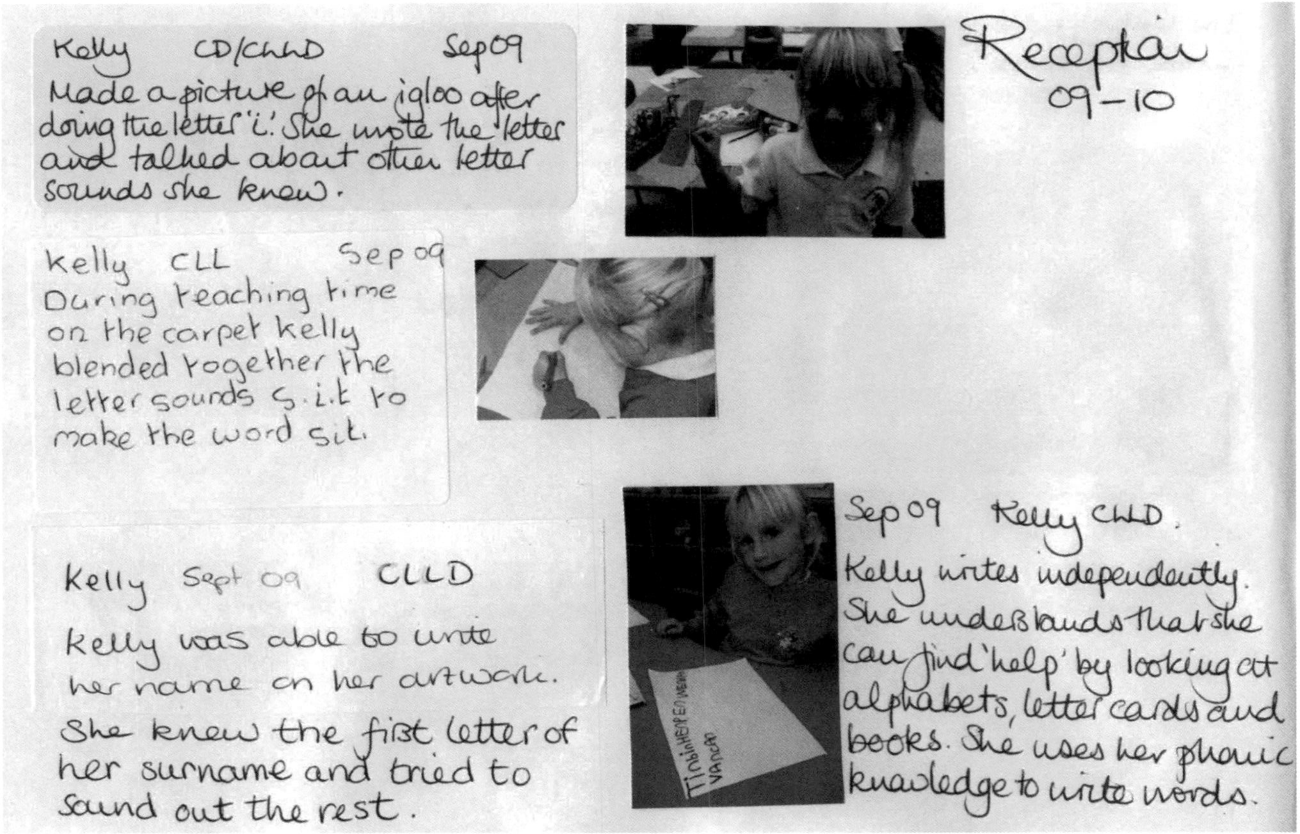

Figure 5.1 Kelly's Learning Journey Diary (1).

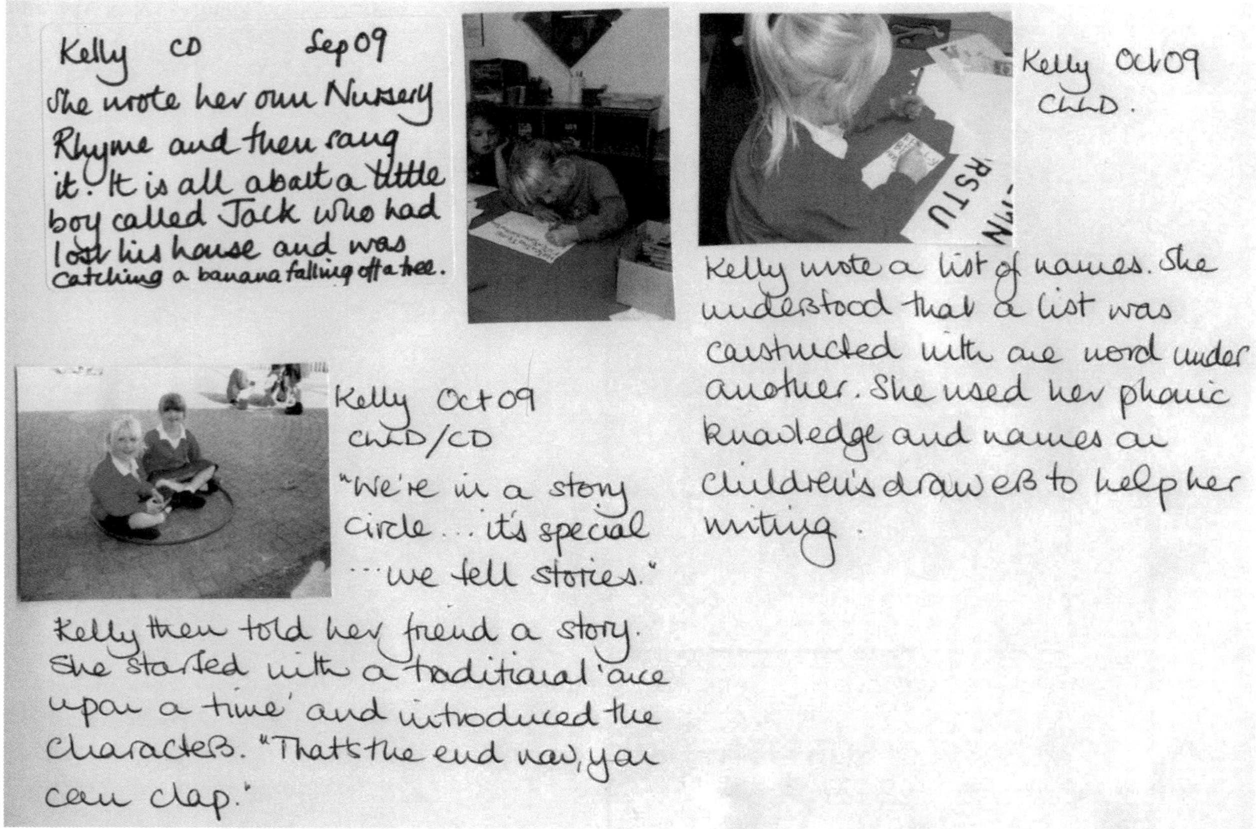

Kelly CI Sep09
She wrote her own Nursery Rhyme and then sang it. It is all about a little boy called Jack who had lost his house and was catching a banana falling off a tree.

Kelly Oct09 CI/CD
"We're in a story circle ... it's special ... we tell stories."

Kelly then told her friend a story. She started with a 'traditional' once upon a time' and introduced the characters. "That's the end now you can clap."

Kelly wrote a list of names. She understood that a list was constructed with one word under another. She used her phonic knowledge and names in children's drawers to help her writing.

Kelly Oct09 CI/LD.

Figure 5.2 Kelly's Learning Journey Diary (2).

Reception 09–10

Feb 09

kelly

kelly when at the creative
table flattened a piece of
Playdough and said "Look,
I've made a pink pancake."

Kelly   CD/K+U   Sep 09
Has an invisible rabbit called Fluff
Tail. She found him a pretend carrot
and carried him carefully round
asking people to stroke him.

Sep 09   Kelly   CD/PSRN

kelly made a birthday cake from
playdough. She stamped a number
3 on, explaining that was the age
of the person.

CD   Sept 09   CD

Kelly was able to
mark a steady
beat with movements
and tapped the
beat on instruments

Kelly   Sept 09   CD
Kelly sang a simple song
from memory and performed
actions to accompany a
song. she named some
percussion instruments and
described the sounds they
made.

Figure 5.3   Kelly's Learning Journey Diary (3).

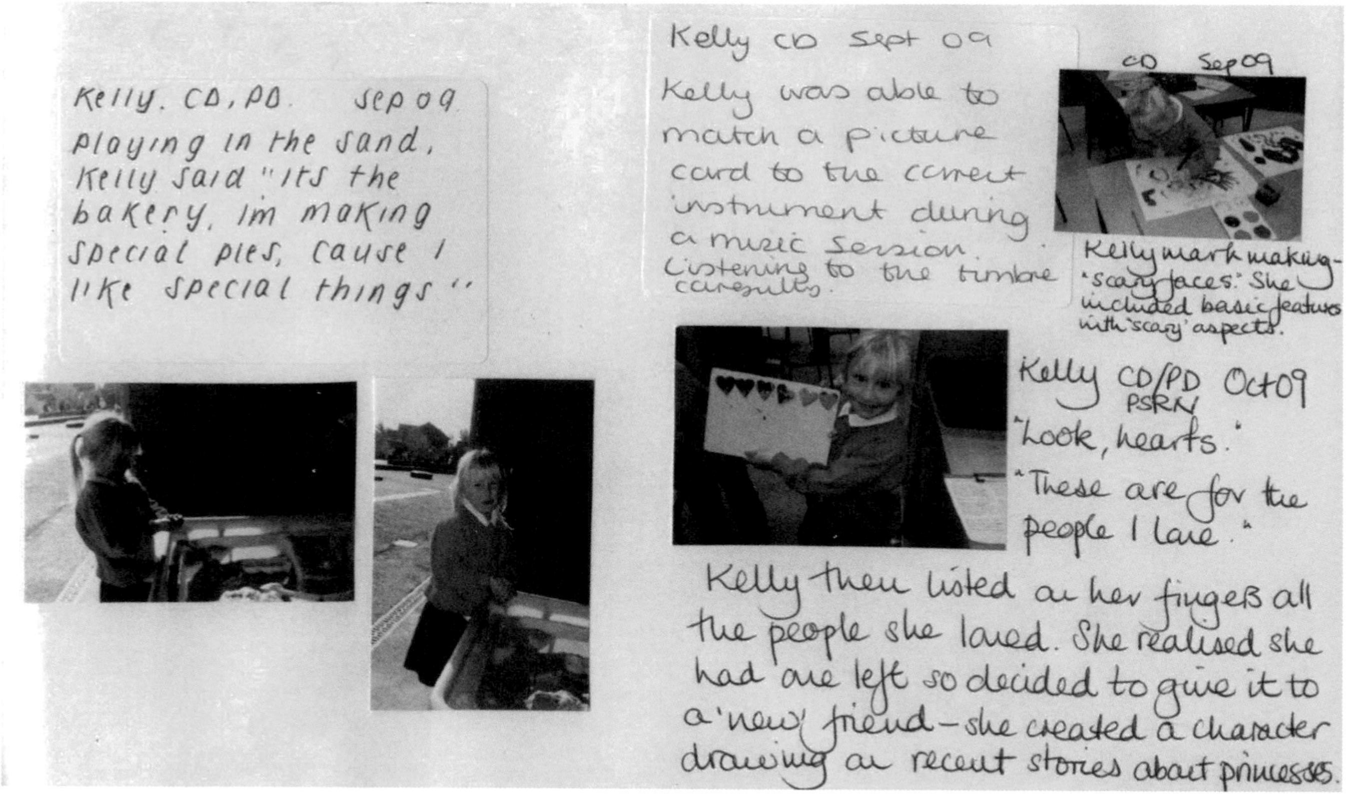

Figure 5.4 Kelly's Learning Journey Diary (4).

their conversations proved extraordinary as they talked of escaping from crocodiles in Africa, being rescued by princes from the dragons that lived underneath the ground and being Olympic gymnasts and winning a gold medal. All six areas of learning were explored during their playful conversations but could have easily been missed.

These Learning Journey Diary observations (see Figures 5.1–5.4) are dated so that we can provide reliable evidence when adding to the children's individual *EYFS* Profiles every half term. As a team we had reflected on how to make the best use of the Profile, as we feel any paperwork undertaken should have a purpose that is in direct relation to our practice and be of benefit to the children. Consequently, where there are gaps in the children's profile graphs, we set personal learning targets for the next half term and the subject component graphs provide an indication of the next areas of learning to be developed. This helps us to resource areas and to consolidate and extend children's learning. This may sound very formalized and here I must emphasize that it is the adult's activities and *not* the children's that are so heavily planned. As professionals we cannot ignore our duties and the requirements of our position but what we do is use reflection as a tool, one that leads us as practitioners to a greater understanding of how to develop our early years practice. Here, reflection on our previous reflections also kick-starts the weekly planning process as we consider what we have observed and try to create conditions that will encourage other children to initiate similar activities for themselves.

At our setting we consider ourselves very lucky as we have large, well-resourced inside and outdoor linked areas. I understand that many settings are restricted by the size of their playful area or by time, and reflection on what they provide and how the children initiate their play, using both resources and the physical area, are very important (see Chapter 10). Featherstone (2006: 8) refers to recent brain research in her article, which suggests practice of a skill develops and maintains links between brain cells:

> Children learn best when they have time to practise the skills we teach them in activities they choose themselves . . . adults are not able to know the activities individuals need to practise so the choice should be as wide as possible and the setting should allow genuinely free choice to individuals and groups.

In a perfect world the children would have everything at their fingertips for as long as they want: as we have yet to discover that world, we can use the process of reflection to help deliver the best possible playful pedagogies to suit the setting as well as the children. Not having the ideal physical setting must not be used as an excuse for not providing the children with daily opportunities for child-initiated play. In fact, Craft (2008: 101) feels some restrictions are necessary as 'total freedom can be confusing. Sometimes it is helpful to suggest some limitations in the way we organize space'. Children's own reflections on issues that directly affect them provide a wonderful insight into what practice could be like. Practitioners should always consult the children on how they would like to use areas or resources, as it is child-initiated play that is to be encouraged.

I cannot write about reflecting on child-initiated play without including here adult-initiated and adult-focused activities and how reflection on these leads the practitioner to a greater understanding of how children in their care learn through play.

In our setting, adult-initiated activities are different to adult-focused activities (see earlier definitions). The adult-initiated activities are playful support given by practitioners during free-flow play, when the children are initiating their own play. The adult may be observing and be invited by the children to join the play; the adult may be working alongside the children and their actions or verbalization of their actions may add a new dimension to the play (what Moyles calls 'playful learning'). The *EPPE* research found that this form of adult support of child-initiated play encouraged 'sustained shared thinking' (Sylva et al., 2003: 36) and these interactions extended the children's play. With these findings in mind a children's daycare centre in Sheffield undertook a Children's Workforce Development Council (CWDC) practitioner research project examining how children learn from following their own interests and consequently developed a children's charter for thinking and learning (Chivers, 2008).

Adult-focused activities are timetabled learning experiences that have a specified outcome ('playful teaching'). These are generally linked to the topic or theme and provide the children with fresh ideas, knowledge and skills that they can incorporate into their play. A particular area of learning is included for any one of a number of reasons: it could have been identified as the next step after considering the half-termly profile subject component graphs; it could be an area that is being revisited (we may have tried it before but had to acknowledge that the children were not yet ready or that our chosen method of teaching was inappropriate at that time) and extended; it could have been identified as we had found few observations in a particular area in the Learning Journey Diaries, or it could have been something we had observed as a child-initiated activity and felt its value and different method of presentation to be perfect for what we were doing. Having 'taught' the focused activity to groups of children during the week, the resources are then made available and we observe how the children use this new knowledge, idea or skill. Sometimes we are delighted by the way the children quickly make it their own activity, extending existing play with the newly learned activity. Sometimes we watch our carefully made resources disappear into a shopping bag in the role-play shop or be buried in the sand or become part of a child's model – we continue to be delighted. Langston (cited in Featherstone and Featherstone,

2008: 11) refers to this process as the children taking ownership and subverting it to a different outcome. Our reflection tells us that it is not the children's fault – they had been very patient with us and sat through an activity that had no relevance or interest to them – but they are now showing us what they are interested in.

So why do we plan?

We are accountable to a range of people and organizations, so we need to produce a written plan indicating that we understand what is needed during a day, week, term or year. It can only be an outline of what is offered as to truly plan what is needed for all the children in your care would take longer to write than to put into action. The plan is to direct the adults, not to produce a tight, restrictive schedule making it impossible for the children to spend the time they need to discover, experiment and practise their developing skills and knowledge. A plan is just that – a plan. It may happen: it may change. Lindon (2008: 9) expresses concerns over the meaning of the word 'planned' as used in the *EYFS Guidance*, suggesting we need to think carefully about what it means to us as practitioners. Our weekly plan consists of three distinct sections, plus a section for reflection and evaluation (see Figure 5.5). What we hope the children will learn (in the six areas of learning) is based on what we think the children will need to learn next, having used evaluations from previous week's planning, from adult-focused activities, whole class 'carpet time' activities, the *EYFS Profile* and, most importantly from our observations, analyses and reflections on previous child-initiated activities. This area of our planning will be supporting and extending what the children have been doing in previous weeks. We then list under activity areas resources to be made available for free use – this is as near as we get to planning for child-initiated activities. These may be supporting a theme or a type of play observed previously or be providing opportunities for the children to move a previously adult-focused activity into the child-initiated range, where it will be changed and used to suit the children's own identified needs and interests.

Lindon (2008: 12) expresses a concern that through some publications, practitioners are being supplied with overdeveloped written planned ideas for child-initiated play so making it 'impossible to see how children will have originated any of the experiences' (p.12). The final section in the plan lists activities to be delivered to whole class or groups in adult-focused sessions and during 'carpet time'. The activities are open, *as are our minds* – if what we are presenting is not working we change it, reflecting where, when or why it failed: we may abandon it or take the lead from something that the children are doing and then we re-present it. Our planning is sufficiently open-ended to be able to do this. We do not stress over it: we *reflect*.

MATCHBOROUGH FIRST SCHOOL EARLY YEARS FOUNDATION STAGE – Reception Class

Week Beginning: 16th November 2009		Topic: All About Me – Senses – sight, taste and smell.

Areas of Learning	What are the Children Learning?		Child Initiated Opportunities and Other Related Activities
PSED	• To work together, to share activities and resources and to take turns and wait patiently. • To manage own personal hygiene needs and changing for PE. • To be aware of own and others preferences and show respect. • To develop an understanding of how to keep themselves safe.	**Planned Focus Activities:** Laura – Exploring the outside area/using senses. Marie – Making perfume. Helen – Mirrors and reflections. Bryonie – Guided reading and writing. Alice – outdoor PE skills. *ICT Suite – Simple City – exploring the program. *Indoor PE – 'Sticky Kids', statues game, moving in different ways along a bench/over a gym table. *Write dance – a walk in the country.	**Home Corner/Role Play:** **Indoors** – The dark tent – provide variety of experiences linked to senses. Outside – home corner. **Creative Workshop:** Cut paper shapes to make patterns – repeating and random. Range of papers and 2D shapes.
CLL	• To segment and blend using known letters. • To recognise and write their names and CVC words. • To hear and say rhyming words. • To listen carefully. • To read tricky/high frequency words. • To learn new letter sounds and use. • To take part in guided writing/reading activities.	*Jolly Phonics, BBC, Big Cat Phonics, Espresso and Education City – songs, activities and DVD. *Adult Led Activities/hear 3 readers – 9.30–10.00 activities to reflect topic and learning needs. **Whole Class/Group Teaching:** Each morning – register, introduce targets, complete calendar and weather activities. introduce Whizzy Wizard. Phonics activities.	**Construction:** Mobilo, Stickle Bricks and Lego. (Stickers on other boxes.) **Sand:** Indoors – Coloured sand for mark making. Outside – Autumn leaves in sand tray with plastic boxes, spades etc.
PSRN	• To write numbers in play. • To recognise, count and order numbers 1–5 and 1–10 and beyond. • To use shapes in creative play and name/describe properties of 4 basic 2D shapes. • To count on one/two more accurately. • To use size, positional and directional language in activities.	Each afternoon – register. Demonstrate an activity. Remind about the CHALLENGE TABLE – to listen to an instruction and follow carefully/to describe things in a feelie bag. Number and shape activities. (See separate planning for CLLD and PSRN)	**Water:** Soapy water and clear water with water wheel – can they hear the water? Pipes and tubes with jugs and bowls. **Books:** A range of interest and story books. Pre-readers and first reading books. Science books.

Ref:
BWW/25.10.07
File:
Planning Matrices

Figure 5.5 Weekly plan.

Meeting the needs and interests of the line manager, head teacher, county adviser and OfSTED inspector

I have met many practitioners in both private and maintained sectors who believe child-initiated play cannot provide the necessary evidence to complete a profile or satisfy the needs for data and statistics of the educational hierarchy. They are nervous to let go of their work sheets and tick lists and feel that if every action and thought is not planned then it cannot have any value. I can only say that 30 years ago I may have felt the same, but by introducing *reflection* into my practice – I am not sure exactly when, I just remember starting to question why we did things the same year after year – there was no turning back. Personal examples of change influenced by reflecting on my own practice include the following:

- When we were 'boy heavy', I changed the layout of the room to create a larger construction area where models could be returned to day after day.
- When one cohort showed themselves to be very creative in model-making but not so interested in painting, tables were moved and an extensive range of resources were provided to accommodate the interests.
- We stopped writing plans for the outside area when, every week in the evaluation box, I was writing comments about what the children had *not* done rather than about the wonderful, creative child-initiated play that *was* happening.
- Establishing the 'café' system for snack time so that we were not interrupting the children's play and those who came in hungry could have their snack straight away.

Reflecting on our practice and understanding the needs of the children means we are continually creating a learning environment that will encourage the children to extend their playful learning and, if that is not happening, we will reflect on why and do something about it.

Our observations and the information that we gather from an adult-focus activity or carpet time and whole class activity (generally held in our heads where they are further reflected upon) inform our planning from week to week. Planning is kept short; we do not need acres of paper explaining how an activity will 'tick' components on an assessment sheet for, as we know, with the best will in the world children do not always do what we expect. To some the unexpected may be a catastrophe; to us it needs recording and reflecting on for it demonstrates individual children's understanding of knowledge and use of skills. We celebrate the things that surprise us. Our planning sheet has a section where we suggest resources for a learning area, based on the observations of the children's current interests: there is no set task – the outcomes are the child's.

The *EYFS Profiles* also provide indicators for what the children need to experience next and this also informs our planning. Graphs can be printed showing each child's individual achievement for each of the components in the six areas of learning. Here we have data to support our practice and, by doing them every half term, over the year we have evidence of the effectiveness of our teaching and learning methods. To accompany this data, I also write a short report that indicates areas of success, those requiring further development and how any innovations introduced to meet the developing needs and interests of the children are progressing.

One of the characteristics of a reflective practitioner is to understand and feel comfortable with the idea that they do *not* have to be in control all the time; that they can admit to being wrong and, most importantly, admit this to the children. Part way through an adult-focused activity, I have stopped and said 'Let's do something else because I don't think this is working': the children will most likely agree and I am happy for them to make suggestions of what we should be doing or how. I have also noted that, initially, practitioners new to working in our setting have to overcome a feeling of guilt when observing child-initiated play and this is a concern of Moyles (1989: 112) who insists that observing is vital, while understanding that practitioners need to justify how they work to others (p.103). We have found that our Learning Journey Diaries provide that necessary evidence for our way of working.

It is important to establish the ethos for learning in your own mind before you attempt to introduce new ways of working. If possible visit other settings who approach the early years curriculum in different ways. Read research reports such as *EPPE* that indicate what good practice 'looks like' and, as Nutbrown (1996: 53) suggests, as adults we must continue to learn. Then, through reflecting on how the children in your care like to learn, you can start to see possibilities for moving furniture to create learning areas, providing continuous provision and operating a free-flow system of play (Bruce, 1991). I always know when a visiting practitioner asks me 'When is play time?' (having observed our day of child-initiated activities as they free-flow between areas) that they have not truly grasped what a child-initiated curriculum or day looks like.

The role of the reflective practitioner in child-initiated play

As I have emphasized, we have to plan but we plan for possible learning opportunities *not* for specific activities. We see our plans as outlines for learning, opportunities provided by the environment, a topic or theme, the range of resources and what the adults can bring to the children, and it needs to be open-ended but within broad learning objectives. Moyles (1989: 87) sees the teacher's role as an initiator, providing a 'framework within which children can explore, play, plan and take responsibility for their own learning'. Fisher (2008: 38) suggests the practitioner's role is complex and divides into five categories – facilitator, observer, responder, protagonist and co-constructor. I also believe that practitioners need to:

- be as informed as possible about research and available good practice, understanding that, with reflection, these will help mould our thinking and directly affect the provision;
- think like a 4-year-old, rather than as an adult;
- look at the 'world' we are helping to create: is this where they would want to play? The best way to facilitate this is to consult the children and then reflect on their insightful comments;
- observe and record, not just to compile records but to celebrate the children's achievements;
- be brave: we have to give up some of our control and allow child-initiated activities to happen without constraint or worry and be willing to stand back and not interfere. Cole (2008: 102) remarks that practitioners 'need to become more comfortable with silence'. Having taken part in 'Nursery Talk' training (Worcestershire speech therapists), I am fully aware of how, in the past, I have filled silence with questions that must have seemed pointless and irritating to the children. This kind of comment and way of thinking can only come from my own reflection on the situation;
- reflect – is child-initiated play actually happening? How do they use the physical environment and the resources? What would help them to extend their play? Are we prepared to ask the children what they want?

How can we improve our reflective practice?

The most obvious answer is to think about and question what we are doing, why we are doing it and what effect it is having on the children's learning. This thinking process may happen during the day or afterwards in a meeting. Paige-Smith and Craft (2008: 174) recognize that practitioners:

> . . . are required to fulfil a range of policy-based expectations within their provision, relating to curriculum, assessment and access to learning opportunities. Policy frameworks offer a focus that brings colleagues and others (including parents) together as a 'community of

practitioners', to develop shared approaches to how they provide for and enhance children's experiences in early year's settings.

Fisher (2008: 190) believes 'practitioners need to have a constantly questioning heart and mind in order to evaluate the quality of children's experiences and the quality of their own contribution to children's learning'. As practitioners, we could take this reflective mode further by starting to explore aspects of the children's learning through small-scale action research projects, as this 'community of practitioners' is aptly situated to observe, record and evaluate. Athey (1990: 19) remarks that teachers generally have research done *to* them as opposed to them actively researching within their classroom and feels they can 'increase professional knowledge of children . . . assist the process of accountability . . .' by identifying an area of interest or need, providing resources, ideas and, by being there, physically as an onlooker or an invited participant, a practitioner can observe and record details of playful learning. This can be used to support the children's profiles or enhance individual's beliefs in a particular way of working. It can provide evidence to a line manager that what is being done is working or can reassure parents that the practice in the setting is good.

What do I, the writer, feel about the contribution of this chapter to supporting critical reflection?

I hope that this chapter has demonstrated that practitioners can meet the needs of the children in their care as well as their professional duties and commitments through play. The most powerful tool to attaining this good, all-encompassing practice, is reflection.

Implications for pedagogy: what might *you*, the reader, reflect on now?

1   Your ethos – how does it shape your practice?
2   Reading and research – how can it provide direction for your thoughts?
3   The children in your care – are you following their interests and needs?

References and further reading

Athey, C. (1990) *Extending Thought in Young Children*. London: Paul Chapman.
Bruce, T. (1991) *Time to Play in Early Childhood Education*. London: Hodder.

Chivers, D. (2008) 'Follow me', *Nursery World*, October, pp. 18–21.

Cole, J. (2008) Our role as adults in enabling independent learning, in S. Featherstone and P. Featherstone (eds) *Like Bees, Not Butterflies: Child-initiated Learning in the Early Years*. London: A & C Black Publishers.

Craft, A. (2008) Creativity and early years settings, in A. Paige-Smith and A. Craft (eds) *Developing Reflective Practice in the Early Years*. Maidenhead: Open University Press.

David, T. (1996) Their right to play, in C. Nutbrown (ed.) *Respectful Educators – Capable Learners: Children's Rights and Early Education*. London: Paul Chapman.

Department for Children, Schools and Families (DCSF) (2008) *Practice Guidance for the Early Years Foundation Stage*. London: DCSF.

Department for Education and Skills (DfES) (2007) *Statutory Framework and Practice Guidance for the Early Years Foundation Stage*. Available at: www.publications.teachernet.gov.uk (accessed 12 September 2009).

Featherstone, S. (2006) A child initiates after an adult plans, *Early Years Educator*, 8(8): 8.

Featherstone, S. and Featherstone, P. (eds) (2008) *Like Bees, Not Butterflies: Child-initiated Learning in the Early Years*. London: A & C Black Publishing.

Fisher, J. (2008) *Starting from the Child*. Maidenhead: Open University Press.

Lindon, J. (2008) *Safeguarding Children and Young People*. London: Hodder.

Moyles, J. (1989) *Just Playing? The Role and Status of Play in Early Childhood Education*. Buckingham: Open University Press.

Moyles, J. (2008) Empowering children and adults: play and child-initiated learning, in S. Featherstone and P. Featherstone (eds) *Like Bees, Not Butterflies: Child-initiated Learning in the Early Years*. London: A & C Black Publishers.

Moyles, J. (ed.) (2005) *The Excellence of Play*, 2nd edn. Maidenhead: Open University Press.

Nutbrown, C. (1996) *Children's Rights and Early Years Education*. London: Paul Chapman.

O'Connor, A. (2008) Don't stop me now! *Nursery World*, 17 September, pp. 18–20.

Paige-Smith, A. and Craft, A. (eds) (2008) *Developing Reflective Practice in the Early Years*. Maidenhead: Open University Press.

Stringer, E., McFayden Christensen, L. and Baldwin, S. (2009) *Integrating Teaching, Learning and Action Research*. London: Sage Publications.

Sylva, K., Melhuish, E., Sammons, P., et al. (2003) *The Effective Provision of Pre-school Education (EPPE) Project: Findings from the Pre-school Period*. London: Institute of Education.

TES Connect (2008) Available online at www.tes.co.uk.

6 Play as an emotional process

Estelle Martin

Summary

When thinking about supporting young children's play experience, it is vital that early years educators reflect on the emotional dimensions of play and children's learning and development. This chapter explores children's emotional development and well-being through a play perspective. The development of a pedagogy of play is explored and the essential quality of relationships that the children experience in enabling their overall holistic development. The contribution of observation, research and reflective dialogues with practitioners is considered.

Key questions as you read . . .

1 How aware are you of the importance of children's emotional development to their learning?
2 What is the relationship between emotional development and play?
3 How can practitioners reflect on the emotional and social development of children in their pedagogies?

. . . and points to consider

- It is important to think about the emotional climate of your setting and how this impacts on children's play and holistic development.
- Observation of children's playful interactions with each other and with adults can supply significant information about their emotional learning.

• Children experience deep levels of emotional satisfaction during prolonged play episodes.

Introduction

> I am certain the children who are told they can't play don't learn as well. They might become too sad to pay attention.
>
> (Paley, 1992: 28)

This chapter begins by exploring the concepts of emotion and well-being as these are central to understanding the holistic nature of children's learning and development. This is recognized in the Statutory Framework for the *Early Years Foundation Stage (EYFS)* in England through its principles and curriculum guidance (DfES, 2007) and the government's *Social and Emotional Aspects of Development (SEAD)* document (DCSF, 2008). There is a discussion about how pedagogies of play can support children's emotional development and well-being in the early years. The interrelationships between children's emerging identities and their emotional well-being is explored, how these relationships are socially and culturally situated and what adults can offer by way of role-modelling to the community of children to support their emotional well-being. The impact on social interactions in play is considered as well as how we think through the emotional experiences that children have during play.

The case for emotional literacy

> There is sound evidence from the literature . . . that work on emotional and social competence and wellbeing has a wide range of educational and social benefits; including greater educational and work success, improved behaviour, increased inclusion, improved learning, greater social cohesion, increased social capital and improvements to mental health.
>
> (Weare and Gray, 2003: 6)

'Emotional intelligence' and 'emotional literacy' are terms that are used in a range of literature to convey the abilities of individuals to develop self-awareness in relation to their own emotional state and to self-regulate and manage those emotional states (see Goleman, 2005; Sharp, 2001). This includes the ability to empathize with others' emotional states, to be socially competent when interacting with others and manage one's own emotions.

As researchers and early years educators, there is the need for us to reflect on the case for emotional intelligence and literacy in their current forms.

Critical reflection on what we observe of children's emotional development and the role of play is a way forward in considering what our perceptions of emotional literacy are and what it looks like in young children when we consider their interactions with each other and with adults. The play of young babies, for example, evolves through interactions with others – parents, carers, siblings and the environment. Through socialization and play, children become more confident and their self-evaluation becomes less dependent on adults' reactions and feedback. Over time they demonstrate their independence and social skills interacting with peers and other people to whom they have attachments (Elfer and Grenier, 2010).

As part of our understanding of the identity and emotional development of children, we need to consider the importance of play and children's rights. The *United Nations Convention on the Rights of the Child* (UN, 1989: *The Children Act* (DoH, 1989; DfES, 2004; DfES, 2006) and the *EYFS*, all recognize, and require, that the child has an entitlement to play. David (1996) highlights Article 31 of the UNCRC as significant to the way in which early years educators and policy-makers make play provision available for children's play. This entitlement to play in England is now subsumed within the National Strategies, the *Every Child Matters* agenda (Her Majesty's Treasury 2004), the *Children's Plan* (DCSF, 2007) and the *EYFS*. Moreover, the early childhood community is encouraged to reflect on the quality and processes of play offered to babies and young children in group- and home-based care contexts to enable positive outcomes for all children. The following Cameo (1) outlines a play episode involving Tanya, aged 7.

Cameo 1

'Perfecto!'

Tanya is playing at being a librarian. She is engaging her mother, father and godparents in the narratives as she plays with her dolls and library books. Tanya gets three books from the shelf and takes them over to the desk where she has transformed a cash register till to a swipe-card machine for library use. [Children will often transform objects in play sequences to symbolize or represent something else in quite novel ways, showing their ability to think in the abstract.] Tanya is using her own public library card to swipe through the machine which makes an electronic noise to indicate the card is accepted. Tanya holds her doll and explains:

Tanya:	You have until the week after next week, ok? Perfecto!
	(*Tanya then looks up at her Dad*)
Tanya:	The library closes early now and we can't go every day.
Godfather:	When do you go with daddy?

Tanya:	On the weekend times – and sometimes with Mummy.
	(Tanya goes over to another bookshelf and explains about her book from Korea that Mummy got when they went to visit at Easter time)
Tanya:	Perfecto! Look, it has stickers inside. This other one has stickers too, about the artists, and the pictures like the horse that Daddy likes.
	(Tanya brings a book to the godmother)
Tanya:	Look, this is like the horse on daddy's book mark.
	(Tanya also shows the pages and pictures of Van Gogh and says she really likes these ones, although she explains:)
Tanya:	Do you know what happened to Van Gogh?
Godmother:	Not exactly, what do you mean?
Tanya:	Well he had his ear cut off! We're not really sure how it happened because he was fighting and it could have been pulled off then.
	(She pauses, looks at her father, then says:)
Tanya:	He could have cut it off himself because he was frustrated, but we are not really sure; it's a difficult, horrible thing, but we can't be sure how it happened and why he was upset.
	(Tanya shows the Van Gogh picture of the vase with sunflowers to her godmother as she speaks. Then she returns to the library desk and swipes the card again to allow the next doll person to take out the books)
Tanya:	Perfecto!

Reflecting on this cameo

In reflecting on this cameo, we can see how much social knowledge Tanya brings to the process: she engages with the adults and commands an audience for the play and the accompanying narratives. Tanya uses the description 'Perfecto!' several times, indicating how she feels about events as she plays in her role as a librarian and as herself. Tanya is able to reveal her logic about Van Gogh and his 'frustration' so she has rationalized that he was upset and understood that his actions may have been as a result of his frustration.

During play children can revisit ideas: Tanya had a chance to reflect on her thoughts and feelings by looking again at one of her books and as part of including others in her play (the adults in this case). She has conceptual language to describe how some feelings may be experienced by other people. In addition, Tanya shows evidence of understanding that how other people may feel is also a tentative process – we cannot always be sure. Tanya seems to be emotionally secure and has an understanding of 'theory of mind' (Schaffer, 1996: 184): she is able to appreciate the views, thoughts and feelings of another person, and once a child is capable of representing to itself the mental states of another person, social interactions assume a much more sophisticated form'; in other words, she has developed *empathy* (Siegel, 2009). Being able to empathize is associated with the ongoing development of knowing and understanding your own feelings and thoughts in order to project these onto the feelings of others (Damasio, 2004). The language children use in conversations and play can also reveal their own feelings and social cognition that is experienced in their familiar cultural context at home and at nursery or school (Brooker, 2002).

Thinking through the language of emotions and the creation of a listening culture

Effective practice requires practitioners to reflect and think through their own expressions and use of the language of emotions. In particular, when children share thoughts and feelings in play – their own or others – adults can create a listening culture where talk about feelings is acceptable and valid alongside other types of description of the experiences children may want to share (Clark and Moss, 2001; Moseley, 1996 for 'Circle Time' activities).

It is important when children are making meaning about behaviour through social interactions that the adult provides a containing element where the child is listened to and feelings are received and accepted as part of understanding the child's perspective and unique development. Gerhardt (2004) promotes the role of the adult in helping children to make sense, to label their feelings and to think about and enable the child to manage their changing emotional states. This can be important in terms of children being able to have positive dispositions to challenging learning situations, thereby becoming resilient through a responsive adult who cares about what happens to the child. This could be the practitioner who is the key person for the child in addition to the parent (Elfer et al., 2003). Children's understanding of their own emotions and emotional development can be influenced by a range of factors:

- the level of family support;
- cultural and social conventions ;
- their individual developmental processes;
- socialization and relationships in early childhood education and care settings;
- the types of pedagogies within the education and care settings.

Creating a listening culture in classrooms and settings (Lancaster and Broadbent, 2003; Rinaldi, 2006) is a huge part of facilitating emotional literacy and social inclusion. Practitioners should provide a range of playful activities to help children to express and represent how they feel, then observe and listen to what children express in these experiences. Examples are as follows:

- conversations with children, actively listening to their views and scribing the narratives of feelings;
- music, movement and drama;
- interactive displays of events and emotions, including descriptions by the children;
- picture books and stories where feelings are a central theme – these can challenge children because they have to 'read' the pictures, helping them to focus on the feelings of the characters in the book;
- puppets, dolls and role-play situations and resources;
- opportunities for free-flow play (Bruce, 2001);
- photographs – documentation using photographs can enable children to conceptualize the ways in which they see their experiences and reflect on their thoughts and feelings;
- photographs and video observations can provide valuable opportunities for reflective discussions with children and will often reveal more to adults about what has interested or motivated the children during a particular learning experience as they reflect on it (a strategy widely used by researchers to illicit children's thoughts);
- creative activities, including digital technologies that enable expression and engage positive emotions; for example, making and creating sculpture, paintings, drawings, music and movement and dance, and use of computers to make marks, engage in interactive games and co-construct virtual worlds (Lancaster, 2003; Marsh, 2005).

These all facilitate the kaleidoscope of children's representations.

Reflective conversations, communication and affirmations

Reflective conversations with children affirm their achievements, offer cultural reference points and enable meaningful sustained shared thinking about what is of interest to the child: see the *Effective Provision of Pre-School Education (EPPE)* Project (Sylva et al., 2004). Implicit within this relationship is an authentic and respectful interaction based on being emotionally present for the child, shown by active listening and consistent patterns of body language (verbal and non-verbal) such as eye contact, facial expression and physical contact where appropriate. Quite often we can recognize that children and babies find it emotionally satisfying when someone who is interested in what they are doing stays alongside the child as an indirect facilitator, encouraging and acknowledging the child's intentions and/or actions (Bruner, 1990; Dowling, 2010). Howes et al.'s (1994) study found that where practitioners demonstrated socialization and modelled positive relationships, the children appeared to be more secure in their setting which, in turn, stimulated more complexity in the children's play.

Through a series of case studies, Pollard (1996) demonstrated how the quality of relationships affects children's learning. The ways in which practitioners develop early relationships influences children's sense of identity and self-esteem. Children are more likely to be motivated and develop positive dispositions for learning through playful and socially secure pedagogies (see Webster, Chapter 7). Accepting the child's individual and unique play patterns supports children's developmental processes, such as self-acceptance and respect for themselves and for others, which is fundamental to the child's personal, social and emotional development (Geddes, 2006).

Play and playful pedagogies

It is during play that children of all ages often express their feelings and experience their emotions, so play can be described as the child's symbolic language of self-expression (Vygotsky, 1978). Informed by psychodynamic theory and educational philosophy, the symbolism represented in play can be observed as spaces for the child's emotions (Oaklander, 1989; Malaguzzi, 1994), which may be experienced like a kaleidoscope of representations. Play allows children to be in control and, therefore, they experience agency and ownership (Moyles, 1989; see Chapter 1). Early educators respect the child's right to make decisions and choices about what, where, how and with whom they play in early childhood education and care (ECEC) settings. This can create a feeling of emotional security, belonging and boost children's self-esteem, giving them a sense of confidence in their own abilities to self-regulate and learn through such responsibility.

The sense of belonging that is nurtured in rich play environments with opportunities to make relationships with peers and adults contributes to the child's sense of identity in context (Martin, 2005). Learning that you are connected to others and belong to this setting is essential to a child's emotional well-being. Identity emerges through the composite of feedback and social interactions in the culture of home, nursery or school and we need to have some understanding of children's culture and society's popular culture as these influences all contribute to the child's identification of self. Understanding this from a social constructivist perspective, where children are seen as active co-constructors of their knowledge, will to some extent allow children to co-construct their identities and shape their culture (Dahlberg et al., 1998: Rinaldi, 2006; see also Chapter 4).

It is known that when children show signs of intense involvement in their play, their learning will be at a high level (Howard, 2010). Observations of a child absorbed in self-initiated play are likely to generate the most accurate information about that child's learning. An assessment of involvement levels (e.g. Laevers, 1994; Broadhead, 2004; Whitebread, 2007) can also help to ensure that what is provided in the environment is effective in motivating children's engagement and social learning.

The perspectives of practitioners about children, their abilities to play and engage in playful pedagogies, and their understanding about the developing child, cultural influences and the architecture of a pedagogy of play for children, can be very influential. The holistic nature of children's learning and development is well documented – this is what makes early years so distinctive (Moyles, 2005). We know that holistic development is most appropriately facilitated through a play-based curriculum – the *EYFS* and the English government's new play policy (DCSF/National Strategies, 2009) wholly support play-based learning – and that emotional processes are integral to babies' and young children's play (Gopnik, 2009).

Being emotionally confident and risk-taking in play

Taking risks in play is invaluable for leading children's learning (Tovey, 2007; Chapter 6). A high-quality curriculum that shows children they are safe and trusted to experiment and discover through multiple play activities – both child- and adult-initiated – creates the conditions for children to feel psychologically secure. This facilitates emotional well-being on three levels:

1   children's sense of being respected and trusted to play and, therefore, their willingness to take risks and feel able to persevere when challenges arise;
2   understanding that making mistakes or doing things differently is acceptable and can produce a desired outcome;
3   learning to do things in different and novel ways.

(Blenkin and Kelly, 1996)

Children who are trusted to play are also able to feel trust in adults, approaching them confidently for help and interacting with them in their play (Scott, 1996: Webster-Stratton, 1999). The relational aspects between children, peers and adults can be emotionally satisfying and provide the support for the ongoing development of social cognition in children, as discussed earlier. Play and playful pedagogies enable children to access the curriculum at their own level with choice for types of play so creating the conditions for ongoing personalized learning and social inclusion (see Chapter 1).

Players and playmates

In play, children are resourceful, using a range of objects and props to construct situations that often mirror their experiences (Roberts, 2006). The child will revisit experiences and ideas to consolidate and make sense of concepts, events and feelings, working through how they manage their emotional reactions and responses. The play will be a powerful vehicle for children to integrate what they have observed and understand about others' emotional reactions. Children in play will progress towards self-regulation and emotional well-being because they have been facilitated to wallow in free-flow experiences that are meaningful to them (Bruce, 2005; Broadhead, 2004). Broadhead's research emphasizes the necessity for practitioners to withdraw from children's play to observe and allow children more time and space to develop their play themes. Research by Elias and Berk (2002) also indicates that the benefits of role playing for children include a greater sense of happiness, ability to self-regulate, sensitivity and emotional awareness. A research project conducted by Rogers and Evans (2008) revealed that 4-year-old children in reception classes, when asked for their perceptions, valued role play highly in relation to interaction on a social level with other children. The children used role play to make sense of starting a new school so this supported their transitional issues and concerns (Fabian and Dunlop, 2010; Chapter 13). The research found that the role play provided a place in which the children could renegotiate terms of friendship, resolve conflicts and try out social strategies.

These studies support my own research (Martin, 2006) focusing on emotional development and learning in two reception and two nursery classes. Findings revealed that relationships, in particular friendships, were very important to the children's sense of well-being and learning. Observations of the children's self-directed play and playful activities initiated by me exposed how competent and insightful the children can be in their social interactions and levels of emotional intelligence. This was confirmed in a later phase of the research, through reflective dialogues with the practitioners in the children's settings. The reflective nature of the dialogues enabled the research to be considered from a range of perspectives and was an essential process in critical analysis of data as in the *SPEEL* project (see Moyles et al., 2002).

Creativity and narratives of play

It is important to recognize that creativity is an emotional process involving the whole child's senses, imagination and feelings (Duffy, 2010). Creativity can be identified in children's play and representations of their inner world, creative thinking and communication. Children will select a range of play media in order to create and reconstruct play scenarios. Play is a strong vehicle for children to express how they feel about themselves, the world, how it is in *reality* and how it could be: *imaginary*. Play empowers a child to be in tune with the whole self and the creative self. Children experience deep levels of emotional satisfaction during prolonged sustained play activities (Laevers, 1994). Imaginative play is essential for children to explore, investigate and realize the possibilities of cause and effect and the use of narratives in constructing social worlds as part of socio-dramatic and role play. Children realize their mastery – which gives them confidence – and ownership during quality play, which is unhurried and which can be developed and extended with peers and adults as identified by the child. The levels of confidence and concentration and achievements in play all contribute to emotional well-being in children.

Paley (1992, 2004) invites readers to reflect on their interactions with children and the ways in which we educate our youngest children. Paley also focuses on the importance of fantasy play in early years classrooms and she has established and developed storytelling and role play/dramatic play techniques with children to encourage imagination and play-based, deep learning. The children's story narratives, given as examples, document the children's powers of thinking, problem solving and their ability to question and work as team players through storytelling and play processes. Paley advocates the need for educators becoming reflective practitioners so that they can inform and enhance experiences for the children and advocates observation as essential to reflective practices in settings as this encourages colleagues to share information about what they have learned from the children and the resources provided – a point to which I now turn.

Observation of children

The ways in which children make sense of their emotions is very individual, as they each have unique experiences influenced by culture and relationships in the family and wider community. A continued study of the literature and research in the field, coupled with close observation and reflection (Ripley, 2007), enables early years educators to understand the sequence of typical development in children's capacities to recognize and manage their own emotions and the significance of social interactions (Schaffer, 1996; Trevarthen, 1998; Dowling, 2010).

The importance of observation of children's social play and the focus of emotional development of the children can be seen as an insight into the children's perspectives, informing our understandings of what matters to children, as we saw with Tanya (Riddall-Leech, 2008). Observation of children's play needs should involve parents where possible and, during play sessions, practitioners can observe parents' awareness of their child's needs. Parents may also be involved in a discussion about their child's development and contribute to the child's profile with their expert knowledge of their own child and that child's learning journey (see Chapter 5).

Observation of personal, social and emotional development and learning in the Foundation Stage may take a variety of forms and each setting will have monitoring and assessment of children as an ongoing part of quality systems and practices that support profiling children's progress. Children may be included and participate in their records of experience by practitioners listening to children and using participatory activities that support children's voices and perspectives about their own development and learning.

Observation of practitioners' feelings and reactions

Another aspect for observation is us, the practitioners. This is part of becoming more reflective and, as we develop more self-awareness in this process, we can gain greater knowledge of how we feel and respond in various situations and the implications of our own emotions and behaviour. This reflection and greater awareness enables practitioners to make choices about how to respond in any situation with more insight and confidence. This is relevant for quality interactions with children and with other colleagues and parents, especially for the children in the class because we have a big influence on them as well as children having an influence on us. We may have strong feelings or reactions to the children and situations we observe: responding with feeling is a natural part of our experiences when working with young children and in life in general. We may respond intuitively to a child, tuning in to them as part of a shared social encounter (see Chapter 1). Recording our feelings and reactions separately from the description and interpretation of children's experiences gives us the opportunity to reflect on our personal responses without distorting the observation. Reflecting with others is also a way of understanding our emotions when involved in working and responding to groups of children who are all individuals with diverse personalities and needs – just like us! Recognizing the way in which we manage our own emotions in relationship to the children can be helpful for, role-modelling behaviour in our interpersonal interactions generally and with colleagues (McLean, 1991; Pascal and Bertram, 1997; Atkinson and Claxton, 2000).

Conclusion

The interrelationships between children's emergent identities and emotional well-being have been discussed through the role of the relationships that children encounter with adults and their peers in learning situations. Cultural and gendered identities can be acknowledged through high-quality play environments that embrace and follow the children's interests and ideas (Browne, 2007). The acceptance of the multiplicity of identities in the community of children is co-constructed within the relationships. Nutbrown and Page (2008) frame loving relationships as 'professional love' in their discussions about working with babies and children from birth to 3 years of age and the relationships required in day care. In fact, all children need to know is that they are loveable: rather than seeing children as being deficient because of their need to feel connected, educators should realize that this is fundamental to children's sense of being themselves. Children really do need to love and be loved as a fundamental human principle if they are to develop as secure emotional and social people.

What do I, the writer, feel about the contribution of this chapter to supporting critical reflection?

I feel that critical reflection is important for my own research and professional knowledge about early childhood and that it is a *process* that is continuous throughout my professional life. Critical reflection underpins a principled and ethical stance to my work with communities of children and practitioners in different ways. There are parallels with the process of observing children's play and their social cognition and emotional well-being. We must reflect on our own values, beliefs and understandings – something promoted throughout this book. I believe these have an emotional component that is providing a compass for our feelings – our intuitive self – which interacts with our professional world and praxis. Supporting children's emotional development and learning through play are essentially related to the construction and reconstruction of social relationships, with the use of theory and research to analyse and interpret them. Moreover, the reflective function in dialogue with colleagues leads to affirmation and new possibilities in the provision of pedagogies of play and social/emotional relationships.

Implications for pedagogy: what might *you*, the reader, reflect on now?

The findings from the research outlined above offer early years educators the chance to reflect on their settings' ethos and planning for a pedagogy of play. In particular, it would be useful to reflect on:

- How relationships with children, parents and colleagues are constructed and sustained.
- The style and quality of interactions with practitioners that are experienced by the children.
- How the emotional development and learning of children progresses during play activity.
- How you make observations of emotional processes in play.
- As members of staff, how you reflect on the emotional well-being of each other.

References and further reading

Atkinson, T. and Claxton, C. (2000) *The Intuitive Practitioner*. Buckingham: Open University Press.

Blenkin, G. and Kelly, A.V. (1996) *Early Childhood Education: A Developmental Curriculum*, 2nd edn. London: Paul Chapman.

Broadhead, P. (2004) *Early Years Play and Learning*. London: RoutledgeFalmer.

Brooker, L. (2002) *Starting School: Young Children Learning Cultures*. Buckingham: Open University Press.

Browne, N. (2007) Identity and children as learners, in J. Moyles (ed.) Early *Years Foundations: Meeting The Challenge*. Maidenhead: Open University Press.

Bruce, T. (2001) *Learning Through Play: Babies, Toddlers and the Foundation Years*. Abingdon: Hodder & Stoughton.

Bruce, T. (2005) *Early Childhood Education*, 3rd edn. London: Hodder Arnold.

Bruner, J. (1990) *Acts of Meaning*. Cambridge, MA: Harvard University Press.

Clark, A. and Moss, P. (2001) *Listening to Young Children: The Mosaic Approach*. London: National Children's Bureau for the Joseph Rowntree Foundation.

Dahlberg, G., Moss, P. and Pence, A. (1998) *Beyond Quality in Early Childhood Education and Care: Postmodern Perspectives*. London: Falmer Press.

Damasio, A. (2004) *Looking for Spinoza*. London: Vintage Books.

David, T. (1996) Their right to play, in C. Nutbrown (ed.) *Respectful Educators – Capable Learners: Children's Rights and Early Education*. London: Paul Chapman.

Department for Children, Schools and Families (DCSF) (2007) *The Children's Plan: Building Brighter Futures*. Norwich: HMSO.

Department for Children, Schools and Families (DCSF)/National Strategies: Early Years (2008) *Social and Emotional Aspects of Development (SEAD)*. London: DCSF.

Department for Children, Schools and Families (DCSF)/National Strategies: Early Years (2009) *Learning, Playing and Interacting: Good Practice in the Early Years Foundation Stage*. London: DCSF.

Department for Education and Skills (DfES) (2004) *Children Act 2004*. London: HMSO.

Department for Education and Skills (DfES) (2006) *Childcare Act 2006*. London: HMSO.

Department for Education and Skills (DfES) (2007) *Early Years Foundation Stage*. London: DfES.

Department of Health (DoH) (1989) *Children Act 1989*. London: Her Majesty's Stationery Office (HMSO).

Dowling, M. (2010) *Young Children's Personal, Social and Emotional Development*, 3rd edn. London: Sage.

Duffy, B. (2010) Art in the early years, in J. Moyles (ed.) *The Excellence of Play*, 3rd edn. Maidenhead: Open University Press.

Elfer, P., Goldschmied, E. and Selleck, D. (2003) *Key Persons in Nurseries: Building Relationships for Quality Provision*. London: National Early Years Network (NEYN).

Elfer, P. and Grenier, J. (2010) Personal, social and emotional development, in T. Bruce (ed.) *Early Childhood: A Guide for Students*. London: Sage Publications.

Elias, C.L. and Berk, L.E. (2002) Self-regulation in young children: is there a role for sociodramatic play? *Early Childhood Research Quarterly*, 17: 216–38.

Fabian, H. and Dunlop, A.-W. (2010), Personalizing transitions: how play can help 'newly arrived children' settle into school, in J. Moyles (ed.) *The Excellence of Play*, 3rd edn. Maidenhead: Open University Press.

Geddes, H. (2006) *Attachment in the Classroom: The Links between Children's Early Experience, Emotional Well-being and Performance in School*. London: Worth Publishing.

Gerhardt, S. (2004) *Why Love Matters: How Affection Shapes a Baby's Brain*. London: Routledge.

Goleman, D. (2005) *Emotional Intelligence*. New York: Bantam Books.

Gopnik, A. (2009) *The Philosophical Baby*. London: The Bodley Head.

Howard, J. (2010) The developmental and therapeutic value of children's play: re-establishing teachers as play professionals, in J. Moyles (ed.) *The Excellence of Play*, 3rd edn. Maidenhead: Open University Press.

Howes, C., Hamilton, C.E. and Matheson, C.C. (1994) Maternal, teacher and child care history correlates of children's friendships with peers, *Child Development*, 65(1): 264–73.

Her Majesty's Treasury (2004) *Every Child Matters*. London: Her Majesty's Stationery Office (HMSO).

Laevers, F. (1994) *The Leuven Involvement Scale for Young Children*. Belgium: Leuven Centre for Experiential Education.

Lancaster, Y.P. (2003) *Listening to Young Children, Promoting Listening to Young Children: The Reader*. Buckingham: Open University Press.

Lancaster, Y.P. and Broadbent, V. (2003) *Listening to Children*. Buckingham: Open University Press.

Malaguzzi, L. (1994) History, ideas and basic philosophy, in C. Edwards, L. Gandini and G. Forman (eds) *The Hundred Languages of Children: The Reggio Emilia Approach to Early Childhood Education*. Norwood, NJ: Ablex Publishing.

Marsh, J. (ed.) (2005) *Popular Culture, Media and Digital Literacies in Early Childhood*. London. RoutledgeFalmer.

Martin, E. (2005) Emotional development and learning, *Early Education*, 45: 11–13.

Martin, E. (2006) Play without prejudice, *Early Years Educator*, 8(9): 32–4.

McLean, S.V. (1991) *The Human Encounter: Teachers and Children Living Together in Preschools*. London: Falmer.

Moseley, J. (1996) *Quality Circle Time in the Primary School*. Wisbech: Learning Development Aids.

Moyles, J. (2005) *The Excellence of Play*, 2nd edn. Maidenhead: Open University Press.

Moyles, J. (1989) *Just Playing? The Role and Status of Play in Early Childhood Education*. Buckingham: Open University Press.

Moyles, J., Adams, S. and Musgrove, A. (2002) *SPEEL: Study of Pedagogical Effectiveness in Early Learning*. London: DfES Research Report No. 363.

Nutbrown, C. and Page, J. (2008) *Working with Babies and Children form Birth to Three*. London: Sage Publishers.

Oaklander, V. (1989) *Windows to Our Children*. Highland, NY. Gestalt Journal Press.

Paley, V. (1992) *You Can't Say You Can't Play*. Cambridge, MA: Harvard University Press.

Paley, V. (2004) *A Child's Work*. Chicago, IL: University of Chicago Press.

Pascal, C. and Bertram, A. (1997) *Effective Early Learning: Case Studies in Improvement*. London: Hodder & Stoughton.

Pollard, A. with Filer, A. (1996) *The Social World of Children's Learning*. London: Cassell.

Riddall-Leech, S. (ed.) (2008) *How to Observe Children*, 2nd edn. London: Heinemann.

Rinaldi, C. (2006) *In Dialogue with Reggio Emilia: Listening, Researching and Learning*. London: Routledge.

Ripley, K. (2007) *First Steps to Emotional Literacy*. London: David Fulton.

Roberts, R. (2006) *Self-esteem and Early Learning: Key People from Birth to School*, 3rd edn. London: Paul Chapman.

Rogers, S. and Evans, J. (2008) *Inside Role-play in Early Childhood: Researching Children's Perspectives*. London. Routledge.

Schaffer, H.R. (1996) *Social Development*. Oxford: Blackwell.

Scott, W. (1996) Choices in learning, in C. Nutbrown (ed.) *Respectful Educators – Capable Learners: Children's Rights and Early Education*. London: Paul Chapman.

Sharp, P. (2001) *Nurturing Emotional Literacy*. London: David Fulton.

Siegel, D.J. (2009) *Roots of Empathy*. New York: The Experiment Publishing.

Sylva, K., Melhuish, E.C., Sammons, P., Siraj-Blatchford, I. and Taggart, B. (2004) The Effective Provision of Pre-School Education (EPPE) Project: *Technical Paper 12 – The Final Report: Effective Pre-School Education*. London: DfES/Institute of Education, University of London.

Tovey, H. (2007) *Playing Outdoors: Spaces and Places, Risks and Challenge*. Maidenhead: Open University Press.

Trevarthen, C. (1998) The child's need to learn a culture, in M. Woodhead, D. Faulkener and K. Littleton (eds) *Cultural Worlds of Early Childhood*. London: Routledge.

United Nations (UN) (1989) *The UN Convention on The Rights of the Child*. New York: UN.

Vygotsky, L. (1978) *Mind in Society: The Development of Higher Mental Processes*. Cambridge, MA: Harvard University Press.

Weare, K. and Gray, G. (2003) *What Works in Developing Children's Emotional and Social Competence and Wellbeing?* London: DfES Research Report No. 456.

Webster-Stratton, C. (1999) *How to Promote Children's Social and Emotional Competence*. London: Paul Chapman.

Whitebread, D. (2007) Developing independence in learning, in J. Moyles (ed.) *Early Years Foundations: Meeting the Challenge*. Maidenhead: Open University Press.

7 Listening to and learning from children's perspectives

Rebecca Webster

Summary

This chapter examines how children's perspectives can be captured, explored and reflected on. It considers the purpose of listening to children's voice, and investigates the advantages and challenges of using video cameras as a tool to facilitate this process. The opportunity for children to explore and share their own perceptions with adults within an educational environment and in the home environment can offer insight into the views of children as individuals and collectively. By drawing on examples from a research project with Year 1 children, this chapter explores some of the practical, theoretical and ethical considerations of using a visual and auditory approach to eliciting children's views and perspectives.

Key questions as you read . . .

There are three key questions that are woven into discussion throughout this chapter. In many ways these key questions are the starting point for discussion, but should also be used as a source of practitioner reflection, following your reading of the chapter.

1   What are the benefits and challenges of listening to the children's 'voice' for both children and practitioners?
2   What strategies can be developed in order to allow for opportunities to enable children to explore and articulate their experiences?
3   How can practitioners adapt pedagogies and practice to reflect the messages children give?

. . . and points to consider

- What are the practicalities of eliciting children's voice from a practitioner or teacher perspective?
- What resources, permissions and dialogue need to occur before embarking on a project that aims to capture children's perceptions?
- What are the potential areas for investigation that are relevant for your setting and practice?
- How will you work with the children, parents and other team members to explore the information that is captured, from both practical and ethical view points?

Introduction

A learner-centred curriculum facilitates an ethos of exploratory and flexible teaching and learning with young children. It should enable the exploration of children's views, interests and attainment within a cyclical and malleable framework. Open-ended approaches and learner-focused pedagogies can empower the collaborative learning between children and practitioners. There are possibilities within the current English *Early Years Foundation Stage (EYFS)* to utilize this way of working as the concept of child-initiated learning is evident within the curriculum framework (DfES, 2007). Indeed, one of the core themes on which this curriculum is centred is the concept of the 'unique child' (DCSF, 2008). This supports the principles of a child-focused approach and values a pedagogy that is responsive, meaningful and often cannot be planned for (see Chapter 5).

There is a stark contrast between the dominance of this flexible child-focused approach within the *EYFS* when compared with the curriculum available for children outside the Foundation Stage. Within the current English Key Stage 1 curriculum, for children aged between 5 and 7, there is less evidence within documentation of the importance of a responsive approach towards learning and teaching. However, this is not to suggest that KS1 teachers do not employ some of these strategies within their practice. Increasingly the term 'personalized learning' is a phrase that has become gradually dominant across all phases of the English National Curriculum. At the core of personalized learning, teachers and practitioners are encouraged to respond to individual needs in order to enable children to achieve at their optimum levels (DfES, 2004). This creates opportunities to work with children in different ways. It also supports the principles of the *Every Child Matters* framework and the *United Nations Convention on the Rights of the Child (UNCRC)* commitment to ensure that children have their voice listened to on issues that impact on their lives (UN, 1990).

Playful methods to elicit children's voice

The ways in which young children's 'voices' can be captured may be associated with participatory research methods. Such methods can enhance the development of pedagogy and practice within schools and settings if the ethos within these establishments values and enables such explorative approaches. However, adult concerns, scepticism, the impact on the authority of the educational system and the effort involved in compliance with the *UNCRC* may hold back some educationalists from working in this potentially more democratic process (Lundy, 2007). There are, nonetheless, some interesting perspectives to be captured by children. These can offer views into aspects of their lives that may not necessarily be otherwise captured (Thomson, 2008). These insights may be used to inform policy and pedagogy, offering tremendous opportunities for reflective practitioners who seek to evolve and develop their work with children.

There are many approaches that enable children's views to be captured and explored. Each approach has its own, often complex and distinctive, strengths and challenges in eliciting children's talk and perceptions. Approaches such as photo-elicitation (see Byrnes and Wasik, 2009) and drawing (see Leitch, 2008) can be replicated and developed with ease in settings. There are other approaches that are directly linked to children's play, such as the use of puppetry (see Epstein et al., 2007). All these methods may produce valuable and interesting results, gathering children's views in different ways. This chapter explores the use of hand-held video cameras to elicit children's voices and consider some of the challenges and insights such an approach may offer.

Video recordings are valuable for several reasons. Not only do these media capture both voice and view from the child simultaneously, which Burke (2008) describes as a 'visual voice', but they also enable the capturing of a sequence of information. Plowman and Stephen (2006) suggest that this portrays the 'big picture' of the child's complex social life. In addition, it is also effective as a tool that can facilitate children to take on a new or different role, placing the capturing of information or evidence in their hands. Thomson and Gunter (2005) suggest that this approach, with children *being* researchers, can have positive outcomes, with children involved with local research for local change.

Aside from the information communications technology (ICT) benefits of using these cameras with children, there are some significant benefits when meeting curriculum demands through the use of this tool. These benefits may be diverse and often unpredictable, from supporting children's social and emotional development, as well as their literacy skills, and, in particular, when developing children's communication and presentation skills. The opportunities for individual or collaborative creative engagement when using video footage are plentiful and the media lends itself well to supporting a cross-curricular approach to learning.

In order to explore this method and the value of video as a tool for capturing children's voice, examples from a research project with Year 1 children (aged between 5 and 6) are used for illustrative purposes. This also enables exploration into some of the issues at both a theoretical and practical level, considering the advantages and challenges when working specifically with children in KS1 or the Foundation Stage.

Working with video: initial considerations and planning

Before embarking on the process of using video cameras with children, there needs to be careful consideration of the practical and ethical implications of using the equipment with young children. Practitioners and teachers need to consider what the focus is for the filming. Is there a specific question or dilemma that is to be considered? There may be many suitable areas to explore such as the development of the transition process between home and school, or children's transitions between year groups (see Chapter 13). Or, is the focus to be based on learning, encouraging the children to record and explore their play using the video? The opportunities are numerous and spread across the curriculum framework, from social/emotional to pedagogical themes (see Chapter 6). Each focus or theme will have its own specific issues that need to be considered and addressed before commencing on a project.

If the focus is very exploratory in its approach, then practitioners and teachers need to be prepared to be open-minded and alert to possibilities arising from children's ideas. Therefore, they should be prepared for the project(s) to move in unexpected directions, which inevitably involves some level of risk. This risk should not be made the reason to abandon the projects or be viewed negatively. As long as there is careful management and ongoing reviews, an element of risk may enable the production of some creative and interesting work. By enabling the children to take the lead, they can work in new ways, planning, articulating and constructing their own learning and documenting the process via the cameras.

The level of adult involvement in the creation and direction of the video projects will inevitably create different boundaries and levels of collaboration between children and adults. This can open out possibilities to explore practice and pedagogy in new ways. Influence can be taken from the Reggio Emilia approach, with the adult and children creating a collaborative partnership (see Nutbrown and Abbott, 2001). This way of working enables children to lead their learning and to negotiate pathways and the direction of their work with adults. The opportunities for practitioner reflection when taking this approach are plentiful and support the notion of personalized learning for the adults (see Chapters 1, 5 and 14 particularly).

While this way of working may provide rich, unpredictable snapshots of the children's perceptions or views, there are inevitably issues concerned with the ethics and boundaries of these flexibly formed projects that need to be given careful forethought. For example, there may be some parents who are happy for cameras to be taken home, while others may see this as a potential intrusion into their private home lives. It is worth considering how the project may be introduced to parents, what expectations they may have in their involvement in the filming process, or use of equipment, the boundaries between home and school or setting and the level of information provided to parents throughout the project.

Home and school shared reflections

Parental involvement when eliciting children's voice and listening to children can be of benefit, not only in strengthening communication and partnerships between home and school, but also for supporting children and their learning. For example, the Year 1 project that enabled children to take the cameras home permitted several constructive outcomes and benefited parents as well as the children and practitioners. There may be opportunities for parents to see their children playing in collaboration with children in the school environment, gaining a glimpse of what is usually unseen. Similarly, parents may film their children playing at home, offering insights to teachers and practitioners about children's interests and communication skills that may not be evident within a classroom context. All these exchanges of information can support and enhance understanding of children's learning and development and enable responsive learning and teaching to develop (see Chapter 12).

The majority of Year 1 children involved in the video project appeared to enjoy the opportunity to use the cameras at home. The inclusive approach and new technology meant that the children were all beginning their work from a similar starting point. Although their levels of ability and experiences of using such technology were different, the work that they were able to produce on the cameras demonstrated their abilities and skills previously unseen in the classroom context. Although the children's level of engagement in the project was evident in their enthusiasm, the end products were not always consistent with their levels of ability. However, there is research to indicate that video-based approaches linking home and school can have a positive impact on children's engagement with settings. A research project completed by Ramsey et al., (2007), which loaned children cameras to document their lives outside their early years provision, found that this often 'represented a watershed in children's engagement with the programme' (p. 26).

Despite great enthusiasm from the children within the Year 1 project, not all children were able to document their lives or perspectives as expertly as others. For some children, there appeared to be a strong parental influence in the decision-making process of what was, and was not, filmed. This was evident within the recorded clips as, occasionally, parents could be heard telling the child what to do. For some, the parental involvement was less audible, but still influential. For example, a parent of a Year 1 child filmed their child at home as he formally introduced his bedroom, while apologizing on camera for the untidy condition of the room. This was in stark contrast to the creative and fast-paced recordings he had filmed with his friends, acting out a story from a popular television programme. Another example of parental involvement was seen as one child read from his school reading book on camera while a parent filmed, with no other recordings being made at home.

Most home-recorded videos provided rich and stimulating lessons to be learned, however. While reflecting on the videos, practitioners and teachers need to be cautious of their own interpretations and potentially biased views. It is easy to draw conclusions, or use the films to confirm beliefs or opinions about the families or home life of children. It is important to use the children's clips in a positive and informative manner. By sustaining a clear purpose and focus, the cameras should be used as a tool to develop and enhance practice, thus becoming a method that enables children to flourish, rather than as evidence which could be used to confirm preconceptions or label children into 'types' (see Brooker, 2008).

The impact of the adult

If teachers and practitioners are to utilize video recording as a method for capturing children's perceptions, views and voice, then we too must accept and be prepared to also be captured on camera, just as other children and parents are. Opportunities for quality interactions with the children and the use of Vygotskian approaches to supporting children's learning can be utilized in this approach, if organization allows for this. Similarly, there are many opportunities for using the recording, either at the time of filming, or at a later date, for some quality shared interactions and sustained shared thinking (Siraj-Blatchford et al., 2002). There are potential links with this method to working with children in a different way, taking influence from the Reggio Emilia approach, and enabling adults and children to negotiate, co-construct learning and move thinking forwards. Shared discourse during the filming process has huge value. Teachers and practitioners may learn about the decision-making processes and perceptions of what is valuable information by listening to and observing the children working in this way. The processes of planning, filming and editing may demonstrate the children's abilities in organizing and representing their views. Equally, it may highlight children's difficulties in these areas, and alert practitioners and teachers to where support is needed.

The process of recording, editing and 'rehearsing' scenes or episodes may allow for insight into the children's perspectives if deconstructed in collaboration with the children. One example of this is the Year 1 boy who was using his camera to take 'photographs' rather than record a film. After discussion with the child, it became evident that the boy did understand what the camera was for and how to use the video function but chose to take 'shots' of places or objects that were important to him. After some minutes working and talking with him about his decisions it became clear that the noise and distractions of the classroom and other children within it were of less importance to him than the order and organization of the environment.

Ethical considerations

Ethically, the cameras pose many issues. The early consideration of these issues is paramount at the beginning of projects and as an ongoing process by teachers and practitioners. Depending on the project focus there may be a number of areas to consider. One such consideration is the accessibility of the video recordings. Videos of children need to be kept within the setting and storage needs to be carefully reasoned. Child protection and safeguarding should be at the forefront of such decisions.

By establishing ground rules at the beginning of the project, teachers and practitioners should consider what the boundaries are for the filming. By collaborating with parents and children in this process, other concerns or questions about the procedures and practicalities of using this media may be raised. For example, there may be some children who do not wish to be filmed, or be unwittingly 'caught' in the camera lens. In order to establish and maintain a positive working ethical framework from the beginning, children should be taught to respect the wishes of others; just as practitioners and parents should be encouraged to respect the views of the children (see Chapter 9).

Burke (in Thompson, 2008) reminds us to be conscious of what rights we have as adults in exploring children's worlds but also to be mindful of the power relationships between adults and children. This is of particular relevance when conducting enquiry into children's lives and attempting to capture, explore and listen to children's perspectives. If we are to embrace the notion of exploring pupil voice in an educational setting, then a positive working partnership between teachers, practitioners and children is necessary. The Department for Education and Skills (DfES) suggests that school councils are one way of achieving this. However, this rather more formal approach does not necessarily include all children. The power relationships that exist between children, which Hart and Tyrer (2006, cited in O'Kane, 2008) attribute to age, gender, ethnicity, birth order, educational attainment, personality and (dis)ability, could potentially be strengthened by such formal and authoritative approaches. The video camera approach is a more inclusive, informal, yet potentially effective way of gathering views.

Negotiation and decisions when deciding on a focus for exploration

A chosen focus or topic may be decided on by the children themselves, or by a combination of child- and adult-led negotiations, or by the adults. Each approach can provide rich insights or may be understimulating and ineffective. One advantage of using individual cameras is that there is flexibility for several projects to be conducted at the same time within the same classroom or setting. If resources do not allow for all the children to be working on a video project at the same time, then a rotation of children using the cameras is a manageable and inclusive way of enabling children to participate.

It is difficult to find a balance between enabling flexibility and supporting children to achieve quality experiences. When the children are the decision-makers and project designers, then they must be given this opportunity to take responsibility and control for their work. Supporting independence and initiative is not only critical to children's learning but also to their confidence (see Chapter 6).

When adults work with children in developing a focus or establishing the project from the outset, the results are often interesting, although there may be some dilemmas relating to ownership of the project. Finding the balance between creating tasks to enable children to explore a particular theme and enabling the children's flexibility and freedom to make their own recording decisions can be a challenge. Some children may wish to please the teacher, creating videos to fulfil hidden or explicit criteria that they perceive, while others may feel anxious about 'getting it wrong', perhaps resulting in capturing very little data. The role of the adult is crucial. Finding ways to establish and maintain a positive and flexible relationship when operating in a different way with children requires careful consideration of both individual and collective needs.

Children's reflections

The use of video within educational settings has often been reserved for special occasions and events. Forman (1999) suggests that we should move beyond this phase, utilizing videos as 'tools of the mind'. He advocates that video cameras enable children to engage with their own actions in a reflective way.

The facility of being able to instantly watch a piece of recorded footage enables the child to move their thinking from beyond the physical and instant action, to thinking about what they have done and why.

While researching with the Year 1 children, the ability to watch playbacks of events either instantly or later, seemed to be of great interest to many of them. This indicates that it could be a useful tool for engaging children in self-evaluation and reflection. Surprisingly, many of the Year 1 children showed little interest in watching each other's videos, but were often seen reviewing and revisiting their own clips, studying what they had recorded. It could be contested that this could be an indication of their egocentric stage of development, as Piaget theorizes. However, some children demonstrated a non-egocentric approach in their recordings. Several children 'presented' their films with an acute awareness of audience, including a 'rehearsal' of scenes. This could be attributed to video as a tool in which to support 'theory of mind' (see Carruthers and Smith, 1996). When considering this, the role of language and communication, particularly with the support of a partner, may sustain the development of a child's understanding. Some children were more successful at this than others, putting themselves in the position of the viewer, as the following Cameo (1) demonstrates:

Cameo 1

The Year 1 boy (Jack) is on camera, entering into an enclosed chicken hutch with his sibling (Ben) filming from behind him and acting as prompt or co-constructor of the dialogue.

Jack: (On camera, walking into large chicken hutch, talking directly to the camera)

This is my chickens, we've got nineteen of them and sometimes I have to feed them and . . . and sometimes when I need to feed them, when I do feed them it's some-it's sometimes . . . um . . . really good because-because every time I feed them they always run to get the food. But right now I'm going to check for eggs. So, so it's going to be quite good, so if you would watch me right now look for some eggs. Okay? Nineteen chickens and I'm looking for eggs, okay, I found one egg so far. Um . . . I'm just going to ask my assistant to open this . . .

Ben: (*Opens box to put egg in*) Yep, hang on a second. [Woah there/Wally/ Oh No!] You dropped it! Oh well, come on! Right, I'll feed 'em. I'm feed 'em, yeah? Woah!

Jack: And, and all these chickens, are some of them . . . the white ones. The white ones are exactly the ones I didn't have.

Ben:	No, leave them because they're laying. I'll check up here. Now we're gonna show you how to do the food.
Jack:	Now we're gonna show you how to do the food. Okay? Now for . . . if I can find the food . . . it's in here . . . (*opens container*)
Ben:	Get a handful of this food.
Jack:	You get a hand full of this food then . . .
Ben:	You chuck it in there . . .
Jack:	You chuck it in. Then they all fly to . . .
Ben:	That gives us a chance to escape, come on, let's escape!
Jack:	Can't I got . . . hold on, we need, if we try an get . . . if I try offering them some food. Come on chickens!
Ben:	They're laying. They're laying! Come on. Let's go!
Jack:	And sometimes it is real fun but if you drop any eggs . . .
Ben:	Like you did just now.
Jack:	Like I did just now . . . it's quite, it's very annoying. So, that's all, bye!

As a practitioner it is worth considering what value this clip may offer to practice or pedagogy. The child in this film demonstrated a different level of confidence and skill at communicating than had been witnessed in the everyday classroom context. In contrast, another child in the same class who appeared to be confident and talkative in the classroom environment recorded no speech on his video at all, choosing to capture only animals and toys at home with no accompanying dialogue.

Learning from and about the individual

Some children seized the opportunity to be independent film makers with great enthusiasm, with several children giving very detailed information about their lives. O'Kane (2008: 125) indicates that such methods enable children to be seen as 'active participants in the construction and determination of their own experiences'. Several children were eager to undertake this self-directional aptitude, often demonstrating good communication skills in their ability to articulate their views.

For one child, a new entry to the class, the video was a way of capturing some personal thoughts. This boy in particular liked to hide with the camera and seemed to whisper into the video camera, commenting at one point: 'I like to be my friend but nobody else wants to'. This was the only speech on this short clip with an almost confessional tone to it. It also opens up debate for the value of the video as a tool in which children may explore feelings as well as learning (see Chapter 6). The video camera in this instance may have reflected the child's individual and private experience that he may not have wished to share in face-to-face discussion.

Practitioner reflections

There were several very unpredictable moments caught on the children's cameras. Several of these involved some sensitive issues. One example from the Year 1 cohort was a captured discussion between two girls about what is cancer, highlighting their misconceptions and concerns about this illness. Much of this dialogue stimulated responsive and necessary discussions between adults and children and enabled the exploration of incidents that may not have emerged from the busy routines of classroom life. Many of these 'episodes' touched on the social and emotional needs of the children in the Year 1 project, raising awareness of issues that needed to be addressed, often at an individual level.

Not all responsive practice came from dialogue-based evidence. Several children, for example, recorded little or no audio on their cameras. However, the data was useful as a starting point for discussions about why particular people, animals or places had been recorded. As a consequence there were numerous opportunities for the practitioner to respond to these clips, thus supporting a responsive pedagogical approach. One such case was one boy who filled nearly 40 minutes worth of video clips without speaking on the video at all. As a tool for gathering this particular child's perceptions, however, this makes an interesting starting point for engaging in discussion and listening to the child. One particularly strong and frequent feature of this boy's video clips was the presence of his pet cat. This could potentially be developed into a range of responsive teaching and learning opportunities for further exploration in partnership with the child.

Watching video playbacks with the children can enhance teacher reflections, not only in understanding the children's learning and points of view, but also in supporting their own reflective practice. Teachers or practitioners may also become involved in capturing their perceptions on camera, to be explored and considered either individually or with colleagues (see Chapters 1 and 3). These videos may be used as a tool for assessment, record keeping, or as an exploratory tool in which to reflect on their own practice through a different lens (see Plowman and Stephen, 2006).

Conclusion

By engaging in reflective experiences with children, there are a great deal of insights which can be used to inform practice and pedagogy. However, it is with caution, careful consideration and sensitivity that practitioners and teachers should reflect on the information that children gather. Such information should be used in a positive way, as a tool for thinking and learning and as a starting point from which dialogue, listening and collaboration begins.

There are potential issues with the interpretation of this type of documentation of children's lives, several of which have been explored within this chapter. However, if we are to work fully with the concepts of 'a unique child' and 'responsive' or 'personalized' teaching and learning, then we must accept that such pedagogical change comes with an element of risk. As with all change, teachers and practitioners will need to strengthen and develop new or different skills. At the core of these skills there must be a willingness and ability to be reflective on both pedagogy and practice.

What do I, the writer, feel about the contribution of this chapter to supporting critical reflection?

By engaging in practices that enable us to see, hear and discuss children's perceptions, there are many opportunities for reflection, either individually or collectively. What *is* crucial when engaging in this reflective process is the time taken to think through the views, perceptions and messages that may have been captured by the children. This means that conclusions should not be drawn early on, or the videos be used to confirm a preconceived view of a child. Instead, time needs to be taken to explore the videos with 'fresh' eyes, reflecting more deeply about the children's perceptions and using this reflection to inform practice and pedagogy in positive ways.

Implications for pedagogy: what might *you*, the reader, reflect on now?

- What value and impact might a project involving listening to children's voice have on your practice and pedagogy?
- How might you set about constructing and developing your own project?
- What boundaries are there for such a project, both geographical and ethical?
- How will you make time to reflect on the management of the project and the ways in which you can disseminate findings to parents and colleagues in order for the outcomes to be both positive and informative?

References and further reading

Brooker, L. (2008) *Supporting Transitions in the Early Years*. Maidenhead: Open University Press.

Burke, C. (2008) Play in focus: children's research voice in participative research, in P. Thomson (ed.) *Doing Visual Research with Children and Young People*. **London: Routledge.**

Byrnes, J. and Wasik, B. (2009) Picture this: using photography as a learning tool in early childhood classrooms, *Childhood Education*, **85(4): 243–8.**

Carruthers, P. and Smith, P. (1996) *Theories of the Mind*. Cambridge: Cambridge University Press.

Department for Children, Schools and Families (DCSF) (2008) *The Early Years Foundation Stage. Every Child Matters. Change for Children*. Nottingham: DCSF.

Department for Education and Skills (DfES) (2004) *A National Conversation about Personalised Learning*. Nottingham: DfES Publications.

Department for Education and Skills (DfES) (2007) *Early Years Foundation Stage*. London: DfES.

Epstein, I., Stevens, B., McKeever, P., Baruchel, S. and Jones, H. (2007) Using puppetry to elicit children's talk for research, *Nursing Inquiry*, 15(1): 49–56.

Forman, G. (1999) Instant video revisiting: the video camera as a 'tool of the mind' for young children, *Early Childhood Research and Practice*, 1(2) Available online at www.//ecr/uiuc.edu/vln2/forman.html (accessed 1 November 2009).

Leitch, R. (2008) Creatively researching children's narratives through images and drawings, In P. Thomson (ed.) *Doing Visual Research with Children and Young People*. **London: Routledge.**

Lundy, L. (2007) 'Voice' is not enough: conceptualising Article 12 of the United Nations Convention on the Rights of the Child, *British Educational Research Journal*, 33(6): 927–42.

Nutbrown, C. and Abbott, L. (eds) (2001) *Experiencing Reggio Emilia: Implications for Pre-school Provision*. Buckingham: Open University Press.

O'Kane, C. (2008) The development of participatory techniques, in P. Christensen and A. James (eds) (2008) *Research with Children, Perspectives and Practices*, 2nd edn. London: Routledge.

Plowman, L. and Stephen, C. (2006) The big picture? Video and the representation of interaction, *British Educational Research Journal*, 34(4): 541–65.

Ramsey, K., Sturm, J., Breen, J., Lee, W. and Carr, M. (2007) Weaving ICTs into Te Whāriki at Roskill South Kindergarten, in A. Meade (ed.) *Cresting the Wave: Innovations in Early Childhood Education*, pp. 29–36. Wellington: NZCER Press.

Siraj-Blatchford, I., Sylva, K., Muttock, S., Gilden, R. and Bell, D. (2002) *Researching Effective Pedagogy in the Early Years*. London: DfES Research Report No. 356.

Thomson, P. (2008) (ed.) *Doing Visual Research with Children and Young People*. London: Routledge.

Thomson, P. and Gunter, H. (2005) From 'consulting pupils' to 'pupils as researchers': a situated case narrative, *British Educational Research Journal*, 32(6): 839–56.

United Nations (UN) (1990) *Convention on the Rights of the Child. UN document A/44/25*. Geneva: UN.

8   Reflecting on children 'playing for real' and 'really playing' in the early years

Deborah Albon

Summary

The observations drawn on in this chapter come from my research, which has been looking at 'food events', real (as in meal and snack times) and pretend (as in role play), in four early childhood settings for the past three years. For the purposes of this chapter, I reflect on observations made in or near role-play areas, which offered the opportunity to observe young children's food-related play. In looking at the numerous observations I have collected of such play, they often seem to fall within two categories: 'playing for real' and 'really playing'. The chapter outlines what I mean, using narrative observations to illustrate these categorizations. Both categories of play, on reflection, are valuable and generate their own challenges for early years practitioners. I conclude by encouraging further reflection on the issues raised in the chapter, as reflection is the key to considering both children's experiences and our own practice.

Key questions as you read . . .

1   What is meant by 'playing for real' and 'really playing' in the context of early childhood practice?
2   What is the value of such play?
3   What challenges might such play pose for practitioners?
4   How might practitioners reflect on such play and, through reflection, extend it further?

. . . and points to consider

1 Think about the differences *you* perceive between playing for real and really playing.
2 Consider the issue of power relationships between adults and children.
3 Reflection will support innovative thinking about children's learning and our own pedagogy.

Introduction

There is a range of ways in which to categorize types of play. Indeed, the topic 'play' has undergone thorough examination and continues to do so; such is its importance in the field of early years education and care. Examples of such categorizations include Hutt et al.'s (1989) taxonomy of play as involving either 'epistemic behaviour', which relates to activity that involves problem solving and exploration, and 'ludic behaviour', which is more playful, repetitive and/or symbolic (see also Chapter 2). In thinking about young children's pretend play, Hendy and Toon (2001) make a distinction between 'socio-dramatic play' and 'thematic-fantasy play', arguing that the former involves the child in pretend activities such as cooking a meal and the latter relates to imaginary worlds that children have invented for themselves, sometimes drawing on cultural narratives available to them and other times derived purely from their imaginations.

This chapter draws on five observations from three early years settings. It should be noted from the outset that I do not claim that *all* play episodes can be categorized exclusively as falling within one of the terms I have called 'playing for real' or 'really playing' and will also include play episodes that are not food-related. Possibly these terms are best thought of as opposite ends of a *continuum* with the observations discussed here viewed as towards the two opposite extremities of this continuum. In addition, as play is often shifting in its focus, a play episode that starts as 'playing for real' can turn into something akin to 'really playing' in a moment – such is the *beauty* of play.

'Playing for real'

The episodes of play that I am characterizing as 'playing for real' are those that seem highly imitative of real life; where the conventions that children may have witnessed at home, nursery, cafés or elsewhere are often highly recognizable to the observer. Hendy and Toon (2001) describe such activity as 'socio-dramatic play'. I have often observed this type of play when children have access to real objects such as real food or cooking equipment and when they have access to a range of materials that they use to stand very directly for something else (as noted in Vygotsky, 1978). Children engaged in episodes of 'playing for real' tend to appear to be 'purposefully' engaged – sometimes for long periods – and seem to be performing an activity in their play at a higher level than might be expected from someone of their age and experience (see also Chapter 1), such as cooking the dinner. I use the term 'purposefully' in inverted commas because it is the type of play that practitioners I have observed and spoken to tend to view highly. It is the kind of play where children seem to want to encounter reality (Moyles, 1989) rather than playfully pushing the boundaries of what is 'real' as we will see in the play episodes I am describing in terms of 'really playing'.

In 'playing for real', children are able to explore aspects of the 'real' world from different angles but without the emotional stress that goes with real life. This is not to say that strong emotions are absent from play but that children are not *really* trying to feed a small baby and get it to sleep and can choose to come out of role when they wish to. When 'playing for real', children may take on different but recognizable roles. In so doing, they are able to experience the world from different vantage points, particularly those of people who have control over them such as parents (Mead, 1967; see also Chapter 7).

In order to illustrate what I mean by 'playing for real', I will now reflect on two observations. The first involves a group of 3-year-old children, one of whom is making roti using playdough in the home corner. The second observation involves a group of 4-year-old children who are using real potatoes as part of their play in the home corner. We will see in these two observations that the play is very recognizable from the real world of cooking and serving food. At the end of this section, I pose a series of reflective questions that occurred to me both at the time of the observations (reflection-in-action) and when reflecting on them further at a later date (reflection-on-action).

Observation 1: Making roti (observation of children aged 3 in a nursery class)

Sarbjeet takes a lump of play dough into the home corner and uses it to make roti, speaking to me in Punjabi but interspersing it with 'special for you'. She demonstrates a high level of skill in forming the flat, round shapes with her hands. Sarbjeet increases the heat on the cooker by turning the knob. Then she stands with her hands on her hips as if waiting for time to pass by, seemingly annoyed at the length of time the roti are taking to cook. To cook them, she places the dough directly onto the 'heat', pressing them down slightly as if they are bubbling up. As she does this, she piles the cooked roti onto a plate very carefully and carries on cooking.

Daspurnima comes over to join her and they both stand at the cooker cooking roti, saying 'wait' as the roti cooks. Sometimes they have their arms folded, chatting together as if gossiping. When all the dough is cooked and a huge pile of roti is made, they bring it over to the table and I am invited to join the group (a group of five children including Sarbjeet and Daspurnima). Sarbjeet gives me a roti on a plate and spoons an imaginary blob next to it saying 'chutney'. She is concerned her roti are too hot to eat at the moment and says 'careful – hot' to make sure we all take care.

Observation 2: Play with potatoes (observation of children aged 4 in a private day nursery)

Today there are real potatoes in the home corner. This is interesting because the children run over to the cook in the kitchen with them and say they have found them and they belong in the kitchen. The cook seems a bit confused about this initially but then laughs and says 'That's OK!' It is very noticeable in this setting that the kitchen is visible to all the children and the children are able to watch the meals being cooked or engage in conversation with the cook about the food they are going to eat.

The children seem to have a very strong sense of real and pretend in the home corner as evidenced by the potatoes. Once they realize that they can have the real potatoes in the home corner, I notice a marked change in the play. Mary gets the toy knife and starts to cut one of the potatoes into pieces and puts the pieces into a saucepan. This is tricky given the lack of a sharp edge. Other children do this too but with a lesser degree of ability and there is a very purposeful air in the home corner. The cook supplies extra potatoes at the request of the children, who run over to the kitchen and tell her what they are doing.

The nursery manager brings over some real knives from the kitchen and the children become engrossed in cutting the potatoes and filling pans. Once full, Mary and Eva say that they need water in the pans to boil the potatoes. They have clearly seen this being done. A practitioner does not question this and puts some water in the water tray to enable the children to fill their pans with water (on top of the cut potatoes). The children are unable to access water from taps themselves owing to the building design. The children spend a long time at play – preparing, cooking and serving up food. The children comment on how the water is dirty now and talk about the need to peel the potatoes. Later, Mary says that she needs to get the water out of the pan like her mum does at home and takes the pans over to the water tray. Mary selects a sieve from a couple offered to her by the cook and takes it over to the water tray and drains her potatoes successfully. She then returns to the home corner.

What follows now are some questions to reflect on in relation to these observations and a consideration of their implications for early childhood practice:

- How willing are practitioners to allow materials to be moved from one part of the room to another, even if it causes a degree of mess? We might view the use of play dough as roti in the home corner positively, but would we *all* value the movement of water into the home corner positively as in Observation 2 owing to the mess it might make?
- How 'real' are practitioners willing to make play activities? In a play situation – one that is likely to be less regulated than a cooking activity, for instance – how willing are we to allow *real* knives, *real* sieving and *real* food, for example, in the home corner? Not all practitioners in this nursery were happy when the manager introduced the knives and removed them when she had left the room, noting that the home corner was likely to be difficult to supervise as practitioners were having staggered lunch breaks.

We might also question the extent to which the second observation, in particular, constitutes play (see also Chapter 2). Arguably, these observations could be likened to an 'in-between activity' (Gura, 1996: 60) as they share many elements from the world of work as much as play. Certainly the skills developed in cutting the potatoes in Observation 2 appear more work-like than play-like (Wing, 1995; Gura, 1996).

- How willing are practitioners to allow children to eat food that has been placed in a play situation? My many observations in this area show that inevitably some children eat what is there.
- If we do allow such activity but are worried about the potential risks for health and safety, are we in danger of regulating such play to the extent that it becomes something that is not play? If so, would this matter (after all, it may be possible to have a work-like approach to our play and a playful approach to our work – see the links with playful pedagogy as described in Chapter 1)?
- Can staff other than early years practitioners become involved in children's play as in Observation 2? In this example, the cook was involved in the children's play.
- Should real food be used as a play material? There are decisions to be made regarding whether this is ethical, given the experience of some people in the world of food insecurity. Alternatively, by having the opportunity to play with real food, children may be able to alleviate any anxieties they experience in relation to food and eating in a relaxed environment (Albon and Mukherji, 2008).

In my observations, the use of real food tends to result in children 'playing for real' whereas plastic food tends to result in play that might be regarded in terms of 'really playing'. Maybe this points to the need for both real *and* pretend items in play situations alongside the ability to mix media from around the play space(s). An example of this might be the child I observed putting dried pasta onto a plate that was available in the home corner and then carefully selecting a piece of red fabric from the workshop area to act as tomato sauce on top of it.

'Really playing'

'Really playing', I wish to argue, differs from 'playing for real' because here, children appear to be stretching conventional boundaries. In my data this relates to *what* food is eaten, but more usually, *how* it is eaten and the kinds of unwritten cultural rules that exist about what is acceptable behaviour during food events. It is play that can be likened to Hendy and Toon's (2001) thematic-fantasy play, but more than this; it is often characterized by its humour and playfulness. For Parker-Rees (1999: 61), playfulness enables us to cope with 'the tension between personal freedom and social constraints that characterizes all forms of interaction'. Further to this, 'really playing' can be linked to 'ludic' behaviours (Hutt et al., 1989) and Kalliala's (2006) notion of 'dizzy' play that turns the world upside down. It should be noted that the *Early Years Foundation Stage* (*EYFS*) (DfES, 2007) lacks reference to such humour and playfulness – the few references there are seem to relate to babies.

'Really playing' can be contrasted with 'good' play, which is encouraged by practitioners as it emphasizes turn-taking and following approved rules (e.g. King, 1992). Bakhtin (1984) discusses the important role played by the carnivalesque in subverting and making fun of authoritarianism, order, officialdom, narrow-minded seriousness, dogma, and 'all that is finished and polished' (p. 3). Carnival is a time when there is temporary liberation from the established order of things and it is always accompanied by laughter. Thus, my conceptualization of some play episodes as 'really playing' seems to fit well with this.

Such playfulness is important as we can see in many examples in this book. Corsaro (1997) argues that playful activity is indicative of children's ability to create and participate in their own peer cultures. In addition to this, the sharing of comic situations and the camaraderie that this engenders may be significant as a precursor to forming close relationships (Dunn, 1988). Given the centrality of developing and sustaining positive relationships in early childhood practice (Elfer et al., 2003; Manning-Morton and Thorp, 2003), it would seem that practitioners should be seeking to maximize opportunities for 'really playing' in their settings.

But are there other benefits to playfulness? Meek (1985) builds on the work of Bateson, who believes that play is important in freeing children from the rigidity of rule-bound games and messages and that this playfulness is essential from an evolutionary perspective as it enables the child to be adaptable and imagine 'what if?' In a similar way, Chukovsky (1968: 97) celebrates the 'intellectual effrontery' and 'topsy-turvy' nature of play. These topsy-turvies have educational value because, as Chukovsky (1968: 99) notes, 'The more aware the child is of the correct relationship of things, which he violates in his play, the more comical does this violation seem to him'.

Thus, in stretching the boundaries of what is possible, children are demonstrating their understandings of 'what might be' and, in so doing, generating new and creative understandings of the world. It would seem, then, that the playfulness and humour indicative in 'really playing' are important in the child's developing awareness of 'sense and nonsense', 'fact from fiction' and that which is 'socially tolerated' (Meek, 1985: 48). Similarly, Egan (1991) argues that in exploring the fantastic, children are able to discover the limits of their world and thus develop a greater understanding of reality.

What follows now are three observations of children 'really playing' where the play bears little relation to what we might, on reflection, view as 'usual conventions' – or are only recognizable in as much as they are opposite to what is usual. In reading these, you will see examples of carnivalesque behaviour and, in Observation 5, children exploring the unthinkable. As with the section on 'playing for real', I conclude the section with a series of questions to stimulate further reflection.

> ### Observation 3: Feeding the pets (observation of children aged 3 and 4 in a nursery class)
>
> Hanan gets a doll and takes it out of the high chair and then puts it to bed saying 'She's asleep now'. This paves the way for the toy cat to come onto the high chair. This results in peals of laughter from Hanan, Sarah and Ben, who has just arrived in the home corner. Ben gets the toy dog and puts it into the larger of the two high chairs and both he and Hanan feed their animals using spoons. All are laughing as they seem to know that this is not how you feed pets. I make a comment about Hanan's cat being in a high chair and Ben jokes 'That's not a high chair, silly – that's a low chair!' This play on words seems highly appropriate in a topsy-turvy world where pets eat at high chairs!
>
> Ben and Hanan have their respective pets in the high chairs and are feeding the pets a range of foods. After trying each one, Ben says 'He [*i.e. the pet*] likes it'. Hanan is copying him. This becomes increasingly bizarre, with ice creams, cups of tea, chocolate cake, babies' bottles of milk and, later, a clock and some clothing (etc.) offered and

sometimes force-fed to the pets. The laughter increases as the food items get increasingly outrageous – as if each child is egging the other on to find something more and more inappropriate. Each time this is reinforced with the language 'He like it' accompanied by laughter at how preposterous this is. After a while a practitioner comes over and tells the children to be quieter.

Observation 4: Sicking up food mum has cooked at a party (observation of a group of children aged 3 and 4 in a nursery class)

In the home corner, Charlie, James, Nina and Furqan are playing together. Charlie says 'Let's pretend we are all eating this food at a party – you're the mum, Nina, and we don't want to eat it 'cos it's horrible and makes us sick'.

Every time Nina, as 'mum', presents food to her 'children', they are sick. James and Charlie shout 'Ugh – horrible' with Charlie making sick noises, with everyone accompanying this with laughter. Sarah and Zara join in as other 'mothers' put on aprons as if to denote this status. All three girls serve up food only to have it refused and a pretence of regurgitation made. Sarah and Zara add a new dimension to the play because they make a pretence of being very offended by this action, telling the 'children' off. 'You just eat it all up and do what I say' says Zara. The more the 'children' are sick or refuse food, the more she and Sarah tell them to 'Eat it'. Their remonstrations with the 'children' are accompanied with wagging fingers and mock cross faces. Maybe the children are also playing out very real anxieties that occur during mealtimes, not least being told to eat foods even when they are not deemed palatable.

The play continues for a while and gets quite raucous. All the children – a cross-language/cultural group – seem to recognize that it is funny to refuse food in this way and that being sick – almost forcing this – is not to be borne. The biggest affront to civility and acceptance is to refuse food or let the cook feel it is horrible in some way. Somehow this is further intensified in the context of a party.

Observation 5: 'Pretend real' eating the dough baby (observation of children aged 3 and 4 in a nursery class)

Farrah is sitting at the dough table where some home corner equipment has been taken and makes a dough baby. She says 'I'm going to make a baby and cut it up and put it in my stew'. I obviously look disgusted and shocked, so she says 'You know it's not real – it isn't even pretend – it's *pretend real*'.

Maybe pretend is pretend, but it *is* real; 'pretend real', it seems, is when all sense of being real is suspended. At least I think this is her meaning. Farrah cuts the dough baby into pieces and puts it into the saucepan. She stirs the pan and Hamid laughs saying it's a 'nice baby' (taking a spoon to the pan).

As with the previous section exploring the notion of 'playing for real', I will now reflect on some of the challenges the observations contained in this section might pose for practitioners.

- Should practitioners get involved in this type of play? This is an interesting question to reflect on because I suspect that often we would not as it is difficult to imagine joining in with play about making a baby stew as it forces us to consider the unthinkable. Yet as Edmiston (2008: 7) reminds us, by not participating in children's play, adults are reinforcing a view of pretend play as a 'special province of childhood; not a space for adults to enter into with children'. The role of practitioners, from this perspective, is confined to encouraging and organizing for play activities as opposed to *participating* in pretend worlds with children.

For Edmiston (2008), when adults and children participate in pretend worlds *together*, there is an opportunity to co-author ethical identities as such play facilitates the exploration of different actions and ways of being in the world. Therefore, in play we can imagine identities that we might like to be or that make us fearful and in doing this, not only *enact* the socially unacceptable, such as sicking up food, but *evaluate* those actions. This is also useful when reflecting on the many observations collected of Farrah's play (such as Observation 5) because as well as exploring the unthinkable in making baby stew, there are many observations of her playing roles where she cares for babies and saves them from 'near death' experiences. When considering Observation 5 now, I wonder what might have happened if I had participated playfully with Farrah and Hamid – maybe as someone with special powers coming to save the baby. As Edmiston (2008) notes, when adults participate directly in children's pretend play, children are not abandoned to think ethically about the actions and feelings explored in their play on their own.

It should be noted that I have observed practitioners engaging in play that I see as 'really playing' – indeed, I recall playing a game with children during the research where every time I was offered some food or drink, I pretended I hated it, making 'Ugh' noises and protested wildly at eating or drinking it. It was in marked contrast to my usual home corner interactions where I am uniformly grateful for *any* offer of food or drink and without fail enjoy it. On reflection, I do not think I would do this with children I do not know as to refuse something in play might seem like rejection, but with children with whom I was very familiar the shared joke was that I had always been grateful for offers of food and drink during role play and was turning this round on its head – something the children seemed to find hilarious; but hilarious in the knowledge that, *in reality*, I cared about them.

- But do *all* practitioners see such playfulness as valuable? Moreover, my observations show a tendency for some practitioners to become overly concerned with the level of noise and the possibility of chaos. One practitioner I observed was very concerned that children were using a plastic orange as something other than a food item eaten by humans and some others were dismissive of such play as lacking any real educational purpose and as only valuable for the immediate sense of fun it engenders. In reflecting on play in this way, we need to ask ourselves whether play is valuable purely in terms of its future benefits for children or whether we should also be valuing the lived-time of children now (Polakow, 1992).

Grace and Tobin (1997) seem to address this issue when they draw on the work of Barthes in relation to pleasure. Barthes distinguishes between *plaisir* and *jouissance*, with the former signifying the more conservative, conformist notions of pleasure and the latter relating to the more playful, anti-authoritarian forms of pleasure. *Jouissance* happens less often in the classroom (or play-space) than *plaisir* as it is focused on the moment. Grace and Tobin (1997: 177) argue that in *jouissance*-like moments in the classroom '. . . the teacher temporarily disappeared, and the children were united in a spirit of camaraderie, a celebration of "otherness" organized around laughter'.

This seems a useful way to think about joining in when children are 'really playing'; a temporary liberation from the usual order of things. Certainly, in my own playful rejection of food and drink in the play episode outlined earlier, I felt a strong sense of truly sharing in the 'dizziness' of the children's play (Kalliala, 2006) in ways that cheerful acceptance of a cup of tea, keeping to the general order of things and 'playing for real' would not have engendered. However, it is interesting to reflect on *when* we might think it is acceptable and if it *is*, the *extent* to which we fully engage with this type of play.

- Is it possible to plan for such play? Would it cease to be 'really playing' if preplanned by adults? I suspect that it would cease to be play (as Bryonie Williams suggests in Chapter 4). Like Gura (1996), I am suspicious of adult constructs such as 'structured play' and think it is possible to plan for episodes of 'playing for real' more than 'really playing'. A strong memory from my own practice was of creating a launderette with a group of 2–5-year-old children following visits to the local launderette with the view that the children could 'play launderettes'. We developed plans around this theme and made washing machines with the children, including drawers for the soap powder and so on. Soon after setting up, the children were using the washing machines as kennels and were enacting their own take on the *'101 Dalmatians'* story. Far from being the pleasant-mannered customer about to have my clothes laundered (a role we had envisaged for ourselves as practitioners), I found myself cast by the children as 'Cruella DeVille' intent on capturing the puppies!

Conclusion

My intention in writing this chapter has been to encourage reflection on play, which I have suggested might be categorized on a continuum of 'playing for real' and 'really playing'. In doing this, my wish has been to highlight the need to preserve both types of play. Each has value and exposes its own challenges for early childhood practice as I have outlined.

My observations and reflections on these show a tendency for practitioners to prize 'playing for real' more highly than 'really playing'. This may be because it is easier to plan for such play and, consequently, it may be more amenable to adult control. Possibly this makes it a more comfortable activity for practitioners to engage in with children when compared to 'really playing'. However, I hope this chapter has encouraged readers to reflect on the challenges 'playing for real' poses for practitioners, not least how 'real' play can be made to be and still be called 'play'.

By way of contrast, engaging in 'really playing' may mean vanquishing the usual order of things. In order to truly be part of such play, practitioners may need to suspend, albeit momentarily, their more powerful position when compared to young children. The *EYFS* (DfES, 2007) pays little reference to such playfulness – to the mercurial ability to turn the world on its head and laugh at it. Maybe this is a good thing, because such playfulness resists easy documentation. But its omission ignores the importance of humour and the role it plays in communality and ongoing relationships.

What do I, the writer, feel about the contribution of this chapter to supporting critical reflection?

I have provided no easy answers to the questions I have posed throughout this chapter. This is because I do not believe there are easy answers; indeed, I am suspicious of 'easy answers' to complex areas of practice. But I do believe that the questions are important to reflect on and constantly revisit as a team. This points to a need for reflective discussions about play in early childhood settings that go way beyond planning meetings merely listing the resources that might be added to an area in order to organize and encourage children's play or that discuss observations of children's play without reflecting on the role practitioners could play in extending or, indeed, inhibiting that play. Rather, it suggests the need to reflect deeply on our own attitudes and values and our individual and collective responses to play; both 'playing for real' and 'really playing'.

Implications for pedagogy: what might *you*, the reader, reflect on now?

Reflect on your own feelings in relation to the play episodes referred to in this chapter.

- Which kinds of play do you feel most comfortable with and why?
- What might your responses have been in these situations. Would you have got some real knives to cut the potatoes, for instance?
- Reflect on observations you have made of young children's play. Where would you put them on a continuum of 'playing for real' and 'really playing'?
- Reflect on the issue of adult (practitioner) power in relation to the above questions; after all practitioners have the power to inhibit and permit all sorts of activity in early childhood settings.

Acknowledgement

I am indebted to the practitioners, parents and children, who made this research possible and who shared their reflections on practice with me.

References and further reading

Albon, D. and Mukherji, P. (2008) *Food and Health in Early Childhood.* London: Sage Publications.

Bakhtin, M. (1984) *Rabelias and his World* (trans. by H. Iswolsky). Bloomington, IN: Indiana University Press.

Chukovsky, K. (1968) *From Two to Five.* Berkeley, CA: University of California Press.

Corsaro, W. (1997) *The Sociology of Childhood.* London: Sage Publications.

Department for Education and Skills (DfES) (2007) *The Early Years Foundation Stage.* Nottingham: DfES.

Dunn, J. (1988) *The Beginnings of Social Understanding.* Oxford: Blackwell.

Edmiston, B. (2008) *Forming Ethical Identities in Early Childhood Play.* Abingdon: Routledge.

Egan, K. (1991) *Primary Understanding: Education in Early Childhood.* London: Routledge.

Elfer, P., Goldschmeid, E. and Selleck, D. (2003) *Key Persons in the Nursery: Building Relationships for Quality Provision.* London: David Fulton.

Grace, D. and Tobin, J. (1997) Carnival in the classroom: elementary students making videos, in J. Tobin (ed.) *Making a Place for Pleasure in Early Childhood Education:* New Haven, CT: Yale University Press.

Gura, P. (1996) *Resources for Early Learning: Children, Adults and Stuff.* London: Hodder & Stoughton.

Hendy, L. and Toon, L. (2001) *Supporting Drama and Imaginative Play in the Early Years.* Buckingham: Open University Press.

Hutt, S.J., Tyler, S., Hutt, C. and Christopherson, H. (1989) *Play, Exploration and Learning: A Natural History of the Pre-School.* London: Routledge.

Kalliala, M. (2006) *Play Culture in a Changing World.* Maidenhead: Open University Press.

King, N. (1992) The impact of context on the play of young children, in S. Kessler and B. Swadener (eds) *Reconceptualising the Early Childhood Curriculum: Beginning the Dialogue.* New York: Teachers College Press.

Manning-Morton, J. and Thorp, M. (2003) *Key Times for Play.* Maidenhead: Open University Press.

Mead, G.H. (1967) *Mind, Self and Society.* Chicago, IL: Chicago University Press.

Meek, M. (1985) Play and paradoxes: some considerations of imagination and language, in G. Wells and J. Nicholls (eds) *Language and Learning: An Interactional Perspective.* Lewes: Falmer Press.

Moyles, J.R. (1989) *Just Playing? The Role and Status of Play in Early Childhood Education.* Milton Keynes: Oxford University Press.

Parker-Rees, R. (1999) Protecting playfulness, in L. Abbott and H. Moylett (eds) *Early Education Transformed.* London: Falmer Press.

Polakow, V. (1992) *The Erosion of Childhood.* Chicago, IL: University of Chicago Press.

Vygotsky, L.S. (1978) *Mind in Society: The Development of Higher Psychological Processes.* Cambridge, MA: Harvard University Press.

Wing, L.A. (1995) Play is not the work of the child: young children's perceptions of work and play, *Early Childhood Education Research Quarterly*, 10(2): 223–47.

PART 3
Reflecting on playful learning environments

9 The pedagogy of play(ful) learning environments

Theodora Papatheodorou

Summary

The question raised in this chapter is what types of playful learning environments do children need for their development and the achievement of their potential? To answer this question, I argue that learning environments are neither neutral nor innocent; they shape and condition how we feel, think and behave. The sensorial, intellectual and social stimuli and experiences they offer and the way they respond and meet, or not, individual and collective needs render meaning to our being, belonging and becoming; to our identity and freedom. I also argue that learning environments are socially constructed: the learning environments we create in early years settings are influenced by our beliefs and values and the relevant theoretical models we embrace.

Key questions as you read . . .

1   If you are asked, would you be able to explain what ideas, beliefs and theories have influenced and driven the design and choice of resources in your early years setting?

2   Reflecting on the learning environment of your setting, would you say that there is a balance between sensory, intellectual and social stimuli? Does the design and planning of the space you have available enable children to engage meaningfully with all stimuli offered?

3   What does your learning environment tell you about your pedagogy and your priorities for children?

4   Would you honestly say that the playful learning environment you have created is a place for children rather than mere space, where they spend a few hours during the day?

. . . and points to consider

- The playful learning environment is influenced and determined by our ideas and beliefs about children and the theoretical models we embrace as policy imperatives prevailing at different times and places.
- A playful learning environment offers a balance of sensory, intellectual and social stimuli that attract children's attention and interests and sustains their active participation in meaningful activities.
- Playful learning environments cater for children's well-being, belonging and becoming; they allow children to transform it from a space into a place, where they can exercise and realize their abilities, capabilities and reach their potential.

Introduction

Historically, the organization of the learning environment of early years settings has been influenced by pedagogical theories and models that dominated the field of early childhood and education. Traditional didactic and teacher-centred pedagogical models meant that the learning environment was organized in a way that asserted the teachers' authority as the knowledge transmitter, while the children were expected to be attentive to their instructions. The classroom had limited resources and its spatial arrangements reinforced such notions further. The seating arrangements, for example, were in orderly rows of desks that limited or prohibited children's interactions.

However, the work of early pioneers such as Froebel and Montessori gradually changed the landscape in early years education. Their pedagogical ideas about the education of young children led to the introduction of learning resources and materials that were purposefully designed to suit children's age and development. For example, Froebel introduced the *gifts and occupations* to enable children to experiment, identify patterns, find relationships and transform images, leading to understanding of themselves and their world, to intuition and discovery (Bruce et al., 1995; Reed, 1992). Similarly, Montessori introduced a range of purposefully designed multi-sensory resources to capture children's attention and initiate a process of concentration for internal formation of ideas and concepts (Montessori, 1912). The influence of early pioneers in the field of early childhood meant that early years settings started to be equipped with a variety of purposefully designed play objects. The pedagogical model was also gradually transformed from didactic and adult-centred to exploratory and child-centred.

However, the greatest impact on the learning environment of early years settings came from Piaget's theory of cognitive development that was linked with children's ages and stages of development. Piaget conceived children as emergent scientists who could become aware of the underpinning principles of phenomena through exploration of appropriate and mentally stimulating resources and materials. Children started to be recognized as active agents in their own learning in a learning environment that offered hands-on experiences and opportunities for exploration and investigation. The idea and notion of play and playful learning gained credibility in the field of early childhood and became the philosophical anchor of practice. Gradually, early years settings were filled with age-appropriate resources.

The developmental model of understanding children's learning and development influenced and dominated the field of early childhood for many decades of the twentieth century across the globe (see Bredekamp, 1987). Advice and recommendations of what makes developmentally appropriate learning environments have been copiously introduced in early years settings across the world, portraying a child whose development and learning were understood as being subject to universal normative criteria and standards (Canella, 2005). As a result, almost identical and homogenous learning environments were designed in early years settings that are culturally and geographically distanced.

In the 1980s, the ecological systems theory and the socio-cultural theories provided us with new insights and understandings of child development, learning and behaviour. Vygotsky's socio-cultural theory influenced the field of early childhood and education, in general, by maintaining that the individual is inseparable from the social and cultural context (Vygotsky, 1978; see also Chapter 4). Bronfenbrenner's (1979) ecological systems theory also suggested that children's development is influenced by complex and dynamic, direct and indirect interrelationships within and between different systems in which the child is located.

Such theorization has led to the idea that learning and teaching are 'context' bound (Jamieson et al., 2000) and, in early childhood, a shift has been observed from emphasis on the availability of age-appropriate playful resources to how they are used and to the wider learning environment, including both its social (e.g. interactions, interrelationships, actions – Chapter 9) and physical attributes (e.g. space, design, resources). Indeed, Malagguzi, the founder of the Reggio Emilia preschools, has notably referred to the learning environment as the third educator (Rinaldi, 2006). However, much of the discussion and debate on learning environments has largely been about social aspects. Time for an example: consider Photographs 9.1 and 9.2 below: what do they tell us about the pedagogy of early years practitioners? What professional assumptions do these playful resources reflect? What do they tell us about the ways professionals work with children?

Photograph 9.1 Classroom environment (1).

What playful learning environments do we need?

There is now much evidence that educational spaces and their design affect children's learning (Penrose et al., 2001). Research has demonstrated that children attending schools with limited space, outdoor facilities and inappropriate play resources, tend to perform less well than children attending schools with better facilities (Smith and Connolly, 1980; Papatheodorou and Ramasut, 1994; Kennedy, 2002). Physical environments that are planned to offer opportunities for shared activity, communication and co-operation (and even conflict) allow children to co-construct their knowledge and understanding of the world (Gandini, 1998; Ellsworth, 2005; Rinaldi, 2006).

In my own research, I asked two groups of primary school age children how they would like their school to be. Their responses, verbal and pictorial, portray an environment that:

- provides multi-sensory and stimulating areas;
- supports real life tasks;

Photograph 9.2 Classroom environment (2).

- encourages active and adventurous play and balances it with quiet play areas and areas for relaxation and rest;
- promotes co-operation, cross-age and gender play;
- takes care of safety, health and hygiene;
- gives a sense of fun and exuberance;
- shows respect to the individual;
- minimizes friction and arguments.

(Papatheodorou, 2002)

Most importantly, children's suggestions were more about playful learning environments rather than play itself, reflecting Dewey's idea and differentiation between playfulness and play (see also Chapter 1). Dewey (1991:162) argued that 'The former is an attitude of mind; the latter is a passing outward manifestation of this attitude'. He explained that the suggestions made in playful learning override the actual act of play, giving a sense of freedom and liberation.

Multi-sensory and stimulating areas – engagement with real tasks

We remember 20 per cent of what we read, 30 per cent of that we hear, 40 per cent of what we see, 50 per cent of what is said, 60 per cent of what we do, and 90 per cent when we see, hear, say and do. (The percentages vary depending on the source.)

The value of multi-sensory experiences has long been acknowledged by philosophers, early pioneers and contemporary educationalists and it has been confirmed by research into neuroscience. The multi-sensorial stimuli, which are repeatedly used to access information, enable the strengthening of connections between neurons in the brain, more accurate thinking, recall of information and faster response times (Wartik and Carlson-Finnerty, 1993). Indeed, early sensory experiences, especially spatial, visual, tactile and smell, are linked with memory and recollection of information and early life events (Papatheodorou, 2010; Grawley and Eacott, 2006). Therefore, the richer the environment the more connections are developed in the brain assisting information processing.

Children's responses in my own research referred to rich and multi-sensory environments that offer them opportunities to engage with a range of playful and meaningful real life tasks and activities that give them a sense of achievement and belonging; tending a garden, creating a bug's home and teaching younger children football skills and swimming are examples of their suggestions. Small or limited resources and places that are safe but boring and unexciting led to arguments among children and friction between adults and children (e.g. being told off; the ball taken by the teacher) (Papatheodorou, 2002).

Cameo 1

On a visit to an early years setting, the head teacher explained that they have a vegetable garden that is maintained by children and staff. The children plant the seeds and weed the plants; they learn when to water the plants according to weather conditions. The early years setting makes its own compost (see Photograph 9.3) by collecting leaves, dried plants and vegetable and fruit peelings from the kitchen. When vegetables are ready, children take them home. The head teacher also explained that, because of limited funds, they had to improvise with the fence and use soft drink cans threaded on to a wire.

Photograph 9.3 Using soft drink cans as a fence.

Note: Photograph taken at the Kwambonambi Pre-Primary School in KwaZulu Natal, South Africa with thanks to Susan Bonney, the head teacher and her pupils.

Cameo 1 is illustrative of the kind of environments that can engage children meaningfully. A garden that is maintained by the children and supported by staff allows children to develop skills as well as knowledge about the physical environment (e.g. when and how to plant seeds, water plants, how to make compost). They also have the pleasure of taking the produce home. Imagination and creativity is also illustrated in the construction of the garden fence. It took, however, the insightfulness of the early years practitioners, and their trust in children's abilities, to embark on this project that required sustained attention and effort over a period of time.

Active and adventurous play

> Children must have opportunities to play both indoors and outdoors
> . . . Providing well-planned experiences based on children's spon-
> taneous play, both indoors and outdoors, is an important way in

which practitioners support young children to learn with enjoyment and challenge.

(DfES, 2007: 7)

The value and importance of access to outdoor play has been explicitly acknowledged in the *Early Years Foundation Stage* (*EYFS*) and is well documented by research that focuses on the experiences of children attending outdoor nurseries. Such research has shown that children with access to outdoors have better concentration, better physical and motor development and varied and imaginative types of play. They were less often ill and, in general, demonstrated better physical and social development (Grahn et al. cited in Williams-Siegfredsen, 2007). Being, feeling and making things outdoors constitute adults' most memorable and favourable recollections of their childhood experiences (Papatheodorou, 2010).

Playgrounds can be exciting outdoor areas that stimulate interest and curiosity, give a sense of adventure and provide opportunities for different kinds of play (including rough and tumble as can be seen in Chapter 10). They allow children to experiment, take risks and control the environment, engage in social activities and learn basic concepts about nature and outdoors (Wardle, undated; Layton, 2001; Chapter 12). For example, areas for football and skipping and equipment such as slides, swings, trampolines, rides and climbing frames can offer opportunities for children to stretch their bodies and emotions to new limits. They also develop dynamic balance, stimulate their senses, manipulate items, explore spaces, interact with others and learn problem solving (National Program for Playground Safety (NPPS) 2002). Children's requests for climbing frames in the shape of birds, tortoises, spiders, birds and cats, and single and multi-seated trampolines and swings, show their sense of fun and opportunity to demonstrate their enjoyment and exuberance (Papatheodorou, 2002).

The key issue here is the availability of outdoor space and its purposeful design to ensure that the necessary stimuli are ever present so as to give the opportunity to every pupil to participate, to set play in motion for a meaningful educational experience (Moore and Cosco, 2000; Doughty, 2001). Yet many children still have limited access to outdoors or playgrounds: these are used as places where children can move and run around in order to get rid of excessive and repressed energy rather than to offer a continuity of experience between indoors and outdoors. There is still often an underlying assumption that outdoor time is a break from learning; a time for children to exert physical energy in order to return to more valuable activities in the classroom (Papatheodorou, 2002).

Areas for quiet play and for relaxation and rest

> sometimes their play will be responsive and boisterous, sometimes
> they may describe and discuss what they are doing; sometimes they
> will be quiet and reflective as they play.
>
> (DfES, 2007: 7)

Children request that adventurous and active play is balanced with quiet areas
for play and areas for relaxation. Children's suggestions for instance, for sand-
pits, igloos, paddling pools, benches, picnic table, shaded areas for cooling off
and a water fountain call for a learning environment that is responsive to their
rhythms, pace and wide spectrum of needs (Papatheodorou, 2002).

Cameo 2

The head teacher explained that they were lucky in their setting to have ample
outdoor space where there is a good range of equipment and areas for active play
such as football, cycling, swings, slides and trampoline. The children, however,
requested a place where they could play quietly, when tired, away from
noisy areas. She explained that they came up with the idea of having a labyrinth
(see Photograph 9.4). Having no funds at all meant that they needed to be
creative. They used plastic bottles from soft drinks that they filled with soil. They
made marks on the ground where the bottles were half-buried; the bottles were
tied with string from around the bottleneck. All the work was done by the
children (with adult help) and they had the pleasure in using it.

The creation of space in Cameo 2 gave children the opportunity to problem-
solve, engage with concepts such as measurement, weight, distance, sym-
metry, painting and mark-making, as well as skills for using tools for digging,
tidying knots, exercising their strength and weight to put the bottles securely
in the ground. It encouraged creative and flexible thinking in using the
resources available rather than the resources that they might ideally like to
have. It allowed children to realize their skills and reach their potential through
a meaningful task (playing for real as defined by Deborah Albon in Chapter 8).

Safe and respectful environments

Today, concerns and fears regarding the risks and dangers involved in allowing
children to play freely outdoors, engage with adventurous play and use real life

Photograph 9.4 Creating a labyrinth.

Note: Photograph taken at the Kwambonambi Pre-Primary School in KwaZulu Natal, South Africa with thanks to Susan Bonney, the head teacher and her pupils.

tools, has been the main reason of providing children a limiting play experience. Children despise and detest the regulations that are put in place and restrict the use of available equipment (Papatheodorou, 2002). Such regulation limits their opportunities for using risky equipment and, in the long term, does not offer children the skills and knowledge to exercise judgement and feel confident in what they can do and understand what they cannot do. As a result, accidents happen when children are older mainly because they have not developed the skills that they need earlier on (Williams-Siegfredsen, 2007).

Cameo 3

Being very aware of health and safety regulations, I was surprised and particularly interested to see that real tools were available in this early years setting. The head teacher explained that these tools were not for display purposes but for use by the children. In her almost 30 years of working life, the head teacher reported no accidents. She explained though that many children are familiar with these tools in their everyday home life experiences (Photograph 9.5).

Cameo 3 perhaps illustrates a situation that may not be observed in English (and perhaps in most European and Western) early years settings. But the photograph shows how these tools can be used to advance children's motor skills, kinaesthetic abilities, concentration and precision as well as mathematical concepts such as linear measurement, qualities of materials and the reaction of materials and tools to their action and handling. Rinaldi (1998: 116, original italics) suggests that in the Reggio Emilia learning environment, 'Many different images could be possible: highlighting what the child *is* and *has*, *can be* or *can do*, or on the contrary emphasizing what the child is *not* and does *not have*, what he or she *cannot* be or *do*'. The potent, wise and insightful child can only emerge if adults trust: our trust is the powerful force for children to behave as we treat them, either explicitly or subtly.

Early years practitioners then are urged to gain a deeper understanding of

Photograph 9.5   Using real woodwork tools.

Note: Photograph taken at the Kwambonambi Pre-Primary School in KwaZulu Natal, South Africa with thanks to Susan Bonney, the head teacher and her pupils.

the value of encouraging and enabling children to use real equipment and tools. The more deprived the physical environment becomes, the more unlikely it is the children will be fully involved with playful experiences that are meaningful to them and the more difficult and challenging the practitioner's task becomes (Cosco and Moore, 1999).

Children also talk about respectful learning environments that are clean, tidy and purpose-built. Premises for multiple purposes may respond to problems of spatial shortage and financial constraints and perhaps do not afford the best experience for children. They also subtly convey negative messages about their expectations from the environment and about their own self-worth and value. For example, children comment that using the same space for both PE (physical education) activity and for lunch 'is not the nicest thing' because 'the floor is wet . . . still people's dinner on the floor . . . and it is not nice standing there . . . it is sticky all the time' (Papatheodorou, 2002: 459).

Playful learning environments

In general, children's suggestions and requests are for playful learning environments that engage their bodies, hearts and minds; an environment that offers sensory, intellectual and social stimuli, allows action and gives a sense of fun and exuberance. Their conception of learning space gives meaning to, and reaffirms, Vygotsky's (1978: 102) argument that:

> Everything that concerns a child is play reality, while everything that concerns an adult is serious reality. A given object has one meaning in play and another one outside of it. In a child's world the logic of wishes and of satisfying urges dominates, and not real logic. The illusionary nature of play is transferred to life.

In the long term, an environment that is not stimulating, inspiring and full of energy, activity and fun will dull children's perceptions and disadvantage their learning (Ceppi and Zini, 1998: n.p).

Documenting action

It is important to have a learning environment that harmonizes purpose, enjoyment and meaning; an environment that offers children the opportunity of seeing the impact of their actions and thus sustaining their interest and motivation, their efforts, perseverance and persistence. Their environment becomes the canvas where their experiences and efforts are imprinted and their lived experience is narrated through story, photographs and other collections of evidence (see also Chapter 14). Children ask for and need 'an environment that not only transforms and conditions them but one that is responsive and transformable because of their actions; an environment where learning is not *learning compliance*, but as absorption and self-presence' (Ellsworth, 2005: 16, original italics).

Revisiting children's responses to my question *how they would like their school to be*, and considering the relevant research and literature, I became acutely aware that children:

- request playful learning environments rather than just play opportunities. They like places that support playful attitudes that set them free to exercise and reach their potential. This, however, requires a modifiable, responsive, transformative and transformable playful learning environment;
- conceive their playful learning environments as holistic and meaningful, where sensory, intellectual and social stimuli are interwoven and inseparable; they affect and are affected by each other. Creating the labyrinth, for example, required as much physical skill as cognitive and mental functions, group effort and collaboration;
- are aware of the age and gender segregation created by their learning environments and they long for less age-related and gendered spaces;
- spurn safety regulations that restrict their play and dislike environments that are disrespectful because of their lack of tidiness, cleanliness and aesthetics.
- understand that playful learning environments are designed and equipped by adults and, in the light of their priorities, for children rather than through consulting children.

The pedagogy of playful learning environments

The previous section clearly indicates that playful learning environments comprise (1) rich and multiple stimuli and (2) an enabling pedagogy whose mediating force sees the child as the main actor – the protagonist – of this environment. The stimuli in playful learning environments vibrate exuberance and zest of life, portray images of fun and enjoyment and offer comfort with their familiarity. They foster thinking, action and collaboration and afford change and growth. They enable interactions, interrelationships and actions. Above all, they create a zone of proximal development, where, to quote Vygotsky (1978: 102), '. . . a child always behaves beyond his average age, above his daily behaviour . . . it is as though he were a head taller than himself . . . play contains all developmental tendencies in a condensed form and is itself a major source of development'.

Playful learning environments are envisaged as safe, caring and welcoming spaces that provide quantity, quality and a variety of resources that are modifiable and responsive. They afford processes and strategies that enable children to engage with processes such as exploration, gathering of information, implementing ideas, reviewing and revising outcomes and products and arrive at conclusions to address incongruent elements to which they may reach as a result of their actions (Reggio Children, 2004; Ceppi and Zini, 1998).

Playful learning environments afford a pedagogy that facilitates and mediates individual and shared activity, forges interaction and interrelationships, generates ideas and action, encourages communication and co-operation and supports independence and interdependence. It considers children's abilities, capabilities and needs, their enjoyment, pace and rhythm, the engagement of their hands, minds and souls (Rinaldi, 2006; Malaguzzi, 1998). This pedagogy demonstrates that the construction of knowledge does not take place in a progressive or linear way but as a developing network, based on dynamic interweaving of interconnected elements. Perception, action and reflection become the fundamental strategies for an individual's knowledge construction as a result of exchange and relationships with others (Ceppi and Zini, 1998).

Above all playful learning environments are seen as relational spaces that provide fluidity of intellectual, social and sensory experiences. They transform and are transformed by the individual; reflect and respond to individual and communal needs for well-being and becoming, as well as to their need for freedom and identity formation (Rinaldi, 2006; Branzi, 1998). According to Malaguzzi, playful learning space '. . . mirrors the ideas, values, attitudes and cultures of people who live within it' (cited in Gandini, 1998: 177).

Playful learning environments – turning spaces into places

Malaguzzi explains that 'the environment becomes part of the individual so that any response to a request we make to the children or a request that children make of adults is facilitated or obstructed by the environment and its characteristics. . .' (cited in Gandini, 1998: 66). These views are also reflected in Greenman (1988: 5) who claims that 'An environment is a living and changing system . . . It conditions how we feel, think and behave . . . The environment either works for us or against us as we conduct our lives'. Therefore, the space we inhabit is neither innocent nor neutral; it has a performative aspect and determines what and how it may occur; it implies a certain order and locates individual's activities. In other words, space lays down the law and either enables or prohibits individual activities (Pouler cited in Jamieson et al., 2000).

Educators in Reggio Emilia preschools speak of space as both 'content' and 'container'. The first refers to educational messages and stimuli being available, while the latter is understood as the processes of exploration, social interaction and constructive learning that are enabled by such messages and stimuli: it is the pedagogy (Filippini cited in Gandini, 1998). The use of space as both content/stimuli and container/pedagogy forges interaction and inter-relationships, stimulates tension and intentions, enables actions and makes play environments come alive. The value of a place comes from its physical qualities (space and stimuli) and the interactions (the pedagogy) that it affords to its inhabitants (Loughland et al., 2002; Cosco and Moore, 1999).

Indeed, many researchers make a distinction between space and place. The first is defined as the mere square footage, the structural and geometrical qualities of a physical environment. The latter refers to the use of space by its inhabitants, their interactions and their lived experience – it reflects a sense of ownership and pride (Cosco and Moore, 1999; Harrison and Dourish cited in Hornecker, undated). Thus, place is more than the physical space; it is a living and changing system, where personal experiences and stories, images and memories unfold and are created to gain meaning and enable a sense of belonging and identity formation (Babacan, 2005). Place is space, plus meaning and identity (Cosco and Moore, 1999).

Conclusion

I have written this chapter being aware that, even today, it is not uncommon for many early years settings to be accommodated in, and operate from, borrowed premises such as church or town halls and school classrooms that provide either large or confined spaces that are fixed and unaltered. Even the learning resources are often brought in for sessional use and then packed away and/or removed from the premises by the end of the session (Papatheodorou, 2008). Children's lived experience is limited and restricted by the primary purpose and function of the premises because there is limited, or no opportunity, for such spaces to change as a result of the interaction and actions of their occupants: no chance for their occupants to leave their mark and see the space being transformed as a result of their being there. This is a situation that offers poor experiences to children and early years practitioners and limited opportunities to transform a space into a place. Whatever space is available can, however, be turned into an important place for children by practitioners who reflect on the possible.

What do I, the writer, feel about the contribution of this chapter to supporting critical reflection?

In reflection, I would like to see the ideas discussed in this chapter as forming the basis for reflection that leads to action; reflection that sets our thinking in motion not only in terms of what an ideal situation might be, but what could be done under certain circumstances and within given resources to provide the best playful learning environments and experiences for all (both children and adults). Most importantly, as Janet Moyles has urged in Chapter 1, to use these ideas for reflection so that they can be utilized as evidence for voicing professional knowledge and wisdom and claim quality playful learning environments for equally playful pedagogy, practices and experiences.

Implications for pedagogy: what might *you*, the reader, reflect on now?

The notion of turning spaces into places has raised a number of questions for reflection. For example:

1   Are playful learning environments in early years settings distinct places that portray the interests and experiences of unique individuals who live there or spaces characterized by some kind of uniformity in terms of resources and their organization that set in motion the same type of playful experiences and learning?

2   Do playful learning environments invite and permit their alteration, so that individual and collective interests and actions, and likes and wants are imprinted in the space to reflect their unique individual and collective personality and identity?

3   Are we conscious and explicitly aware of the implicit and subtle messages conveyed by the space available for playful learning and its design and resources?

4   Do playful learning environments focus mostly on children's becoming at the expense of their well-being and belonging?

References and further reading

Babacan, H. (2005) Locating identity: sense of space, place and belonging. Paper presented at the Diversity Conference, Beijing, China, 30 June to 3 July.

Branzi, A. (1998) Education and relational space, in G. Ceppi and M. Zini (eds) *Children, Spaces, Relationships: Metaproject for an Environment for Young Children.* **Milan: Reggio Children and Domus Academy Research Centre.**

Bredekamp, S. (1987) *Developmentally Appropriate Practice In Early Childhood Programmes (Rev. edn.).* Washington, DC: NAEYC.

Bronfenbrenner, U. (1979) *The Ecology of Human Development: Experiments by Nature and Design.* Cambridge, MA: Harvard University Press.

Bruce, T., Finlay, A., Read, J. and Scarborough, M. (1995) *Recurring Themes in Education.* London: Paul Chapman.

Cannella, G.S. (2005) Reconceptualizing the field (of early care and education): if 'Western' child development is a problem, then what do we do? In N. Yelland (ed.) *Critical Issues in Early Childhood Education*. Maidenhead: Open University Press.

Ceppi, G. and Zini, M. (1998) *Children, Spaces, Relationships: Metaproject for an Environment for Young Children*. Milan: Reggio Children and Domus Academy Research Centre.

Cosco, N. and Moore, R. (1999) Playing in place: why the physical environment is important in playwork. Paper presented at the 14th Play Education Annual Play and Human Development Meeting: Theoretical Playwork, Ely, England, January.

Department for Education and Skills (DfES) (2007) *Practice Guidance for the Early Years Foundation Stage*. Nottingham: DfES Publications.

Dewey, J. (1991) *How we Think*. New York: Prometheus Books.

Doughty, D. (2001) Playgrounds: the final frontier, *Times Educational Supplement*, 2 February.

Ellsworth, E. (2005) *Places of Learning: Media Architecture Pedagogy*. New York: RoutledgeFalmer.

Gandini, L. (1998) Educational and caring spaces, in C. Edwards, L. Gandini and G. Forman (eds) *The Hundred languages of Children. The Reggio Emilia Approach – Advanced Reflections*. Greenwich, CN: Ablex Publishing.

Grawley, R.A. and Eacott, M.J. (2006) Memories of early childhood: qualities of the experience of recollection, *Memory and Cognition*, 34(2): 287–94.

Greenman, J. (1988) *Caring Spaces, Learning Spaces: Children's Environments that Work*. Redmond, WA: Exchange Press.

Hornecker, E. (undated) *Space and Place – Setting the Stage for Social Interaction*. Available online at www.informatics.sussex.ac.uk/research/groups/interact/previousSite/papers/pdf/hornecker.pdf (accessed 8 January 2010).

Jamieson, P., Fisher, K., Gilding, T., Taylor, P.G. and Trevitt, A.D. (2000) Place and space in the design of new environments, *Higher Education Research and Development*, 19: 221–37.

Kennedy, M. (2002) By design, *American School and University Magazine* (January).

Layton, R. (2001) The great outdoors, *American School and University Magazine*. Available online at www.asumag.com/mag/university_environmental_great_outdoors/ (accessed 25 October 2009).

Loughland, T., Reid, A. and Petocz, P. (2002) Young people's conceptions of environment: a phenomenographic analysis, *Environmental Education Research*, 8: 187–97.

Malaguzzi, L. (1998) History, ideas and basic philosophy: an interview with Lela Gandini, in C. Edwards, L. Gandini and G. Forman (eds) *The Hundred languages of Children. The Reggio Emilia Approach – Advanced Reflections*. Greenwich, CN: Ablex Publishing.

Montessori, M. (1912) *The Montessori Method: Scientific Pedagogy as Applied to Child*

Education in 'Children's Houses' with additions and revisions by the author (trans. by A.E. George), Available online at www.digital.library.upenn.edu/women/montessori/method/method.html (accessed 7 November 2009).

Moore, R.C. and Cosco, N.G. (2000) Developing an earth-bound culture through design of childhood habitats. Paper presented at the International conference on People, Land and Sustainability, University of Nottingham, 13–16 September. Available online at www.naturalearning.org/docs/Earthbound Children.pdf (accessed 17 January 2010).

National Program for Playground Safety (NPPS) (2002) *Playground Safety News*, 5(3): 1–3.

Papatheodorou, T. (2002) How we like our school to be . . . pupils' voices, *European Educational Research Journal*, 1(3): 445–7.

Papatheodorou, T. (2008) Turning spaces into places: children as designers and implications for practice. Paper presented at the Workshop at the Happy, Healthy Children Play Outdoors Conference, organized by the Early Childhood Research Group, Anglia Ruskin University and Essex Early Years and Childcare Service, 26 April.

Papatheodorou, T. (2010) *Sensory Play*. Research Report submitted to Play-to-Z, Chelmsford.

Papatheodorou, T. and Ramasut, A. (1994) Environmental effects on teachers' perceptions of behaviour problems in nursery school children, *European Early Childhood Education Research Journal*, 2(2): 63–78.

Penrose, V., Thomas, G. and Greed, C. (2001) Designing inclusive schools: how can children be involved? *Support for Learning*, 16(2): 87–91.

Reed, J. (1992) A short history of children's building blocks, in P. Gura with the Froebel Blockplay Research Group directed by T. Bruce (eds) *Exploring Learning: Young Children and Blockplay*. London: Paul Chapman.

Reggio Children (2004) *Children, Art, Artists: The Expressive Languages of Children, the Artistic Language of Alberto Burri*. Milan: Reggio Children.

Rinaldi (1998) The space of childhood, in G. Ceppi, and M. Zini (eds) *Children, Spaces, Relationships: Metaproject for an Environment for Young Children*. Milan: Reggio Children and Domus Academy Research Centre.

Rinaldi (2006) *In Dialogue with Reggio Emilia: Listening, Researching and Learning*. London: Routledge.

Smith, P.K. and Connolly, K.J. (1980) *The Ecology of Preschool Behaviour*. Cambridge: Cambridge University Press.

Vygotsky, L.S. (1978) *Mind in Society: The Development of Higher Psychological Processes*. Cambridge, MA: Harvard University Press (eds M. Cole, V. John-Steiner, S. Schriber and E. Souberman).

Wardle, F. (undated). Outdoor Play: designing, building, and remodeling playgrounds for young children. Available online at www.earlychildhoodnews.com/earlychildhood/article_view.aspx?ArticleID=65 (accessed 25 January 2010).

Wartik, N. and Carlson-Finnerty, L. (1993) *Memory and Learning*. New York: Chelsea House Publishers.

Williams-Siegfredsen, J. (2007) Developing pedagogically appropriate practice, in R. Austin (ed.) *Letting the Outside In: Developing Teaching and Learning Beyond the Early Years Classroom*. Stoke-on-Trent: Trentham Books.

10 Thinking it through
Rough and tumble play

Pam Jarvis and Jane George

Summary

This chapter outlines the structure, qualities and consequences of 'rough and tumble' ('R&T') play, moving on to advocate its vital importance for healthy human development. In doing so, we introduce a new model of the developing human being, drawn from the 'biocultural' perspective described in the philosophical literature. The chapter concludes by reflecting on the lack of reference to such play in current policy documents and within contemporary practitioner training. It also disseminates some ongoing action research undertaken by the authors that attempts to engage practitioners in the concept of the 'biocultural model' and the central importance of genuine free play within an outdoor environment for children in the early years.

Key questions as you read . . .

1   What do you understand by R&T play?
2   Why do you believe that R&T play might be important?
3   What are your professional reactions to R&T play?
4   How and why should we facilitate rough and tumble play in contemporary early years environments?

. . . and points to consider

•   We hope that readers will be led to review their practice through the biocultural model of the developing child and thence to consider what value genuine free play is given within the provision within their setting.

- While this chapter focuses on outdoor R&T free play, there are also links that can be drawn to active play that may occur both indoors and outdoors, particularly among group of boys.
- If restrictions on 'war' and 'superhero' play are lifted, research shows an ultimate enrichment in free play activity, particularly that undertaken by boys.

Introduction

R&T play can be observed in most primary school playgrounds. A well-known example is the generic chasing and catching game known to generations of British children as 'He', 'Tig' or 'Tag', depending on regional origin, which has also been internationally and cross-culturally observed, for example, by Konner (1972) among Zhun-Twa (!Kung) children in the Kalahari desert; by Fry (1987) among Zapotec Native American children in Oaxaca, Mexico; as 'El Dimoni' in Spain; and 'Oni' in Japan (Opie and Opie, 1969: 20).

This chapter focuses on the developmental role of R&T play with particular attention to the narratives that children use to underpin such activities. The four questions posed above are used as headings to explore the issues.

What is R&T play?

R&T play is an evolved behaviour that has been observed in young animals across a vast range of mammalian species, and can be defined as follows:

- *behaviour*: a physically active set of behaviours, e.g. run, chase, jump, play fight;
- *affect*: positive emotional engagement, indicated in primates by a play face (open mouth smile) – see Photograph 10.1;
- *consequence*: friendship – which clearly differentiates R&T from real aggression;
- *structure*: reciprocal behaviour, in which children swap roles during the activity (e.g. being chased and chasing).

(Pellegrini, 2005)

Between April 2002 and December 2003, one of the authors of this chapter carried out a schedule of detailed observations of children's R&T in their primary school playground. During this time the participants were aged between 4½ and 6. When the literature was reviewed prior to starting this study, it was

Photograph 10.1   The human play face.

found that, while there had been a lot of previous investigation of children's physical action in R&T, there was very little focus on the language and play narratives they used. The principal reason was due to the way that play researchers categorized play behaviours; many appeared to presume that, as soon as a child attached language to physical play, it should cease to be categorized as R&T. However, what was observed was that, particularly with respect to outdoor play between boys and mixed gender groups, there were many interactions where the observed physical actions were those that would be described as R&T if they had been observed between young non-human animals. However, the children nearly always imposed some type of narrative over these actions in order to make sense of what they were doing. Through such narratives, which tended to be a mixture of fantasy and rule negotiation components, they began to independently negotiate issues such as social and gendered roles, original collaboratively created rules, and in a very simple way, fairness and 'justice'. This seemed to me to be a hugely important aspect of their development, in that they were engaging in experiences that led them into the early stages of becoming socially independent beings who were increasingly able to engage in the complex web of competition and collaboration that typifies not just human, but primate behaviour in general.

Within R&T, the children observed continually negotiated who should chase and catch who and why and what the consequences were of being caught. Fantasy and rule construction were mixed in many ways. For example, in a game that was partially R&T and partially rudimentary football play with highly simplified rules, the children (all boys) negotiated concepts such as handball, time-wasting and a very simplified concept of 'offside', while frequently evoking the name of 'Beckham' and claiming either to be him, or to be 'like' him. R&T play also typically involved gendered behaviour; for example, R&T between all-girl groups was not a commonly observed play style but, where it did occur, the accompanying narratives tended to be originally created by the players and based on a 'caring' theme. Two examples included saving a magic rabbit from a cruel witch, and putting a noisy, hyperactive baby to bed. R&T between all-boy groups was one of the most commonly observed play styles: the associated narratives were usually based on 'battle' or 'superhero' themes drawn from the media culture of the time, for example, Beckham as outlined above, Beyblades and Robot Wars.

Boys' R&T narratives tended to deal with a group coming together to repel threat, be that the French football team or putting out a fire; girls' narratives tended to focus on care and concern for others, banding together to protect the vulnerable against people who they perceived as 'cruel' or 'mean'; for example, a nasty witch. Boys, therefore, competed to be the 'toughest' individual in group, while girls were focused on appearing the 'nicest' or 'kindest'. In general boys seemed to be concerned about being perceived as 'weak', while girls were very careful not to appear 'mean' or unkind. This also led to gendered relationships being created between the children and the staff, girls seeking to appear 'good', while boys walked a less direct line of appearing slightly rebellious without being deemed seriously naughty. While boys seemed to relish mild admonishments in passing from adults, they appeared to perceive the 'time out' punishments that were meted out in this particular playground for seriously bad behaviour as a loss of status in the eyes of their peers. All these complex relationships were largely mediated through play that contained a substantial R&T component.

A key example was the football play in which the boys engaged, which was at this stage essentially a 'hybrid' activity, described in my notes as 'R&T with a ball'. There was no concept of teams; children joined and left the games at will, taking it in turns to keep 'goal'. Once, when an adult engaged with this activity and tried to instigate conventional team-based play, the game quickly broke down due to the children's huge confusion. They did, however, know enough about teams to vie with each other to claim the name of 'England' and scoff at the name of 'France'! This led me to deep reflection on the sometimes surprisingly sophisticated understanding of 5-year-old children, and how they used their independent outdoor free play to explore and experiment with such intricate cultural ideas, remaking them as their own in a highly Vygotskian fashion.

Overall, my observational findings (see Jarvis, 2007a) indicated that boys and girls aged between 4½ and 6 created sophisticated and clearly gendered narratives to script their single gender R&T play in which they could compete and collaborate, constructing subtle hierarchies within their peer group. The gender roles that they took had a highly simplified correspondence with adult-gendered behaviour described by evolutionary psychologists (e.g. Buss, 1994).

Boys and girls also took highly gendered roles within mixed gender R&T play, specifically:

- girls initiated and organized mixed gender chasing, with most episodes beginning when a girl 'tagged' a boy as an invitation to chase her;
- boys acted as chasers, while girls were chased;
- girls collaborated to organize the games and competed to be 'most chased';
- boys collaborated in chasing activities, while competing to be 'best chaser';
- girls frequently 'told' on boys, who appeared to experience a raise in status among peers following minor (but not major) adult reprimands, indicating an unwitting role for supervising adults in the children's R&T play scenarios.

These mixed gender games were all generally labelled 'kiss chase' by the children, but they had various underlying narratives, which were closely calibrated to the weather and other environmental conditions. For example, a game played on a wet tarmac playground involved girls pretending to be escaping prisoners, while the boys tried to 'capture' them; a game played on grass on a warm sunny day was based on the fantasy that a boy's touch would put a girl to sleep, while a girl's touch would awaken her. Mixed gender R&T play was not as common as all-boy play of this genre but it was observed more frequently than all-girl R&T play.

In conclusion, the children created a socially complex, gendered society within their playground environment. Where adults attempted to mentor children's R&T play, they seemed to struggle to address the players' meanings and intentions, with the result that the children struggled, in turn, to absorb the invading adult concepts (e.g. that of fixed teams in football play), as they tended to be poorly matched to the children's current social 'zones of proximal development' (Vygotsky, 1978). This finding intrigued me, and I went on to ask the adults within the setting to reflect on the children's outdoor free play; the results are summarized below. First, however, we consider what children might actually be doing in their play that is developmentally important and why it can be proposed that independent engagement in collaborative R&T play may be as vital to children's healthy development as learning to read and count.

Why is R&T important?

Human infants are born at a much earlier point in their neuronal development than their nearest primate relatives and are equipped by nature to build a substantial number of neuronal connections in response to the physical and social environment. Human beings evolved within the environmental niche of a hunter-gatherer. Due to the long periods over which evolution operates, the basic blueprint for a human being has not changed for many thousands of years; our basic psychology and physiology is still the same as that of ice-age nomads and early Mesopotamian agriculturalists. As hunter-gatherers, we evolved to use our long developmental period to build technological and symbolic acuity, foresight, stamina, agility and, most importantly, the highly developed social cognition required to engage in intricate, gendered patterns of collaboration and competition (see also Chapter 6). In common with other, albeit less cognitively complex mammalian young, children principally achieve such development through free play activity, which provides essential practice experience for young animals, developing skills and independence that they will require in adulthood: 'the play of children (and of animals) has an essential functional value . . . preliminary training for the future activities of the individual' (Piaget and Inhelder, 1969: 60).

The more complex the adult society, the longer animals spend in their developmental period and the more complex the play activities in which they engage. The most socially and technologically sophisticated societies on earth are those created by human beings, underpinned by our unique ability to collaborate on intricate technological tasks, which in turn is rooted within our ability to communicate highly abstract thoughts through the medium of language. A human being is, at the same time, therefore, both an evolved organism and the product of development within a language-based culture. The theoretical perspective that emerged from this premise, which allocates equal importance to evolved and environmental factors, was dubbed the 'biocultural' approach by philosophers Mallon and Stich (2000: 143) who state that the 'biocultural model [of the human being]. . . . reflects a confluence between innate and learned influences'. We take the view that the only effective holistic way to explore complex sequences of human behaviour (such as R&T activity) is within the wide theoretical arena of the biocultural perspective.

As the physical qualities of R&T had been very thoroughly investigated by previous researchers, the emphasis that one of the authors created within her PhD research was principally on the language and resulting narrative associated with R&T play. Human beings are the only creatures on Earth (as far as we know) who principally communicate in a deeply symbolic language that uses a sequence of sounds to communicate highly abstract ideas; for example, 'that is not fair' and 'sometimes I love him and sometimes I hate him'. Children obviously need to undertake a huge amount of environmental learning to cope with such a sophisticated form of interaction and, given that they have evolved from earlier species along the way, they also learn to use other, more subtle and subconscious forms of communication alongside verbal language. The Reggio Emilia philosophy of pedagogy proposes that children use at least 100 'languages' in their play activities (Brock, 2009: 73) and it is not only obvious verbal narratives that are utilized and further developed in R&T play. For example, the importance of the human 'play face' in signalling playful intent during R&T behaviours was initially identified by Konner (1972). This was subsequently emphasized by several later researchers in the field and linked to firm evolutionary roots; for example, Van Hooff (1976) noted that an open mouth display is associated with play fighting and chasing in the young of all primates species (see Photograph 10.2).

This led us to wonder what experiences children need in order to learn to use and understand subtle gestures and why some appear to learn to use them more effectively and/or at a much younger age than others. Levels of experience

Photograph 10.2   Pearson photo of chimps' play face.

in social interaction are logically a crucial factor and this was precisely what Pellegrini and Blatchford (2000) found. They conducted a study on outdoor free play in early years, in this case focusing solely on boys. They concluded that for 5-year-old boys, the amount of time spent in active social play with other boys directly predicts their level of success in social problem-solving one year later. Braza et al. (2007: 209) proposed that R&T interaction underlies the social hierarchies that children create in the playground, reducing aggression and helping children to develop 'social intelligence'.

In conclusion, it can therefore be posited that young children's access to independent free play (preferably in a natural outdoor arena where they can run around freely), in which they collaborate to construct play narratives, is critical if they are to learn the extensive range of complex human communication skills. The narratives they create may at times seem silly or lacking in understanding to adult carers, but what must be grasped is that the principal value of such interactions are not in the development of children's intellectual knowledge, but in the social learning that occurs between peers. R&T activities, therefore, have a particularly important role in the development of shared meanings, providing opportunities for children to practise the complex social skills required for the mixture of collaboration, co-operation and competition that characterizes human adult societies. If children do not have opportunities to engage in such play in early–mid childhood, they may later experience problems in social interaction due to poorly developed social competences.

What do practitioners say about R&T play?

In the early 2000s, Bishop and Curtis (2001: 182) proposed 'Many teachers . . . found it hard to accept . . . evidence of video recordings of positive (playground based) play, many having observed nothing but bad behaviour'. This was exactly what Jarvis (2007b: 254) found when undertaking interviews with child participants' teachers; for example:

> *Teacher:* 'I don't really know [what imaginative ideas children use in their outdoor play], I am too busy sorting things out in the playground . . . often dealing with complaints or injuries . . . you'd know better than me'.

And from field observation notes:

> *I decided to walk around with the teacher on duty on this morning and try to get an idea of 'how it feels' from that perspective. I immediately perceived the 'fish bowl' problem, constant target of child complaints – 'He pushed me' or 'He hit me', more or less continually. . . . I asked the teacher on duty*

> *'What is playground duty like'? She said, 'Well, sometimes it is a night-mare, if you get several accidents at once and still the children are trying to talk to you. Often the little ones pat or tug at your sleeve or coat to get your attention, and if there are several pulling you in several directions at once it can get really stressful'.*

> (Jarvis, 2005: 181)

Overall, the adult interviews indicated that the school staff tended to have an exclusive focus on the problems arising from outdoor play, due to being over-whelmed by the number of children they were required to supervise during their playground duties, and problems relating to the everyday hazards that arise when a large group of young children play energetically on a hard surface (see Jarvis, 2007b).

This gives some indication of why supervising adults may find it so very difficult to inhabit the role of 'playmate', given that it sits very awkwardly against the crucial role of invigilator within the outdoor play situation. I fre-quently observed adults trying to engage with the children's play but, as in the example of the football play outlined above, if the intervention was extended it tended to lead to the imposition of adult constructions on the children's play, with the result that the children disengaged. One such episode involved a teacher patiently showing a group of boys how to use a skipping rope 'prop-erly' when it was clear – at least to a non-participant observer – that they were clearly using it in a chasing play narrative. They later described their activity to me as 'fire engines'.

In England, the *Early Years Foundation Stage (EYFS)* statutory guidelines (DCSF, 2008) emphasize the potential value of play-based learning both indoors and outdoors for children in early years settings. Practitioners in England should, therefore, be much better informed in this respect than they were in the pre-*EYFS*, pre-*Foundation Stage* period during which my research was conducted. Considering the content of the *EYFS*, however (see below), in my more recent collaborative work with Jane George, we began to develop some concern that the guidelines, and in particular, the profile targets might lead to an increasing focus on adults closely planning children's activities in *all* environments, which was not the case during the period of Jarvis's original research. At that time, interacting below a rather indifferent adult 'radar', beyond the odd sporadic intervention, the children were in general quite free to organize their own outdoor play.

With regard to the current role of the adult, the current *EYFS* practice guidance document (DCSF, 2008: 7) communicates a mixed message that leaves itself very open to individual interpretation, proposing that, while chil-dren should be allowed to play spontaneously both indoors and out, adults should continually monitor and attempt to 'extend and develop'. However, early play researcher Newell proposed: 'children's amusement, directed and controlled by grown people would be neither childish nor amusing' (Newell [1883] 1963: 12), and Jarvis's observational findings, gathered over a century later, also indicate that adult intervention in R&T play, however well-intentioned, is prone to become problematic via the unwitting destruction of the narratives that children created to script their play activities. A logical conclusion is that effective outdoor free play supervision must therefore address a difficult balance between children's need for a physical and psychological 'space' to make and learn from social successes and mistakes alongside a dichotomous, emergent need for protection against serious physical and psychological harm.

As such, we are currently engaged in research focused on the attitudes of trainee practitioners to children's outdoor play. In the period directly following the publication of the *EYFS*, while we were working as higher education lecturers in education and early years, we noticed a dramatic increase in the number of independent dissertation proposals that were focused on the topic of outdoor play. We initially saw this as a great improvement on the days during which one of the authors (Jarvis) was asked by a fellow teacher why she was studying outdoor free play due to the fact that it had nothing to do with learning! While it is too early to formally report results, we have, however, found from small-sample research that there seems to be a movement towards adult direction in the outdoor environment that we find rather troubling. For example, one participant reflected:

> I hope [my research] will give me the ability to explain why I want to make alterations and the confidence and determination to ensure the improvements (assuming there are any) are continued and that the outdoor area becomes an area that is planned for. I think I will be recommending more creative and imaginative outdoor play and that staff become more interactive with the children more outdoors and it develops from being a 'space for children to run around in.

This last point in particular appears to indicate that perhaps practitioners have not necessarily moved on from the idea that children are 'not doing very much' when they are running around in an outdoor area and that the change that has been engendered by the current *EYFS* guidelines is to indicate to trainee practitioners that they are required to remedy this (apparent) 'issue'. We plan to undertake further research in this area, exploring the 'model of the child' that contemporary practitioners are typically using when considering their practice within the outdoor play arena and whether (as we suspect may be the case) the biocultural model is a completely new concept for them. It will be interesting to see if they revise their ideas to any extent if this model is introduced into their professional reflections. If we consider the biocultural nature of the human being, it seems obvious that young primates from such a deeply social species need frequent opportunities to engage in truly independent interaction with peers in order to learn the deeper lessons of independent social behaviour.

We now move on to engage with the contemporary question of how practitioners might facilitate independent R&T activity under the statutory guidelines of the *EYFS*, allowing children enough 'space' to independently explore their social environment, while intervening to prevent dangerous situations unfolding.

Facilitating R&T play in the early years

The body of research outlined above builds a very persuasive argument for R&T play for young children. The evidence presented explains its value, especially the significant contribution it can make to supporting social and emotional development; it presents a strong theoretical case for encouraging and supporting this type of play. But what does current national guidance for practitioners in England tell us?

The *Statutory Framework for the Early Years Foundation Stage* (DCSF, 2008), which replaced the National Standards documents, outlines for us the space requirements, the minimum standards; that is, clean, well ventilated and well lit, heated to a suitable temperature and with personal hygiene facilities. It also states that 'wherever possible, there should be access to an outdoor play area, and this is the expected norm for providers' (DCSF, 2008: 34). Within the practice guidance, the themes and commitments direct us to the importance of the learning environment (card 3.2) and active learning (card 4.2) (see DCSF, 2008). Three aspects of the learning environment are noted:

- the emotional environment;
- the outdoor environment;
- the indoor environment.

And three are components for active learning:

- mental and physical involvement;
- decision-making;
- personalized learning.

But there is no mention of rough and tumble play. As individuals some of us may intuit the links between the research and the practice guidance but some may not and, if we accept what the research is telling us, this is far too important a link to be left to chance.

Since the early 1990s we have seen many changes in the activities and resources we offer to young children and the role of the adult in supporting early learning. Outdoor areas were rare and, where they did exist, they were used for play too big or too messy to have indoors. Very few would have had the safe surfaces we now expect, so rules for safety would have been the norm, with adult direction and intervention to prevent accidents. More enlightened practitioners would have offered crates and large blocks for large-scale construction activities often with fabrics and canvas to support den building. These resources that are open-ended and can be used in any way the child desires would have supported holistic development through creativity and facilitated the child to create their own learning plan. Transfer of resources and activities from indoors to outdoors may also have occurred but this would have happened under strict control of the supervising adult and quality learning opportunities may have been lost through inopportune intervention. Jane George in particular, as an early years practitioner with over 20 years experience in settings caring for and educating children under 5 years old, wonders if some practitioners reading this now are sharing the 'guilty conscience' that she had when writing this section!

The contemporary 'outdoor area' looks very different. It has safe surfaces under climbing frames, designated areas for different activities, floor markings to support specific types of play, garden areas, outdoor sand/gravel pits and many of the indoor activities replicated in a covered area. It is often very appealing to a parent's eye but possibly less so to the young child as it offers little scope for child-initiated, self-directed play and may not be that attractive when viewed from a height of less than one metre! Jane George looks back across her experience of practice and comes to the conclusion that she has always tried to offer children 'safe adventures' creating artificial environments that she perceived to be safer than the real world. But one aspect of making the environment safer is that it has rules and codes of conduct and to enforce these the area is under the adult gaze. Having already directed play through designing the environment and selecting the resources, some adults may further disrupt play by untimely and insensitive interference.

Probably the most suitable environment for supporting naturalistic R&T play is offered through the 'forest school' approach, so valued in the Scandinavian countries but something of a treat available to a small but increasing number of settings in the UK (see Knight, 2010). Here with a natural 'safe surface', child-initiated play can develop with minimal 'adult gaze' as children explore the unique environment around them (see Jarvis et al., 2010). R&T play may also be promoted in 'soft play areas' where young children may engage in strenuous physical play that they have initiated and which they negotiate with other children using the resources but away from the adult gaze.

The recent Children's Society report *A Good Childhood* (Layard and Dunn, 2009) supports the argument for children playing in a self-initiated fashion with adults respecting the children's play by keeping a 'discreet distance'. One of the recommendations is that: 'public authorities should give priority to open spaces where children can play unsupervised' (p. 48). The report stresses the importance of friendship to children's all round development and notes that 'children who make friends early do better later. They have greater moral sensibility and better understanding of social relationships' (Layard and Dunn, 2009: 36).

Conclusion

If R&T play has the potential to support holistic development, but especially if it offers the opportunity to promote social and emotional development, it is something that all practitioners should value and become expert in. But at the moment, it can be posited that researchers and practitioners do not share a common language; R&T as such is not mentioned in the *EYFS* so the intricacies of supporting quality R&T play are missed. The responsibility seems to lie with experienced practitioners to lead practice but can we be sure they are fully informed and heading in the right direction? We hope this chapter, and our ongoing research and training with practitioners and trainee practitioners, will be of use in this endeavour, some of whom will be reading this book and preparing to lead practice by developing their skills and knowledge through higher education study including foundation degrees, honours degrees and gaining *Early Years Professional Status*. These are the people who are working at the interface between research and practice and transforming practice in their settings through reflection and practitioner research projects. It is our hope that by introducing and reflecting on the biocultural model of the child to this generation of practitioners they will become a significant force for change as, by carefully thinking through both the theoretical and practice issues, they will be the translators and interpreters moving contemporary research into practice, to the huge benefit of children in their care.

What do I, the writer, feel about the contribution of this chapter to supporting critical reflection?

In this chapter we have reflected on some empirical data relating to children's complex activities within R&T play and linked it to evolutionary concepts, identifying the links between the play of young creatures of many species, and the significant impact on the ways in which they learn species-specific behaviour. It has introduced a new model of the developing child and considered how the biocultural paradigm can be used to enrich practitioners' understanding of the vital importance of genuine free play for children in the early years.

Implications for pedagogy: what might *you*, the reader, reflect on now?

- How, where and when do children engage in R&T play in your setting?
- How does the design of the outdoor area in your setting facilitate children engaging in genuine free play?
- How might an understanding of the 'biocultural model' of the child change and/or develop your ideas relating to the provision of outdoor free play?

References and further reading

Bishop, J. and Curtis, M. (2001) *Play Today in the Primary School Playground*. Buckingham: Open University Press.

Braza, F., Braza, P., Carreras, M., et al. (2007) Behavioral profiles of different types of social status in preschool children: an observational approach, *Social Behaviour and Personality*, 35(2): 195–212.

Brock, A. (2009) Curriculum and pedagogy of play: a multitude of perspectives? In A. Brock, S. Dodds, P. Jarvis and Y. Olusoga (eds) *Perspectives on Play*. London: Pearson.

Buss, D. (1994) *The Evolution of Desire*. New York: Basic Books.

Department for Children, Schools and families (DCSF) (2008) *Statutory Framework for the Early Years Foundation Stage*. Nottingham: DCSF.

Fry, D. (1987) Differences between play fighting and serious fighting among Zapotec children, *Ethology and Sociobiology*, 8: 285–306.

George, J. (2010) Safe and equal in the setting and beyond, in P. Jarvis, J. George and W. Holland (eds) *The Early Years Professional's Complete Companion*. Harlow: Pearson Longman.

Jarvis, P. (2005) The role of rough and tumble play in children's social and gender role development in the early years of primary school. Unpublished PhD thesis, Leeds Metropolitan University.

Jarvis P. (2007a) Monsters, magic and Mr. Psycho: rough and tumble play in the early years of primary school, a biocultural approach, *Early Years: An International Journal of Research and Development*, 27(2): 171–88.

Jarvis, P. (2007b) Dangerous activities within an invisible playground: a study of emergent male football play and teachers' perspectives of outdoor free play in the early years of primary school, *International Journal of Early Years Education*, 15(3): 245–59.

Jarvis, P., George, J. and Holland, W. (2010) *The Early Years Professional's Complete Companion*. Harlow: Pearson Longman.

Knight, S. (2010) Forest school: playing on the wild side, in J. Moyles (ed.) *The Excellence of Play*. Maidenhead: Open University Press.

Konner, M.J. (1972) Aspects of the developmental ethology of a foraging people, in N. Blurton Jones (ed.) *Ethological Studies of Child Behaviour*. Cambridge: Cambridge University Press.

Layard, R. and Dunn, J. (2009) *A Good Childhood: Searching for Values in a Competitive Age*. London: Penguin.

Mallon, R. and Stich, S. (2000) The odd couple: the compatibility of social constructionism and evolutionary psychology, *Philosophy of Science*, 67: 133–54.

Newell, W.W. ([1883] 1963) *Games and Songs of American Children*. New York: Dover Publications.

Opie, I. and Opie, P. (1969) *Children's Games in Street and Playground*. London: Oxford University Press.

Pellegrini, A. (2005) *Recess: Its Role in Education and Development*. Mahwah, NJ: Lawrence Ehrlbaum Associates.

Pellegrini, A. and Blatchford, P. (2000) *The Child at School*. London: Arnold.

Piaget, J. and Inhelder, B. (1969) *The Psychology of the Child*. London: Routledge & Kegan Paul.

Van Hooff, J. (1976) A comparative approach to the phylogeny of laughter and smiling, in J.S. Bruner, A. Jolly and K. Sylva (eds) *Play: Its Role in Development and Evolution*. New York: Basic Books.

Vygotsky, L. (1978) *Mind in Society*. Cambridge, MA: Harvard University Press.

11 'This is a *different* calculator – with computer games on'
Reflecting on children's symbolic play in the digital age

Maulfry Worthington

Summary

This chapter explores data from research into children's imaginative (symbolic) play, from a cultural-historical, social-semiotic perspective as they explore, make and communicate personal meanings. It begins by focusing on children's play and 'sign-making', introducing the research background and highlighting the value of such play for children's learning. Several case studies explore children's interest in popular culture, new media and technologies through their representations or 'signs', evident in their 'superhero' play and in their models and drawings. The chapter raises questions about early childhood cultures and practices, emphasizing the importance of reflective teaching to help understand and support children's play and cultural interests at a deep level. Data has been drawn from observations of 3- and 4-year-old children in a nursery. The findings provide pedagogical points for practitioners to use for critical reflection in their support of children's interests in popular culture and digital technologies.

Key questions as you read . . .

1   What can we learn about children's interests and understandings of new media, popular culture and contemporary technologies from observations about young children's imaginative play?
2   Why are children's own meanings so important? What is the value of such play?

3   Which pedagogical strategies can enhance and support young children's meaning-making?

. . . and points to consider

- Play is valuable in many ways and provides rich contexts for young children's learning. It is within pretend or imaginative play that children use a range of representational means and artefacts to make and communicate personal meanings. This semiotic (i.e. meaning-making) perspective has been developed in recent years by Kress (1997) who refers to young children's 'multi-modality' as the many ways and diverse media and materials they use to make meanings. Researchers recognize the significance of children's symbolic play for literacy and it is understood to also underpin mathematics and *children's mathematical graphics*.
- The socio-cultural contexts of children's homes have a considerable influence on their understanding of the world and are evident in the technologies available in homes and many other aspects of their worlds. Modern media is beamed directly into all our lives to an extent previously unknown and cultural icons from magazines, video games and television have social currency among even the youngest children. These influences impact on children's play, drawings and model-making.
- Play is not always well understood with the result that children's experiences may sometimes be limiting. Children need to know their imaginative play and interests are understood and valued by adults in their nursery or school. When teachers and practitioners reflect on their values, beliefs and practices and develop their pedagogy, children's play and meaning-making can be particularly rich and complex.

Introduction

In his book, *How we Think*, Dewey (1933: 9, italics in original) wrote of the significance of 'reflective teaching' defining it as '*Active, persistent, and careful consideration of any belief or supposed form of knowledge in the light of the grounds that support it and the further conclusions to which it tends* constitutes reflective thought'. When considering children's play, reflection can help teachers consider issues of the (sometimes different) cultural values and expectations of the children's homes and their educational settings, values that are bound 'to influence and be influenced by the perspectives of parents, children and teachers' (Pollard and Tann, 2005: 27).

The role of reflective teaching has been explored by early childhood researchers (e.g. Heaslip, 1994; Adams, 2007) and in two large studies, the *Study of Pedagogical Effectiveness in Early Learning (SPEEL)* (Moyles et al., 2002) and the *Study of Primary Interactive Teaching (SPRINT)* (Moyles et al., 2003). This chapter aims to promote critical, reflective pedagogy in support of effective imaginative play.

Play

Among researchers the importance of play is well recognized (e.g. Huizinga, 1950; Moyles, 2005; Pellegrini and Smith, 2005; Athey, 2007), highlighting its value for cognitive processes and skills and affective behaviours (Wood and Attfield, 2005; Goswami, 2008). Vygotsky (1978) showed that through children's meaning-making with gesture and actions, artefacts, speech and drawing, imaginative (symbolic) play underpins symbolic languages such as writing. Representing meanings with open-ended materials is an integral aspect of this 'multi-modal' meaning-making (Kress, 1997; Pahl, 1999; Worthington, 2007).

Following many years in which play has often been marginalized, there appears to be renewed interest (in England) in play in early years settings. The curriculum for the *Early Years Foundation Stage* (DfES, 2007) supports and promotes play for children from birth to 5 years (see also Chapter 1). Teachers and practitioners are encouraged to continue to provide play opportunities for children in Year 1 (5- and 6-year-olds) (QCA, 2002) and the final report of the *Cambridge Review* also underlines its significance (Alexander, 2009). Heaslip (1994) addressed ways of 'making play work in the classroom' arguing 'Professionals need to be able to justify though their practices, how play is the supreme way through which young children learn, and . . . be able to articulate this to others' (pp. 101–2).

However, in spite of curricular guidance, teachers and practitioners – particularly in schools – must justify their pedagogy in the light of tests, 'standards' and inspections, making it particularly important that teachers develop a good understanding of play and can justify its role. Since play is complex and difficult to define, observations of play can be difficult for teachers and practitioners to understand, with the result that children's experiences of play may be brief, fleeting and unfulfilling. And without adult–child dialogue to scaffold their meaning-making in play, children's own meanings often fail to develop.

Imagination in play: making meanings, making signs

Semiotics (i.e. 'sign-making' or meaning-making) explores the relationship between meanings, signs, and socio-cultural influences (e.g. Vygotsky, 1978;

Jewitt and Kress, 2003; Kress and Van Leeuwen, 2001), reflected in the growing research on 'multi-modality' in early childhood (e.g. Kress, 1997). Children's communicative sign-making practices are powerful psychological tools that allow them to signify meanings to 'mean' something': they support a complex interplay of thought that is rooted in children's imaginative play (Vygotsky, 1978; Van Oers, 2005). In his study on the 'potentials of imagination', Van Oers (2005: 5) argues that 'The need to make sense of one's environment is probably one of the most basic drives of humans'.

For Vygotsky, 'play' is imaginative or pretend play within which children make connections between 'first-order' and 'second-order' symbolism (Vygotsky, 1978), representing (re-presenting) externally their internal, mental representations. Vygotsky's research (1978) showed how, through gesture, actions, sound and speech, artefacts and drawings ('first-order symbolization'), children make and communicate meanings. While, for example, a child uses a shell to signify an ice cream or draws circles to signify a car (i.e. the wheels), they are only *symbols* or representations of real things (see Worthington, 2010).

In contrast, 'second-order' symbolism refers to symbolic 'written' languages such as writing and mathematical notation. The processes of assigning meanings in play and in writing are closely related and, from this perspective, Vygotsky (1978: 116) argued 'make-believe play, drawing and writing can be viewed as different moments in an essentially unified process'. Kress (1997: 108) has a similar semiotic perspective, emphasizing:

> Imagination is a form of sign-making in which the boundaries to sign-making, the chains of signs, are potentially unlimited ... It is dependent on and enhanced by the ability to engage in free movement among forms of (internal) representation – not confined, for instance, to staying within language, or the visual, or the tactile, but able to range freely across modes.

Providing open-ended opportunities and resources offers children 'different potential' for realizing imagination (Kress, 1997: 29).

Children of the digital age

Marsh et al. (2005: 9–10) define the digital technologies and related aspects explored in this chapter:

- *Popular culture* 'refers to those cultural texts, artifacts and practices which are attractive to large numbers of children and which are often mass produced on a global scale' ... such as 'toys; games; media; and artifacts related to popular narratives, characters and icons'.

- *Media* 'is a term used for materials and resources in a range of formats and modes which are used for communication' including 'books, comics and magazines, newspapers, television programmes and films'.
- *New technologies* 'refer to technological innovations that have been made possible through digitisation. It can include "old" technologies, such as radio and television, which have been transformed by the digital signal' in addition to computers, console games, hand-held computers and mobile phones'.

Characters from popular culture influence children's imaginative play (Paley, 1984) and the examples of models and play in this chapter are populated by characters such as 'Power Rangers' and 'Batman', American wrestlers; monsters and 'CBeebies'.

New technologies explored by the children include calculators, video and computer games and palm-held games such as 'Nintendo', televisions and remote controls. And, in significant leaps of imagination, the children also created their own imaginary technologies: such 'productions are a mix of different ideas and influences that they put together to form objects which are entirely new' (Pahl, 1999: 24). They made 'switches' to 'control' Power Rangers that could alternatively kill and control daylight and darkness. One child made a 'spy gadget' with codes and a protected password: another drew a 'world' that can be controlled (to rotate) and another, a 'magic watch'.

Marsh et al. (2005: 1) writes of 'children of the digital age', showing how rapidly childhood cultures are changing and proposing that research into these aspects 'is of central importance in the provision of educational, social and cultural experiences that are appropriate for children in contemporary societies' (2005: 12–13).

Parker (1997: 3–4) argues that reflective teaching can change teachers' roles from being a 'lone operator' to engaging in not only reflection but also in action-research and critical thinking. Critical reflection is particularly relevant if we are to consider both the challenges of the twenty-first century and the particular contexts of individual early childhood settings and local needs of teachers, children and families.

Research methodology and analysis

The chapter draws on some of the data collected for the first phase of my research, an extension of research into children's mathematical graphics (Carruthers and Worthington, 2005, 2006) that charts the emergence of children's mathematical graphics from its genesis in imaginative play. The

focus of this chapter is on children's play and representations relating to popular culture media and technologies. The data is drawn from 16 children of 3–4
years of age, of whom 12 are boys and four are girls. Their models, cut-outs and
drawings were gathered through observations of children's self-initiated play
in one of two nursery settings that collaborated in the research and include
two short observations from the reception classes to which two children
moved. The data is qualitative, drawing on the children's spontaneous play
without adult direction.

Analysing imagination

I used Van Oers 'functions of imagination' in order to analyse and better
understand the observations, adding a new function 'imagination as dynamic
change' that supports children's understanding and meaning-making of
popular culture, new technologies, media and sometimes magic.

In his research, Van Oers endeavoured to understand 'the novelties in
children's [play] activities or verbal narratives', discovering that the 'products
of imagination served special functions' (2005: 8). He developed two 'functions of the imagination', 'imagination as etcetera-act' (abstract thinking) and
'imagination as an act of generating alternatives' (divergent thinking).

Imagination as etcetera-act

This function of imaginative play refers 'to the invisible, by suggesting – with
the help of some symbolic means – that a given series or rule can be continued'
(Van Oers, 2005: 8). During the first phase of research (Worthington, 2010),
I identified several examples of 'imagination as etcetera-act'. For example,
Hamzah drew a series of brown and black dots, explaining it was a 'car'. While
his drawing lacked recognizable 'car' features such as the body of a car or
windows, Hamzah's verbal explanation allows us to continue the 'car' rule for
ourselves. Kress (1997) includes a similar example from a 3-year-old child's
drawing of a car (p. 11).

On another occasion, Finley removed a portion of a paper plate and
folding the remaining portion in half, he made a series of short cuts across
the fold. Finally, he added several short lines and marks, explaining that
he'd made a puppet of 'a man'. The children had been looking at models
of skeletons and talked about the ribs: the short cuts and lines on Finley's
puppet appeared to suggest ribs. Rather than the children's play, drawings
or models providing complete symbolic representations that are immediately
accessible to adults, this example shows that it was knowledge of the context
and Finley's explanation that provided the 'etcetera' information. Van Oers

(2005) proposes that we have to continue the 'rule' for ourselves in order to understand their meanings. The important point to recognize is that, rather than attempting to replicate or make an exact copy of something, young children's models and drawings effectively capture their internal, mental representations that can become clear when we take the time to listen and understand.

Imagination as an act of generating alternatives

This function of imagination 'consists of making alternative representations of objects, situations, and actions . . . of how the world *could* be' (Van Oers, 2005: 9). Identifying Vygotsky's example of a child substituting a stick for a horse (1978), Van Oers emphasizes that the object (or other representation) chosen by the child depends on its affordances (i.e. the possibilities or qualities that a gesture, action artefact, material or mark offers) and the extent to which the child's choice is compatible with their intended meaning.

Examples of this function of imagination from my data included a child engaged with her friend in playing 'moving house'. Putting lots of books in a bag (pretending this was a 'suitcase of clothes'), Felicity dragged the heavy bag to their 'new house'. In another instance, Nathan used an envelope and some coloured paper to make 'an astronaut' and announcing 'Blast off', lifted it above his head to make it 'fly to the moon'. The lack of visual details was completed by his actions and words and was sufficient to ensure that others understood his meaning.

Imagination as an act of dynamic change

As I analysed and reflected on collected examples, I became aware that some observations did not fit neatly in either of the two categories above. They showed children assigning specific powers or functions to their artefacts, models and drawings, using them to 'operate' imaginary 'technological gadgets'. This led to an additional 'function' that I created, 'imagination as an act of dynamic change'. Vygotsky (2004: 20) refers to the 'association between imagination and reality' which 'may represent something substantially new'. In certain respects this new category appears to be related to Vygotsky's (p. 20) fourth 'law governing the operation of the imagination' that:

> a construct of fantasy may represent something substantially new, never encountered before in human experience and without correspondence to any object that actually exists in reality [which] once it has been externally embodied, that is, has been given material form, this crystallized imagination that has become an object begins to actually exist in the real world, to affect other things.

Vygotsky's examples include 'any technical device, machine, or instrument . . . created by the combinatory imagination of human beings' (2004: 20–1): they follow 'an internal logic of their own' (p. 24). Pahl (1999: 90) emphasizes that such play involves 'complex stories of transformation' and that artefacts and models 'added realism to dramatic play' and 'enabled the wearers to feel "more real" in the roles they were adopting' (p. 48).

'Switches for Power Rangers'

A group of boys were engaged in 'superhero' play about 'Power Rangers', excitedly running outdoors, swinging from the tree and climbing on and through a tunnel (Photograph 11.1). Marsh et al. (2005) comment how important such 'media icons are to young children'; parents often described their

Photograph 11.1 Mason's 'switches for Power Rangers'.

children as being 'obsessed with them and were aware of the pervasiveness of their consumer culture' (p. 45). Noticing some red bricks Mason put one in the end of his sleeve so that it was partly hidden; then added several bricks, and some to his other sleeve.

Ignoring the colour of the bricks in his sleeves, Mason urged his teacher 'Press that one and I turn red; that one – green and this one – blue! I'll leave them on until I see monsters!', then pressing one of the bricks he shouted 'Kill!' After a short interval with two friends in the hammock, Mason climbed out and pressing one of the bricks announced, 'It's morning so I have to turn the lighting speed up!' Next he added another brick to his sleeve and admiring the effect said 'This looks like a *real* Power Ranger one' before running off.

'Paper calculators'

Alfie watched Mason use pages from a notebook to make 'calculators' and decided to join in. Having drawn shapes on his page, Alfie ripped it off the pad and then made more symbols, saying '6, 7, 8, 9, I've done a number 10', followed by a third sheet, announcing '9, 10, 11, 12'. In 20 minutes Alfie had made a total of seven paper 'calculators' (Photograph 11.2).

This play began several weeks earlier when Mason was playing with a real calculator: he seemed to be using it as a digital game, pressing the buttons and commenting excitedly 'Fighting games! Video games!' It was Mason who first decided to use a small notebook to make 'paper calculators', explaining as he tore off a sheet, 'This is a *different* calculator with computer games on'.

Several of Mason's peers joined in and developed their own 'paper calculators' and, making another calculator, Alfie announced 'Lots of fighting!' A week later Mason explained he'd made a calculator with 'Batman' on it. Pahl (1999: 17) emphasizes 'Children's modelling needs to be carefully watched. It is often different from what we suppose'. The boys returned again and again to this play over a period of two terms, making rapid scribble marks, drawing 'buttons' on their 'calculators' and occasionally writing numerals. This interest allowed the children to adapt, co-construct and negotiate symbolic meanings so that layers of meanings evolved over time.

'Televisions for boys'

Several boys had been talking about their favourite American wrestlers on television. Mason decided he was going to make 'a TV for wrestling' and Keon joined him, adding 'I'm doing a TV for boys – not for girls!' Alfie drew the

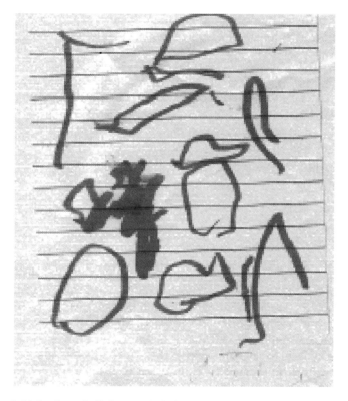

Photograph 11.2 One of Alfie's paper 'calculators'.

outline of a television screen, a 'TV for boys *and* girls', adding knobs so it could be turned on and off. It seems likely that Mason had not known televisions with controls on the set at home, but perhaps their representation emphasized the physical potential of being able to control his 'television' (Photograph 11.3).

Sophie joined in this play explaining that her television was for 'CBeebies' (a television channel currently broadcast for young children): she drew a figure on her 'screen', suggesting that she understood 'CBeebies' as more appropriate for girls – or at least not specifically aimed at boys.

Mason announced he needed a 'clicker' (a remote control) (Photograph 11.4) and poking a pencil into a 'multilink' cube pointed it at his 'television', pretending to turn it on and off. Developing Mason's earlier idea, Alfie moved his hand up and down the wall where the children had stuck their 'televisions', pretending to press the (sometimes imaginary) knobs, then extending Mason's idea of a remote control, he mimed the actions of using one. Extending this play further, Mason later made a (paper) wrestler's belt with a large buckle for his friend Keon.

Photograph 11.3   Television control knobs.

While paper might seem an unlikely material to represent calculators or televisions, in both contexts it suited the expression of children's ideas. Kress (1997: 31) argues that 'this conceptual "what is to hand" is significant, because it sets limits to and provides possibilities for imagination, opens up categories . . . and cultural differences of various kinds'. Additionally 'It provides materials for the differentiation of gender'.

Social and individual play

The examples of *imagination as an act of dynamic change* were often highly social and may in part reflect children's home experiences of similar technologies where they sometimes watch or play with other family members or friends. However, it is worth acknowledging that some of today's technologies such as CD players with headsets, mobile phones and computer use emphasize individual rather than shared interaction: these experiences appear to be reflected in other examples of drawing and models gathered from this data. For example, Lewis described his drawing (Photograph 11.5) as 'the world – and it goes round!' He explained that his home was in the top left-hand corner and near that, the nursery. Lewis pointed to a winding route between nursery and his

Photograph 11.4 Mason's remote control.

home, suggesting a map of the route he had physically moved through many times, and explained that the black circles (lower right) 'make it go'.

On other occasions Nathan made a 'magic watch' (a strip of paper with a zigzagging line on it) that enabled magic to be channelled through his fingers to an object or person at which he pointed, and Mason made a 'spy gadget' (Photograph 11.6) for which he created a code (a string of combined letters and numerals) to 'protect the password' to access his gadget; reversing the code enabled him to turn his gadget off.

Gender issues

Like the examples in this chapter, in Pahl's research it was largely boys who engaged in such play, 'Boys are often less confident with pen and paper than

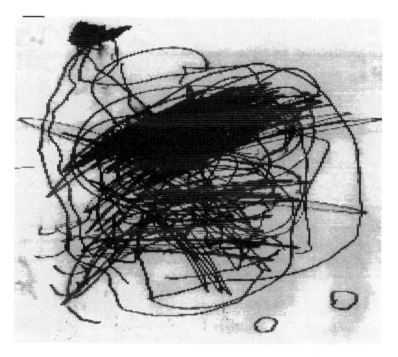

Photograph 11.5   'To make the world go round'.

girls . . . Model making is a way of expressing ideas in space and extending their thoughts . . . expressing concepts in the third dimension' as 3D models (1999: 94).

In their large-scale research project into 'digital beginnings' Marsh et al. (2005: 71) observed that 'boys in particular appeared to respond to the increased use of popular culture, media and new technologies . . . a pattern which has been noted in other studies'. In the examples in this chapter, power and control appeared to be a significant factor for boys. Kress (1997: 120) proposes that:

> children are not interested in just everything, but are selective in their interests from an early age . . . These selections lead to specialisms . . . One effect of such specialization is the establishment of gender . . . Some selections seem to be quite gender-neutral . . . others are not.

Cultural differences: pedagogy

The examples included in this chapter are drawn from a city nursery with the exception of Mason's spy gadget and Nathan's watch that were from their first

Photograph 11.6 Mason's 'spy gadget'.

few weeks in Year R. The research aims to be collaborative, the researcher and teachers reflecting and co-constructing understanding together. While the two nursery settings studied used the same play-based curriculum, adults understood and interpreted play and their pedagogical roles differently and engaged in different levels of critical and reflective discussion during the research.

In the city nursery the teachers focused considerably on the children's own meanings, sensitively listening, closely observing and 'tuning into' the children's symbolic actions, play behaviours and representations. The teachers' attention to detail was reflected in their written observations that informed their subsequent plans to further support the children's thinking (see also Chapter 14). This interest and attention impacted on the children's play, evidenced by numerous rich examples of their meaning-making that often revealed complex meanings and 'signs' that they elaborated and transformed.

Staff in the rural nursery encouraged and valued 'free play' that the children clearly enjoyed and the data included several examples of children exploring and representing personal meanings within role play (see also Chapter 5). There was considerable evidence of children making models with plastic construction materials such as 'Lego' but, since such resources limit what can be done with them, their models generally had only one meaning. In this nursery children made almost no representations that they transformed or adapted. Perhaps because there was no culture of making models with various media and found materials, no examples of 'imagination as an act of dynamic change' were found from this setting.

The children had extended periods to play freely indoors and during these times adults were often busy with individual children, engaged on an 'assessment task'. Adults in this setting seldom engaged in discussion with the children about their play or representations: 'meaning-making' was not explicitly discussed and written observations were brief and seldom used to inform planning. An extended period of free play outside was clearly enjoyed by the children but at this time adults supervised, watching and ensuring safety rather than observing and engaging in children's play (see Chapter 10).

Findings

The play episodes explored in this chapter show that:

- the children spontaneously initiated their own play, making independent decisions about the 'modes' and materials that would enable them to best signify and communicate their meanings;
- the children's imaginative play was considerably influenced by their knowledge and understandings of technologies, popular culture and new media, crossing the boundaries between home and their setting;
- the data showed considerable gender bias with almost all examples of 'imagination as an act of dynamic change' from boys' play;
- the setting's culture and pedagogical practices influenced the children's meaning-making; the extent to which they made models and whether they explored popular culture and digital technologies.

Conclusion

These examples highlight the importance of rich imaginative, symbolic play in which meanings combine with culture to shape children's narratives, supported by adults observing, reflecting and tuning into children's 'voices'. It is hoped that the examples (and analysis) of the play episodes will encourage practitioners to explore and critically examine imaginative play in their own settings, reflecting on their roles in supporting this. This chapter offers new insights into the influence of children's 'digital childhoods' on child-initiated play. The research has also highlighted the gender bias in play. However, we should not assume that girls have no knowledge or interest in contemporary technologies and popular culture: indeed, 'both boys and girls respond to these themes' provided adults are aware and make appropriate provision (Marsh et al., 2005: 62). Significantly, the findings have also shown how differing perspectives, values and levels of critical reflection contribute to contrasting outcomes for children's play.

What do I, the writer, feel about the contribution of this chapter to supporting critical reflection?

Through my research and writing, I have reflected that in our global, digital age the fast-paced change of life suggests that it is even more important to consider and re-evaluate my values, beliefs and practices in early education, to go beyond 'routine action' and engage in '*reflective* action' involving 'a willingness to engage in constant self-appraisal and development' and implying 'flexibility, rigorous analysis and social awareness' (Dewey cited in Pollard and Tann, 2005: 9). Marsh et al.'s (2005) study found that their involvement effected practitioners' earlier 'mixed views about the role and importance of popular culture and media in children's lives' (p. 48), impacting on their attitudes and approaches to 'open everybody's eyes' (p. 71). Early childhood practitioners like me have the means to engage in reflection and critical discussion to support children's imaginative play and 'digital childhoods'.

Implications for pedagogy: what might *you*, the reader, reflect on now?

- Focus on children's meaning-making throughout their imaginative, symbolic play and engage in dialogue with children to scaffold their meanings, enabling them to negotiate and co-construct understandings.
- Critically examine the extent to which children's explorations of popular culture, new media and technologies are noticed and valued.
- Consider gender bias and the extent to which your provision supports the interests of both boys and girls regarding their 'digital cultures' (see also Chapter 7).
- Reflect on your provision of open-ended resources for model-making and drawing materials and of the space children have to explore these materials. What might you add or change?
- Meet with colleagues to share and reflect on your observations of children's play so that you can co-construct your understanding and deepen insights into children's imaginations.

References and further reading

Adams, S. (2007) Putting the bananas to bed! Becoming a reflective teacher, in J. Moyles (ed.) *Beginning Teaching: Beginning Learning in Primary Education.* Maidenhead: Open University Press.

Alexander, R. (ed.) (2009) *The Cambridge Review of the Primary Curriculum: Children, their World, their Education. Final report and recommendations of the Cambridge Primary Review.* London: Routledge.

Athey, C. (ed.) (2007) *Extending Thought in Young Children*, 2nd edn. London: Paul Chapman.

Carruthers, E. and Worthington, M. (2005) Making sense of mathematical graphics: the development of understanding abstract symbolism, *European Early Childhood Education Research Association (EECERA) Journal*, 13(1): 57–79.

Carruthers, E. and Worthington, M. (2006) *Children's Mathematics, Making Marks, Making Meaning*, 2nd edn. London: Sage Publications.

Department for Education and Skills (DfES) (2007) *Practice Guidance for the Early Years Foundation Stage.* London: DfES.

Dewey, J. (1933) *How we Think.* Boston: D.C. Heath and Company

Goswami, U. (2008) *Cognitive Development: The Learning Brain.* Hove: Psychology Press.

Heaslip, P. (1994) Making play work in the classroom, in J. Moyles (ed.) *The Excellence of Play.* Maidenhead: Open University Press.

Huizinga, J. (1950) *Homo Ludens.* Boston, MA: Beacon Press.

Jewitt, C. and Kress, G. (2003) (eds) *Multimodal Literacy.* New York: Peter Lang.

Kress, G. (1997) *Before Writing: Rethinking the Paths to Literacy.* London: Routledge.

Kress, G. and Van Leeuwen, T. (2001) *Multimodal Discourse: The Modes and Media of Contemporary Communication.* London: Arnold.

Marsh, J., Brooks, G., Hughes, J., et al. (2005) *Digital Beginnings: Young Children's Use of Popular Culture, Media and New Technologies.* Sheffield: Literacy Research Centre, University of Sheffield.

Moyles, J. (ed.) (2005) *The Excellence of Play*, 2nd edn. Maidenhead: Open University Press.

Moyles, J., Adams, S. and Musgrove, A. (2002) *SPEEL: Study of Pedagogical Effectiveness in Early Learning.* London: DfES Research Report No. 363.

Moyles, J., Hargreaves, L. and Merry, R. (2003) Interactive teaching, digging even harder into meanings, in J. Moyles, L. Hargreaves, R. Merry, F. Paterson and V. Estarte-Sarries (eds) *Interactive Teaching in the Primary School.* Maidenhead: Open University Press.

Pahl, K. (1999) *Transformations: Meaning-making in Nursery Education.* Stoke-on-Trent: Trentham books.

Paley, V.G. (1984) *Boys and Girls: Superheroes in the Doll Corner*. Chicago, IL: The University of Chicago Press.

Parker, S. (1997) *Reflective Teaching in the Postmodern World*. Buckingham: Open University Press.

Pellegrini, A.D. and Smith, P.K. (eds) (2005) *The Nature of Play: Great Apes and Humans*. New York: Guilford Press.

Pollard, A. and Tann, S. (2005) *Reflective Teaching in the Primary School*. London: Cassell.

Qualifications and Curriculum Authority (QCA) (2002) *Continuing the Learning Journey*. London: QCA.

Van Oers, B. (2005) The potentials of imagination, *Inquiry: Critical Thinking across the Disciplines*, 24(4): 5–17.

Vygotsky, L.S. (1978) *Mind in Society: The Development of Higher Psychological Processes*. Cambridge, MA: Harvard University Press.

Vygotsky, L.S. (2004) Imagination and creativity in childhood, *Journal of Russian and East European Psychology*, 42(1): 7–97.

Wood, E. and Attfield, J. (2005) *Play, Learning and the Early Childhood Curriculum*. London: Paul Chapman.

Worthington, M. (2007) Multi-modality, play and children's mark-making in maths, in J. Moyles (ed.) *Early Years Foundations: Meeting the Challenge*. Maidenhead: Open University Press.

Worthington, M. (2010) Play is a complex landscape: imagination and symbolic meanings, in P. Broadhead, L. Wood. and J. Howard (eds) *Play and Learning in Educational Settings*. London: Sage Publications.

12 A place for play
Creating complex learning environments

Pauline Trudell

Summary

This chapter proposes that imaginative play has a powerful impact on young children's learning, and goes on to consider what practitioners need to put in place if deep and complex play is to develop. Physical space, time, resources, routines, relationships and interactions between adults and children are all considered, as well as the principles on which to establish an environment for play and learning. The link between imaginative play and other forms of symbolic representation such as language and literacy is explored. Imaginative play also fosters the development of social and emotional literacy, of moral concepts and problem solving, but, important as this learning is, play is valid in its own right and can transform and integrate experience, knowledge, thought and feeling.

Key questions as you read . . .

1   What is meant by 'teaching' at Foundation Stage level? What do practitioners need to know?
2   What do you understand by continuous provision and workshop organization; open-ended materials and open-ended questions?
3   How might adults be deployed to lead planned experiences; observe; and participate in child initiated activities? How might they extend those activities?

. . . and points to consider

- Literature and research validate the distinctive form of education for young children that has developed over decades in nursery schools and classes in England.
- This practice can only be maintained and strengthened if practitioners are confident about those principles of learning and teaching that underpin it.
- Staff teams must include in their planning time to reflect on what they understand about play and learning.
- Reflection and analysis impact on the way in which we organize an environment for play and learning.

Introduction

> . . . in play, under a table or up in a tree, alone, or in small groups, expressing themselves in words, or with blocks or music or miniature world materials, children think and feel and act in ways of utmost importance for their learning.
>
> (Drummond, 2000: 59)

This quotation tells us something about the high seriousness of play, and, at the same time, draws our attention to a location in which play might thrive. It sets before us a place where children may climb trees, choose to be alone or with others and where their thoughts and feelings can be expressed in many different ways. It conjures up not only an idea of the material resources available but also of the use of time and space and the role of the practitioner. It captures the complex interconnection between learner, teacher and place. A learning environment in which imaginative play can flourish cannot be achieved in isolation from those other closely related elements with which it forms an integrated whole. So, before examining the context in which playing, thinking, and learning occur, we should first pay critical attention to what we think about learning itself (see also Chapter 9).

What we believe about young children and how they learn will determine the conditions in which that learning takes place and the ways in which we support and extend learning (see Chapters 1, 2 and 5). All early childhood practice in this country has been shaped by a constructivist philosophy of learning and play that stems from the work of Piaget and Vygotsky and those theorists and academics who later reinterpreted and commented on their work (see Chapter 4). The practical application of that philosophy over decades produced a distinctive form of practice based on clear principles of early learning. These principles include:

- A view of learning as a process in which children actively construct understanding.
- Learning is believed to be social and collaborative: individual understandings and interests can be shared with other children and with engaged and responsive adults so that knowledge becomes co-constructed.
- Young children, like adults, experience their lives and learning as simultaneous and integrated. All aspects of children's learning and development are important and complementary.
- Relationships and feelings, communication, problem solving and investigation, creativity and imagination, thread through every area of learning and cross-curriculum boundaries.
- Representation is essential to the learning process and play is a key system of representation.
- Learning is most effective when children are able to make decisions about how to go about it and have time to reflect on new experiences.
- Children learn in individual families and specific social and cultural contexts: personal, social and emotional development and sense of identity affect learning;
- Children have different and variable attitudes and dispositions towards learning.

The counter side of learning is teaching, the two constituting 'pedagogy' as we have seen in Chapter 1. What practitioners believe about learning directly influences their interactions with children and their provision of an environment that aids children in their efforts to play and learn, for example:

- If practitioners' work is grounded in the principles already outlined then their professional understandings will begin with a knowledge of child development, early learning and pedagogy.
- A good understanding of curriculum content is important; as is the planning of provision, space, time and learning experiences to support and extend learning for individuals and groups of children.
- Such practitioners are fully involved in the project of learning, responding to children's efforts to solve problems and sustain ideas, and scaffolding learning (see Chapter 5).
- They recognize the critical importance of consistent relationships between children, teachers and children, and teachers and parents.
- They acknowledge individuality and are able to recognize and build

on children's existing understandings and intrinsic motivation to extend learning.
- They are aware that children's access to the curriculum is uneven and draws on a variety of teaching strategies for those who need additional support.

Listening, observing, analysing, recording and assessing learning in order to plan for each child's progress is at the heart of early childhood practice and practitioners will document the processes as well as the products of children's learning (see Chapter 14). The difficulty for practitioners currently is not that these principles of learning and teaching have been overturned but that they are becoming detached from practice. The rhetoric has been retained in successive curriculum documents in England and the USA but made increasingly irrelevant by a contradictory emphasis on goals and measurable outcomes. A perception of children as individuals with their own personal histories, interests, aspirations and ways of interpreting and understanding the world, will lead to systems of education different from those that start from an external curriculum and the expectation that children will reach age-related goals in predictable stages.

The collective English view of young children's learning contained in recent funding policy (*Early Years Funding Formula Guidance*, July 2009) disregards those essential but subtle aspects of early childhood practice, such as consistent routines and relationships and planned settling-in procedures. This means that curriculum guidance on personal, social and emotional education becomes remote from lived experience and practitioners are faced with an impossible contradiction. A blurring of the distinction between education and childcare, formalized by *The Childcare Act* 2006, has been accompanied by a corresponding shift from pedagogy (how they should learn) to curriculum (what they should learn): curriculum guidance is substituted for the shared professional understandings reached by teams of principled practitioners.

The highest level learning is initiated by the child and sustained with the help of adults who are able to observe and recognize children's persistent interests and present understandings and who can open the way to new worlds of knowledge. In these muddled times it is more than ever important for practitioners to clearly recall the reasons why they provide young children with the resources, time and space that they do in order to continue to develop their practice.

Defining the learning environment

The learning environment has been variously regarded as an aspect of the curriculum – '. . . the most neglected and misunderstood dimension of the planned curriculum is the creation of an environment or setting in which education is to take place' (Blenkin and Whitehead, 1987: 35) – or of pedagogy. In truth it is both. Siraj-Blatchford et al. (2002) distinguish between pedagogical interactions (specific behaviour on the part of adults) and, pedagogical framing (the 'behind-the-scenes' aspects of pedagogy that include planning, resources and establishment of routines). A key aspect of 'pedagogical framing' is a learning environment that supports children in their efforts to think and learn (p. 43).

In an 'instructive' and 'constructivist' learning environment the arrangement of space, time and resources is important (see Chapter 4). Practitioners should also be looking to establish:

- consistent relationships, experiences and routines;
- opportunities for children to:
  - actively explore, investigate, speak and listen, and develop ideas and language in their own time and their own way;
  - have playful encounters with people and with a range of materials;
  - control their own learning through choice of activity and availability of resources (this assumes a workshop environment);
- a climate, or atmosphere, which encourages questioning and where understanding is 'co-constructed'.

(based on Blenkin and Whitehead, 1987: 36–52)

Children's self-chosen play activities reveal their preoccupations and schemes of thought, as do monologues, questions, conversations and storying while they are involved in those activities (Photograph 12.1). The responsive adult who listens, observes and (sometimes) intervenes is the vital resource here (see Chapter 2).

Within such an environment children take responsibility for the decisions they make; for example, returning resources they have selected. They can only be expected to do this if the material resources are coherently arranged and clearly labelled and if the routines of the day are organized so they have time to do so. This 'bread and butter' aspect of maintaining the learning environment should not be underestimated if children are to work independently and make meaningful choices (Whitebread et al., 2007; Chapter 9).

When considering the learning environment we probably think first of the resources and equipment we provide; the continuous provision, that is:

- the materials that children can investigate and examine and to begin to classify and explore the relationships between;
- the sites we provide for socio-dramatic play and talk;

Photograph 12.1 Active exploration.

- the paint, clay, blocks, books, paper, pens, musical instruments and small world play that allow children to explore many different modes of representation and to develop ideas across a variety of media;
- the 'open-ended' resources that can stand in for other objects, events, and ideas.

Early pretence substitutions in play; for example, making 'tea' in the sandpit, or using a cylindrical block as a doll's feeding bottle, are thought by cognitive psychologists to be a reflection of a general capacity for symbolic representation. Symbolic play allows a child to manipulate ideas (see also Chapter 8). In order to think about anything we must represent it in some way. Language is *the* key signifying practice in which we represent and make sense of experience. It is through language that meaning is produced and exchanged, within specific cultural contexts (Hall, 1997) but there are many other ways of representing thoughts, ideas and feelings that include music, the visual arts, dance, drama, imaginative play and movement.

The learning environment, crucially, includes space, inside and outside. The younger the child the more likely it is that representation will be through motor actions which, in turn, generate new learning through the interplay between movement and perception. Early representation is an attempt to hold in the mind actions, events, people and objects in order to make sense of experience. 'But ... it is not a copy of that experience. Representation is an essentially dynamic, constructive act which shapes the experience itself' (Matthews, 2003: 24). Matthews argues that young children's drawing and painting represents dynamic patterns of action – the movement, shape and location of objects – and that 'Early mark-making is a member of a family of interrelated expressive and representational actions' which are made possible through play (p.37; see also Chapter 11). Thinking about this will influence our attitude towards children's drawing and painting; the provision we make for it and how we talk with children about their visual representations. Most importantly it should encourage a way of thinking about the learning environment as an environment for play and playful pedagogies.

In almost all nursery settings the home area is perceived to be the natural habitat of imaginative play. In the home area, as children pretend to be mothers and fathers, brothers and sisters, babies, and, often, cats and dogs, imaginative and socio-dramatic play can combine and connect with making up stories in the mind and a narrative mode of thought. In the following extract (Cameo 1) the head teacher of a London nursery school observes and describes play in the home area during the early weeks of the autumn term where some children are new to full-time attendance and some children are settling in. It perfectly illustrates how all the separate elements of a good learning environment – the resources, including people, the space and the time – come together to transform what might otherwise be commonplace, easily overlooked play into a learning process for practitioners as well as children:

Cameo 1

For the past couple of weeks there has been a lot if interest in play with domestic themes. All day, every day there are eight to ten children in the space with not all having the same agenda. Staff changed their plans for the focussed activity, so that the home corner became the focus. The adults' role is to help children share the space and accommodate different plot lines, using talk and growing empathy to incorporate and tolerate each other's ideas. Adults will also take on a role in the play if allotted to them by the children. Several children are interested in being Mum or Dad so staff are usually given roles as a baby or sister.

One particular day, I [HT] got caught up in watching play from the other side of the room. Four children were seated at a table having a meal, others dressing, cooking etc. One older girl (M) had wrapped a piece of sparkly fabric around her shoulders. She paced the floor in the home corner, then into the rest of the room, out and along the corridor and back again, all the while talking out loud, though not addressing anyone in particular 'I've got so much to organise, so much to do. I have to clean the sitting room, sort out the shopping, I've got the whole party to organise, so much to do, so much to organise and no one to help me. I don't know how I'm going to do it all. So much to organise, I've got to do everything, I have to organise it all' and so on, repeating this idea over and over as she paced the rooms.

After about ten minutes, the member of staff in the home corner suggested to M that she send someone shopping for the party. M attended to that briefly and went back to her pacing and litany.

Meanwhile a new boy (J) was putting three rucksacks on his back and going off to school. He said goodbye to the family – no one in particular – and walked over to the book corner, which was empty. He stood there, silent, face calm, for a minute and then said (not directed to anyone) with a slight note of pleading in his voice, 'Mum, I'm waiting for you to come and collect me. . . . Mum, come and get me, please.' HT suggested he ring her. He went back to the home corner, found a phone and returned to the book area 'Mum, Mum. Oh no, voice mail. Mum, text me please'. He then went back to the home corner, where M was still pacing and complaining about how much she had to do. He watched her closely. He then said, again to no one in particular, but near to HT 'I don't know, she's angry . . . She's angry 'cos I didn't eat my breakfast but I wasn't hungry. . . . I said "I'm sorry Mum" but she didn't say "That's okay"'. The HT said 'Well she seems very busy, and she keeps saying she needs help and she has so much to organize. Maybe she was worried about you, not angry'. He replied 'I need a Daddy'.

The head teacher's tentative assessment is given below.

> All the children remained deeply engaged in this play for an hour or more. There was no quarrelling. All were exploring something very important to them as individuals in this scenario. We can only make tentative guesses at what that might be. Talks with parents might shed further light.
>
> J, as a new boy, probably would be thinking about being collected, not being able to communicate with his Mum. We know that his parents have both recently been away on business and his carer has changed. He is enjoying nursery very much but there is still much to sort out about contact with those he loves, perhaps. Maybe nursery gives him a safe space to explore this. Maybe it only arose because of M's concerns, maybe they triggered his role, maybe her response

reminded him of his own busy parent. Maybe he wanted the plot to go differently – maybe he wanted M to respond to his call to be collected – perhaps he wanted to represent that aspect of his experience – but she didn't pick up on that and he wasn't yet at the stage when he could direct play by saying something like 'Pretend I'm the boy, yeah, and I'm at school and I say . . .'). M loves to organise – she spends hours arranging materials when she paints, or uses the workshop, she likes to have tools and props in just the right place when she plays offices etc.

And from the same source:

> Since the beginning of term a large group of children having been playing dogs, with an occasional handful of cats . . . They behave like dogs barking, crawling, jumping, and sleeping in a basket. One child in particular is interested in being the dog owner: she likes to control them so staff have told her about some command words – sit, heel, lie etc. She is also fascinated by connections and makes elaborate three pronged leads (she started with one prong and has now moved on) so that she can take three dogs for a walk at the same time. She uses the karabiners, and works out how to join them to three dogs and then feed into one lead in her hand [imagine a 'y' with an extra up stroke]. These are predominantly an older group of [nursery] children and the play takes place outside. The children are all skilled at collectively developing the plot and the play is peppered with 'Pretend I'm the puppy and I run away, right and you're the Mum and you say, "Oh, no, the puppy has run away". And I'm called Russell, okay?' Another consistent theme is the building of homes for the dogs – from boxes, baskets, hollow blocks.
>
> It is hard to be sure what this play represents for the children. One of the present children has a new puppy – that's one trigger. But I'm not sure if actually representing real life experience is all there is to it. There are always children engaged in this type of play – to greater or lesser degrees . . . Is it about a generic need to think about being 'other'? To what extent is the crawling significant? . . . There are always elements of domestic play in the animal play – there's always a mum, babies . . . there's always running away, naughtiness, punishment, being cross, danger, being saved, being sorry.

The physical resources in this school's home corner facilitate the play. Here the head teacher describes them.

> The home corner is a large area, in a corner, so that play isn't interrupted by people walking through or past it. It contains a sink,

washing machine, cooker, fridge, cupboards, table and four dining chairs for the kitchen area. Crockery and utensils but no toy food – instead we have containers of open-ended and easily replaced materials such as corks, conkers, buttons, pebbles. These can be used as the children wish – to stand in for food, to be playthings for the babies or pets or bones for the dogs – or simply explored by children more interested in heuristic play. A small table with a chair and writing and reading materials appropriate to a home – A–Z street guide, calendar, diary, pens and pencils, envelopes, writing paper, cards, pin board. Two beds with two dolls, a small chest of drawers with a change of clothes for the dolls, nappies and scarves, gloves and hats for children. On top, a collection of bangles, necklaces. A basket with mobile phones. A rocking chair. Dressing up clothes – waistcoats, trousers, jackets, and lots of unspecified items i.e .lengths of fabric, some very beautiful, which can be used imaginatively by the children as their thinking dictates, e.g, shawls, veils, blankets, robes. Shopping bags, hand bags.

The dog and cat play can develop because we have lots of open-ended resources in the garden available daily – a pile of blankets/ rugs, a trolley full of things to connect – karabiners, giant clothes pegs, ropes, etc., boxes and blocks. Children can play outside all day, every day.

Equally important are the involved and engaged adults and the simultaneous access to outside space and extended space inside, not that 'pacing the corridor':

As adults it is important that we provide the space, time and props for children to develop these themes. That we don't rush to analyse, that we don't dominate the play. Adults observe. They join in as the children want, that is, to be the mum or the owner and to extend the play by adding vocabulary e.g. the dog commands. A small group of children were also taken to the local park to watch the dogs in the canine walking area.

Domestic role play is only one kind of play, but it is perhaps a starting point for many children into more complex imaginative play and the arrangement of the home area needs careful thought (see Chapter 8).

Hall and Robinson (1995) have been influential in supporting the idea of a 'print flood' in the home corner so that children gain knowledge of the purposes of print and of the social contexts in which that knowledge is embedded. Children need the opportunity to behave as readers and writers. They make an explicit link between imaginative play and literacy and draw a parallel between children negotiating the roles and dialogue of such play and a writer drafting and redrafting a piece of work – the idea of such play as authorship.

The home corner has been seen as an arena where gender-differentiated play is acted out (Paley, 1984) and recognized as an imaginative world where girls see themselves as powerful and in control (Walkerdine, 1990). In role play children 'try on' positions in a variety of discourses in which they have never participated in real life. They take up roles, and their corresponding rules, spontaneously and can adopt a dialogic narrative, taking on two or more roles. In role play a metaphoric, associative principle (where one word stands for another and one object stands for another) emerges, and this principle leads to the capacity to generalize abstract and formal ideas (Walkerdine, 1990).

Play and the learning environment

There are many theories and analyses of play and much writing that acknowledges its importance in early learning, but there is no agreed definition of play in an educational setting (see Chapter 2). A study carried out by Bennett et al. (1997) examined teachers' understanding and use of play. Most teachers identified free, imaginative play as a curriculum priority for 4-year-olds but, in practice, they were more comfortable with the 'cognitive learn-as-you-play model' (Drummond, 2000: 52)

The *Researching Effective Pedagogy in the Early Years* (*REPEY*) study (Siraj-Blatchford et al., 2002: 43) found that 'the most effective settings . . . achieve a balance between the opportunities provided for children to benefit from teacher initiated group work and the provision of freely chosen yet potentially instructive play activities'. This finding is important if it helps to redress a too teacher-dominated model of early learning but the qualifying phrase, *potentially instructive*, is likely, in some cases, to perpetuate what Wood (2008) has referred to as the reification of an educational model of play: 'the gaze is regulatory (focused on outcomes), rather than hermeneutic (focused on children's meanings, understandings, play and activity choices)'.

Moyles's idea of a 'play spiral' (1989) encourages a balance between teacher-initiated play scenarios and 'free' play, suggesting that such scenarios may influence and enrich children's spontaneous play in the same way that story and oral or written narrative does. Play and literacy are crucially related. Both are systems of representation: both are forms of thought (Piaget, 1951). If our aim is to extend and deepen children's thinking, we know that the development of spoken language is vital to this. Early words accompany actions and language, once acquired, is itself a major means of extending the range and complexity of thought – words can be used for things not present, events not actually experienced: they can be used *in place* of things.

We also know that through reading and telling stories we are able to influence not only spoken language and early literacy but also children's capacity to represent their experience, understanding and feelings through play: constructing stories in the mind – or storying, as it has been called – is one of the most fundamental ways of making meaning; as such, it is an activity that pervades all aspects of learning (Wells, 1986: 194).

If storying is a way of making meaning then the adult input is storytelling. Paley (1990) writes of play and its necessary core of storytelling. The make-believe world of stories, read and told, connects with the multiple texts of children's everyday life – conversations, televisual and filmed stories and the impact of new technologies (Browne, 1999). The initial reading of a literary text gives itself up to children's rereadings in the world (Wolf and Brice-Heath, 1992). Practitioners need to be aware, too, that learning practices such as narrative experience and active engagement with play provision are culturally specific, and children will experience a diversity of linguistic, cultural and reading practices (Gregory, 1996, 1997). Adult involvement and sensitive intervention in imaginative play is crucial if all children are to gain access to it.

There is a link between being read to and narrative competence. A rich experience of hearing stories read and told influences children's spontaneous narratives (Whitehead, 2010). Children weave together stories from books, their own lives, and make-believe and this enables them to make meanings in language in a particularly rich, complex and powerful way (Fox, 1988, 1993). Literary texts are thick with possibilities: those of ordinary language are thin by comparison (Wolf and Brice-Heath, 1992). Oral story and anecdote constitute a primary way for children to enter the 'possible world' of abstract thought and language; moving from the 'here and now' to the many possibilities and interpretations that underpin written language.

Meek makes implicit use of Bruner's possible worlds metaphor when she writes about children exploring the boundaries of real and not real, sense and nonsense (Meek, 1985). Drummond employs it explicitly to develop the idea that in play children leave the everyday world and pass through invisible doors into alternative worlds (Drummond, 2000).

Tess Robson, the head teacher whose home area observations and reflections are quoted earlier, uses stories to push back the boundaries of imaginative play and open the door to alternative worlds. Observing three boys engaged in increasingly repetitive and frustrating superhero play she says:

> I sat near them with an illustrated encyclopedia of mythology. They joined me and we looked at a few pictures. It was Baba Yaga, gruesomely depicted, who caught their imaginations. I outlined her story and they adopted her as a villain.

Thus began an imaginative play project that extended over three terms and became an intense and transforming learning experience.

> The children's imaginative play was dominated by acting out its themes – good and evil, power and vulnerability, strength and weakness, bravery and fear, danger and rescue.

The play was sustained throughout by the passionate involvement of the head teacher as an active play partner, contributing ideas, stories and music. She comments on the play:

> Something called imaginative play happens in all settings. Predominantly it will be role play around children's everyday experiences – home corner, shops, hospitals, garages etc. It's important that we give children opportunities to represent their experience and knowledge and practitioners are confident about providing and supporting this type of play. But that's not the imaginative play that I'm talking about here. I'm talking about a wilder play, play that is dangerous and challenging, both to children and to us, play that grapples with concerns that have engaged human beings in all cultures, in all ages, play that deals with big themes – life/death, good/evil, heroes/villains, courage/fear, power/weakness. Themes that are enshrined in creation stories, myths, legends, folk and fairy tales around the globe . . . I believe that if we fail to nurture this deep abiding need of children to play in this way, we do them harm . . . it is a powerful way for children to learn very deeply about the nature of friendship, to understand emotions, to represent, to create, to think, to empathize, to develop as talkers, writers and readers.

Conclusion

The *REPEY* study identified criteria that are particularly important when working with young children. One of these is the quality of adult–child verbal interactions. The researchers coined the term 'sustained shared thinking' where 'each party engages with the understanding of the other and learning is achieved through a process of reflexive "co-construction" ' (Siraj-Blatchford et al., 2002: 10). The practitioner who enters the world of children's play – and reflects deeply on its implications – has the chance to sustain thinking in the most powerful way. Preparing an environment for play, which means weaving together everything we know about young children and learning, is the first step.

What do I, the writer, feel about the contribution of this chapter to supporting critical reflection?

Through my own practice over many years and reflection on the literature and research validating a distinctive form of education for young children that has developed over decades in nursery schools and classes in this country, I now appreciate that this practice can only be maintained and strengthened if practitioners are confident about those principles of learning and teaching that underpin it. The physical and cultural environment – for example, how it is planned, maintained, acknowledged – has a key role in children's and practitioners' learning. I hope readers have gained insights into the nature of play and early learning in order to encourage a reflective approach to practice, and the development of thoughtful and creative practitioners and pedagogies.

Implications for pedagogy: what might *you*, the reader, reflect on now?

1   How should physical and social space be arranged if children are to be supported in their efforts to:

- engage in complex play;
- problem-solve, think creatively, investigate and discover;
- use their imagination and represent their thoughts and feelings in many different ways;
- learn and play alone and with others?

2   Do you offer children enough time to develop their ideas through play? Is there enough space?

Acknowledgement

All observations and commentary on observations were provided by Tess Robson, Tachbrook Nursery School, Westminster. Photograph supplied by Wendy Scott (Jasper, aged 2 years and 3 months).

References and further reading

Bennett, N., Wood, L. and Rogers, S. (1997) *Teaching Through Play: Teachers' Thinking and Classroom Practice*. Buckingham: Open University Press.

Blenkin, G. and Whitehead, M. (1987) Creating a context for development, in G. Blenkin, and A.V. Kelly (eds) *Early Childhood Education: A Developmental Curriculum*. London: Paul Chapman.

Browne, N. (1999) *Young Children's Literacy Development and the Role of Televisual Texts*. London: Falmer Press.

Drummond, M.J. (2000) Perceptions of play in a Steiner kindergarten, in L. Abbott and H. Moylett (eds) *Early Education Transformed*. London: Falmer Press.

Fox, C. (1988) Poppies Will Make Them Grow, in M. Meek and C. Mills (Eds) *Language and Literacy in the Primary School*. London: Falmer Press.

Fox, C. (1993) *At the Very Edge of the Forest: The Influence of Literature on Storytelling by Children*. London: Cassell.

Gregory, E. (1996) *Making Sense of a New World: Learning to Read in a Second Language*. London: Paul Chapman.

Gregory, E. (ed.) (1997) *One Child Many Worlds: Early Learning in Multicultural Communities*. London: David Fulton.

Hall, N. and Robinson, A. (1995) *Exploring Writing and Play in the Early Years*. London: David Fulton.

Hall, S. (1997) The work of representation, in S. Hall (ed.) *Representation: Cultural Representations and Signifying Practices*. Buckingham: Open University Press.

Matthews, J. (2003) *Drawing and Painting: Children and Visual Representation*, 2nd edn. London: Hodder & Stoughton.

Meek, M. (1985) Play and paradoxes: some considerations of imagination and language, in G. Wells, G. and J. Nicholls (eds) *Language and Learning: An Interactional Perspective*. London: Falmer Press.

Moyles, J. (1989) *Just Playing? The Role and Status of Play in Early Childhood*. Buckingham: Open University Press.

Paley, V.G. (1984) *Superheroes in the Doll Corner*. Chicago: University of Chicago Press.

Paley, V.G. (1990) *The Boy Who Would Be a Helicopter*. Harvard, MA: Harvard University Press.

Piaget, J. (1951) *Play, Dreams and Imitation in Childhood*. London/New York: Heinemann.

Siraj-Blatchford, I., Sylva, K., Muttock, S., Gilden, R., and Bell, D. (2002) *Researching Effective Pedagogy in the Early Years (REPEY)*. London: DfES Research Report No. 356.

Walkerdine, V. (1990) *Schoolgirl Fictions*. London: Verso.

Wells, G. (1986) *The Meaning Makers: Children Learning Language and Using Language to Learn*. London: Hodder & Stoughton.

Whitebread, D., Bingham, S., Grau, V., Pino Pasternak, D. and Sangster, C. (2007) Development of metacognition and self-regulated learning in young children: the role of collaborative and peer-assisted learning, *Journal of Cognitive Education and Psychology*, 6: 433–55.

Whitehead, M. (2010) Playing or having fun? Dilemmas in early literacy, in J. Moyles (ed.) *The Excellence of Play*, 3rd edn. Maidenhead: Open University Press.

Wolf, S.A. and Brice-Heath, S. (1992) *The Braid of Literacy: Children's Worlds of Reading*. Harvard: Harvard University Press.

Wood, E. (2008) Unpublished presentation, *Challenging Play*, London: NUT Early Years Colloquium, November.

PART 4
Reflecting on playful contexts

13 Thinking through transition, pedagogy and play from early childhood education to primary

Kevin Kelman and Linda Lauchlan

Summary

The term *transition*, for the purposes of this chapter, means the process of movement from one educational setting into another. The transition for children from one setting to another is much more complicated than simply changing buildings. It may require adjusting to a new peer group, a new role, new teachers and new expectations. Children may be expected to cope with many new demands: they may meet new academic challenges, have to adapt to new school and teacher expectations and, perhaps, gain acceptance into a new peer group. Transitions between educational settings can often mean a change in location, educators, curriculum and philosophy. This chapter aims to look at the impact and opportunities these changes can have on children.

Key questions as you read . . .

1 If you were a child making the transition from early childhood settings to primary school, what pedagogical differences would you be likely to experience?
2 What impact may these differences have on you as a learner?
3 From your experience, what have you noticed as the main differences in pedagogical approaches between early childhood education settings and primary school settings?
4 As a reflective practitioner, how can you ensure that you articulate to parents, carers, colleagues, managers and external bodies the importance of a more playful approach at the transition?

. . . and points to consider

- Children experience a numbers of transitions in their educational experiences that can challenge them, their families and communities in many different ways.
- Just as you would not uproot a seedling without thought as to where it would be placed, so children should not be uprooted without thought and sensitivity.
- Pedagogical differences between early childhood education and care (ECEC) and primary schools can appear vast for young children and parents/carers and they will all need support.
- Sustaining playful pedagogies can significantly help children with major transitions.

Introduction

A number of transitions occur throughout a child's educational experience. These transitions have been described as *horizontal* and *vertical* (Kagan, 1992). For example, vertical transitions occur when children first move from home to a playgroup, from playgroup to a nursery, from nursery to a primary school, and so on. Horizontal transitions occur when children move from one setting to another during a day or week; for example, from playgroup to nursery, from childminder to nursery, from primary school to after-school, and so on. This chapter focuses solely on the vertical transition for young children from an early childhood education setting to a primary school setting.

Examining the challenges and opportunities around transitions

As practitioners, it is worthwhile for us to examine and reflect on the challenges and opportunities around transitions as part of our professional discourse. If we have a clear understanding of the impact that this juncture in children's educational experiences can have on their future progress and development, we can use this knowledge to maximize the potential benefits and minimize the risks for the learners.

All transitions are important and, as Edgar suggests, are a source of major change in an individual's life:

> Transition from home to pre-school, from pre-school to primary school, from primary to secondary and from school to work or

from youth to adulthood are always characterised by challenges, uncertainty and tension.

(Edgar, 1986 cited in Yeboah, 2002: 54)

The transition from early childhood education settings to primary school is a potential source of difficulty for young children (Cryer and Clifford, 2003). Studies from Australia (Dockett and Perry, 2004), Germany (Griebel and Niesel, 2005), Iceland (Einarsdottir, 2006), New Zealand (Peters, 2000) and the UK (Fabian, 2002) suggest that there are many global similarities in the issues that arise in relation to the transition that takes place at this stage in a child's development. Fabian (2002) summarizes these as:

- Physical discontinuities, such as the types of furniture, size of the building and layout of the learning environment.
- Social discontinuities, for example, new friendships, loss of friendships and availability of adults because of the changes in staffing ratios.
- Philosophical discontinuities, which may include: differences in pedagogical approaches; the change in balance between work and play; and more subject orientated timetabling.

As well as the challenges that arise at this transition, it is also important to reflect on the positive impact that transitions can offer. Taking on a new identity can stimulate feelings of excitement, anticipation, curiosity and pride. When transitions are supported well, children can develop transitions' capital (Dunlop and Fabian, 2007), providing children with the skills to adapt to change and thrive in new situations in the future. Working relationships for staff can be enhanced as practitioners work together to support children's transition to school. In addition, positive transition experiences for children can provide a real opportunity to sustain and enhance previous cognitive and social development. Wood and Caulier-Grice (2006) suggest that some of the value of early childhood education may be diminished during later childhood if it is not built on progressively. Wood and Caulier-Grice go on to suggest that 'it is sustaining these gains through primary school years which will have the most impact on their adult life chances' (p.19).

Cleave et al. (1982) drew parallels between the work of the educators at the transition and the work of gardeners when they stated that: 'When a seedling is transplanted from one place to another, the transplantation may be a stimulus or a shock. The careful gardener seeks to minimise shock so that the plant is re-established as easily as possible' (p.19).

Therefore, those working with young children at the transition from early childhood education settings to primary school should, perhaps, seek to learn from gardeners and try to lessen the shock for young children as they are 'transplanted' from early settings into school settings. Indeed, this may be an opportunity to enhance children's growth if the transition experience is supportive and nurturing. To continue with this analogy, perhaps practitioners should consider that, during transition, some of the previous supports should remain in order to nurture development and allow opportunities to thrive.

Pedagogical differences across the transition

One of the main findings from research focusing on this transition for children is the lack of continuity and progression in learners' experiences. The discontinuity between pedagogical practices – the play and child-centred methods in early childhood education settings, and the subjects and lessons emphasis in primary schools – has been widely recognized (Buchanan et al., 1998; Brostrom, 2002; Fabian and Dunlop, 2002; File and Gullo, 2002; Griebel and Niesel, 2002; Margetts, 1999). Many authors have noted that children's adjustment during transition may be affected by the discontinuity between early childhood education and formal school education (Cleave et al., 1982; Ledger et al., 1998). For this reason, it is suggested that transitions should involve practices that will ensure a smooth transition for the child from one setting to another (Myers, 1997; Dunlop, 2002; Sanders et al., 2005).

Much of the literature on transitions has been from the perspectives of teachers and parents. However, a number of researchers have tried to focus on the children's perspective (Dockett and Perry, 1999; Perry et al., 2000; Clyde, 2001; Einarsdottir, 2003; Sharpe, 2002; Potter and Briggs, 2003). The children who were involved in some of these studies reported a clear dichotomy between work and play in the primary school settings. In Corsaro and Molinari's (2000) Italian study, first grade children saw primary school as more work-focused than play-focused. In one Swedish study (Pramling et al., 1995) first grade children were asked about what they saw as the differences between early childhood settings and primary school settings. The findings indicated that children saw primary school as a place where you work and the early childhood settings as somewhere you play. They saw play as something they choose themselves (see Chapter 2) and they did not see what happened in school as play because they did not organize and choose it for themselves. Peters (2000) found that, on entering school, children did not like their outdoor play being more limited; having fewer opportunities to choose when they could play and being directed by adults. Similarly, Ledger et al. (1998) found in their New Zealand study that the transition was problematic for some children, as they found there was more teacher direction and fewer opportunities to initiate their own learning in primary school settings.

As practitioners, it is important for us to consider the pedagogical differences in early childhood education settings and primary schools. Although challenging, we may gain a new perspective by considering what it may be like for a child to have to navigate between these two pedagogical approaches. In order to do this, practitioners need to have a clear understanding of appropriate pedagogical approaches to support children's learning (see Chapter 12).

Overcoming the pedagogical differences

It has been established that transitions are crucial times of opportunity and that they must be managed well in order to support positive experiences and to maximize potential learning opportunities. Despite this understanding, early childhood education has often been seen, traditionally, as a separate chapter, with a new chapter starting in the first year of primary in terms of continuity of learning environment, pedagogy and often progression. It is, therefore, crucial to identify and explore the deep-rooted factors that continue to challenge the success of effective transitions between early childhood education settings to primary school and how to overcome some of these.

In many countries across the world, educators are facing pressure to start teaching formal and academic skills to children at a younger and younger age. Bodrova (2008) suggests that this pressure has developed due to societal concerns that have emerged over the perception that children are falling behind in their academic work later in their school career. However, she states that an early focus on academic skills not only proves to be ineffective in the longer term, but can also actually create difficulties around social and emotional development in the future (see Chapter 6).

Contrary to many people's perceptions, some countries viewed as academically high achieving as a result of their formal approaches to learning, actually have informal approaches to early learning. This is reinforced in the recent report by Miller and Almon (2009: 2) that states:

> China and Japan are envied in the U.S. for their success in teaching science, math, and technology. But one rarely hears about their approach to schooling before second grade, which is playful and experiential rather than didactic. Finland's children, too, go to playful kindergartens, and they enter first grade at age seven rather than six. They enjoy a lengthy, playful early childhood. Yet Finland consistently gets the highest scores on the respected international PISA exam for 15-year-olds.

In recent years, some countries' policy developments have had an increased focus on the impact of pedagogy on learners' experiences in the first years of primary. In addition, there has been more emphasis on valuing the importance of transitions and the need to overcome some of the pedagogical differences. As a result, several countries have recently developed new curricula with the intention of addressing some of the challenges and opportunities outlined earlier in this chapter. These adapted curricula often focus on altering the pedagogy in the early years of primary from a more product- and outcome-focused, adult-led environment to a more playful pedagogy that is similar in approach to early childhood education pedagogy. Some examples of curricula that have tried to develop continuous learning experiences for children across the transition from early childhood education settings can be found in the suggested websites at the end of this chapter.

These developments have resulted in practitioners taking a closer, reflective look at how learning environments and methodologies can support continuity and progression. Stephen (2006) suggests that to continue the playful and more experiential pedagogical approaches from early childhood education into early primary enables new learning experiences to be introduced in a more familiar and developmentally appropriate way. Martin-Korpi (2005) captures this philosophy of trying to blend the pedagogies by identifying the need to create a pedagogical meeting place, where children experience a more harmonious approach and more similar learning environments at the transition from early childhood settings to primary school. It is therefore vital that, as reflective practitioners, we consider the impact of pedagogy on effective transitions and continue to work towards creating pedagogical meeting places within our settings.

Some barriers to overcoming pedagogical differences

Although several countries are working to enhance the learning experience across the transition, as highlighted earlier, some experts identify a number of persistent barriers to continuity. Stephen (2006) reports that these attempts are still vulnerable to the different contexts that the curriculum operates in and of the attainment focus in primary school. Bertram and Pascal (2002) and Mooney et al. (2003) go on to suggest that one of the most significant barriers is the separation between early childhood education and primary education, which can manifest itself in having different cultures, separate workforce development and continuing professional development (CPD) opportunities, budgets and professional bodies.

A further crucial reason for the ongoing barriers to continuity and progression that we must consider is that parents, children and practitioners have often developed cultural expectations of the shifting identity of a 'nursery child' to a 'school child'. This can result in clear differences in what they perceive should happen when a child begins primary school. Some examples may include:

- Parents expect to see visible examples of their children learning to read, write and count through worksheet evidence or a reading book being sent home. This may have been developed through personal experience of when they themselves were at school or the experiences their older children had in early primary.

- Children may have expectations about starting primary through parental and external influences on what will happen when they begin primary school. Children often have expectations about learning more, 'working hard' and playing less (Dockett and Perry, 2004).

- Primary teachers may feel pressured to produce more tangible and visible forms of evidence of formal learning. They can feel under pressure to demonstrate academic achievement and attainment to parents, school management and other colleagues. As Stephen (2006) suggests, primary practitioners are often affected by the dominance of these expectations within the wider school culture.

These set cultural expectations can impact on all involved in the transition from early childhood education settings to primary school and, therefore, impact on the flexibility of practitioners being able to develop a progressive and more playful early primary pedagogy. Having established an understanding of the move to create more similar learning environments and better continuity in pedagogy across the sectors, it is now crucial for us to reflect on our role in achieving this goal.

Playful pedagogy supporting transitions

One-off transition strategies are inadequate. Stronger, more sustained and substantive approaches to encourage greater alignment should be developed. A real opportunity exists for practitioners to enhance transitions by developing more coherent and playful approaches to learning.

Countries that are creating new curricula to develop more continuous learning experiences for children advocate a more playful approach. For example, the *South Australian Curriculum Standards and Accountability* framework has developed a common curriculum framework across early childhood settings and the initial primary school years. Similarly, in Scotland, the new curriculum, *Curriculum for Excellence*, encourages greater alignment of early childhood education and primary school pedagogical approaches.

Inevitably, within any professional context, there are contrasting views and, as stated earlier in the chapter, a pressure remains to formalize learning in the early years. There are many definitions and much discussion around play and interpreting it (see Chapter 8). Concerns about the diminution of the educational value of play are shared by many practitioners. Sutton-Smith (1997) argues that play is progressive and can facilitate the development of knowledge and skills but acknowledges that it is not the only determinant of learning. Stephen (2006) highlights the work of Bennett et al., (1997) who demonstrated the need to explore play not only as 'an opportunity for children to learn but also for adults to teach, or at least to pro-actively contribute to children's learning' (p. 7). Recently, Miller and Almon (2009: 1) stated that:

> In spite of the fact that the vital importance of play in young children's development has been shown in study after study, many people believe that play is a waste of time in school. School, they say, should be a place for learning. There's plenty of time for play at home.

Practitioners are often able to express the 'What?' and 'How?' of their day-to-day practice. However, it is vital that they are also able to articulate 'Why?' they offer a playful approach to learning in order to validate it to others. In order to articulate one's professional practice, consideration should be given to a range of evidence-based perspectives. Indeed, McLane (2003) urges educators to 'know enough about play to be both its advocates and sceptics . . . [to] recognize play's potential without romanticizing it and reducing it to fuzzy, simplistic slogans'. This sets the challenge for reflective practitioners to really consider their philosophical stance on the value of play in children's learning beyond early childhood education settings. Practitioners need to have the confidence to openly share their reflections of their playful pedagogy (see Chapter 3). An effective way of doing this is to engage in reflective dialogue with colleagues who can support and challenge one another as critical friends (see Chapter 1). As a consequence, practitioners may feel more empowered to challenge some of the cultural expectations addressed earlier in the chapter; for example, the value some parents place on formalized approaches to learning and the more traditional role of the teacher.

Playful learning and the adult role

Many practitioners are grappling with their role in supporting children through playful learning in the more structured environments of primary schools. Playful learning is generally well embedded within early childhood settings and recognized as an appropriate methodology to support children's development though may not always be practised. The *Effective Provision of Pre-School Education (EPPE)* study suggests that good early years practice provides a balance of child- and adult-initiated learning experiences (Sylva et al., 2003). The challenges for practitioners lie in continuing this balance into early primary while, at the same time, providing continuity and progression in children's learning experiences.

Helpfully, the *Key Elements of Effective Practice (KEEP)* (DfES, 2005: 11) suggest that: 'There should be opportunities for children to engage in activities planned by adults and also those that they plan or initiate themselves. Children do not make a distinction between 'play' and 'work' and neither should practitioners'.

Currently, the Department of Children, Schools and Families (DCSF) in England published a helpful document entitled *Learning, Playing and Interacting: Good Practice in the Early Years Foundation Stage* that explores the adult's role in supporting children's playful learning (DCSF, 2009). Figure 13.1 is a useful tool to consider the balance of adult direction and child-led activity within the learning environment.

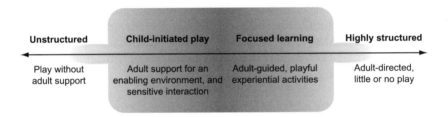

Unstructured	Child-initiated play	Focused learning	Highly structured
Play without adult support	Adult support for an enabling environment, and sensitive interaction	Adult-guided, playful experiential activities	Adult-directed, little or no play

Figure 13.1 Balancing adult- and child-led activities.

According to Waller and Swann (2009) a new debate has opened up around the role of practitioners shaping and controlling children's play. They suggest that play will be determined by the space, time and resources within the learning environment that the practitioner creates. In addition to the learning environment, the interactions between practitioners and children will have an influence on progression and continuity. Examples 1 and 2 below demonstrate a willingness in recent policy developments to reconsider the adult's role in the early primary classroom:

Example 1

In Queensland, Australia, recent guidance for practitioners suggests that they must give consideration to their different and shifting roles including the roles of co-player, observer, listener, initiator, responder, facilitator, scaffolder, modeller, questioner, challenger and mediator.

Example 2

A framework to support continuity of learning in primary one was developed by Stirling Council, Scotland. It set out core features based on sound early years practice and required in school to support children to be effective learners and to achieve their potential. Early primary practitioners were set the challenge of considering: appropriate learning spaces and environments; play; participation; and appropriate structure and organization of the day. This aimed to extend the approaches which are used in nursery into the early years of primary.

As can be seen, when considering the adult's role, the range of challenges require extended professional dialogue and consultation with a range of stakeholders including colleagues, children, parents and carers. Moyles (2008: 35) states that:

> there are many skills required of practitioners . . . It is clear that what is needed is a very special kind of practitioner who can be extremely playful and flexible, but who also has specific knowledge and excellent communication skills. A practitioner who thoroughly understands child development and early years curricula in general and, in particular, each unique child who comes under his/her responsibility in the setting.

The importance of the role of the practitioner cannot be overemphasized; the challenges are great. However, an effective transition supported by a playful approach may reap the reward of a positive and lasting impact on the child throughout the rest of their life.

Conclusion

In this chapter, transitions from early childhood education into primary have been identified as crucial times of change for children, parents and practitioners – full of challenges and opportunities. It is, therefore, vital that practitioners continue to reflect on their role in supporting effective transitions in order to maximize the potential opportunities and to overcome some of the barriers to progression and continuity.

It has been strongly asserted that a positive experience at this crucial time will develop individual capital to flourish in future transitions and deal well with times of change. Positive transition experiences can impact positively on life chances. Indeed, Ghaye and Pascal (1989) suggest that transitions can be a critical factor in determining children's future progress and development. Therefore, practitioners have an important and challenging responsibility to provide enriching and supportive learning environments, which ensure meaningful progression and minimize discontinuity. Dunlop and Fabian (2007: 156) reinforce the view that 'transitions have the capacity to transform both positively and negatively, and further, if they are not always positive, if they are even just a little too challenging for any given child, then the transition itself needs to be transformed'.

This chapter has asked readers to consider and reflect on the need to transform early primary pedagogical approaches in order to support more effective transitions across early childhood education settings and early primary. The different curricula identified earlier in the chapter have gone some way to creating pedagogical meeting places in those contexts; where there are more similar learning environments and more familiar approaches to learning through play. However, as Stephen (2006) suggests, there are persisting barriers to maximizing these opportunities.

To fully embrace more playful approaches in early primary settings in order to enhance effective transitions, we must tackle the notion of unrealistic existing cultural expectations of the shifting identity of a 'nursery child' to a 'school child'. It is, therefore, vital that practitioners are well equipped to understand and articulate the value of playful pedagogy in the early years of primary, in order to develop a shared understanding and similar expectations with colleagues in early childhood education settings, children, parents, carers and others. It is only through joined-up thinking, a partnership approach and developing a shared understanding of the importance of playful approaches and the impact of transitions, that the true pedagogical meeting place will be found.

What do we, the writers, feel about the contribution of this chapter to supporting critical reflection?

In reflecting on transitions as the focus of this chapter, we have reaffirmed our belief in the importance of practitioners being able to consider the opportunities and challenges of the transition to school from a child's perspective. Writing this chapter has also reinforced how crucial it is that practitioners have a deep understanding of play as a vehicle for learning, in order to communicate effectively with all stakeholders and move forward together with a shared understanding of the benefits of playful pedagogy for young learners. There are clear policy developments that practitioners can seize to create successful pedagogical meeting places within their settings. And, it is increasingly apparent that knowledgeable, flexible, creative, open-minded and effective practitioners are the key to overcoming the continuing challenges for young learners to experience effective transitions.

Implications for pedagogy: what might *you*, the reader, reflect on now?

- Can you identify some of the opportunities that arise for children as they make the transition from early childhood education settings to primary school?

- How do the learning experiences that you offer provide a more harmonious learning environment between early childhood education settings and primary school settings?
- As a reflective practitioner, how can you ensure that you articulate to parents, carers, colleagues, managers and external bodies the importance of a more playful approach at the transition?
- How can you support parents, carers and others to nurture children's positive expectations of school as they make the transition?
- How can you structure the learning environment to maximize play, real life situations, investigations, transitions and routines, and focused learning and teaching?

Some useful websites

Examples of curricula that attempt to develop continuous learning experiences for children across the transition from early childhood education settings are as follows:

- The *Foundation Phase*, Wales (www.wales.gov.uk/topics/education andskills/curriculumassessment/arevisedcurriculumforwales/ foundationphase/?lang=en)
- The *Early Phase of Learning*, Queensland, Australia (www.education. qld.gov.au/strategic/advice/earlychildhood/)
- *Curriculum for Excellence*, Scotland (www.ltscotland.org.uk/ curriculumforexcellence/index.asp)
- *The South Australian Curriculum Standards and Accountability Framework* (www.sacsa.sa.edu.au/splash.asp)
- *Aistear*, the Irish Early Childhood Curriculum Framework (www. ncca.biz/Aistear/)

Helpful websites that may extend your knowledge of pedagogical approaches

- Learning and Teaching Scotland – Early Years Online (www.ltscotland. org.uk/earlyyears)
- Training, Advancement and Co-operation in Teaching Young Children (www.tactyc.org.uk)
- Effective Provision of Pre-School Education (EPPE) Project (www.eppe.ioe.ac.uk)
- Key Elements of Effective Practice (KEEP) (www.teachernet.gov.uk/ docbank/index.cfm?id=11033)
- Early Education (www.early-education.org.uk)
- Study of Pedagogical Effectiveness in Early Learning (www.dcsf. gov.uk/research/data/uploadfiles/RR363.pdf)

References and further reading

Bennett, N., Wood, E. and Rogers, S. (1997) *Teaching Through Play: Teachers' Thinking and Classroom Practice*. Buckingham: Open University Press.

Bertram, T. and Pascal, C. (2002) *Early Years Education: An International Perspective*. Birmingham: Centre for Research in Early Childhood (CREC).

Bodrova, E. (2008) Make-believe play versus academic skills: a Vygotskian approach to today's dilemma of early childhood education, *European Early Childhood Education Research*, 16(3): 357–69.

Brostrom, S. (2002) Communication and continuity in the transition from kindergarten to school, in H. Fabian and A.-W. Dunlop (eds) *Transitions in the Early Years*. Abingdon: RoutledgeFalmer.

Buchanan, T.K., Burts D.C., Bidner J., White V.F. and Charlesworth, R. (1998) Predictors of the developmental appropriateness of the beliefs and practices of first, second, and third grade teachers, *Early Childhood Research Quarterly*, 13(3): 459–83.

Cleave, S., Jowett, S. and Bate, M. (1982) *And So to School: A Study of Continuity from Pre-school to Infant School*. Cheltenham: NFER-Nelson.

Clyde, M. (2001) Children's responses to starting school: some Victorian studies, *Journal of Australian Research in Early Childhood*, 8(1): 23–32.

Corsaro, W. and Molinari, L. (2000) Priming events and Italian children's transition from pre-school to elementary school: representations and action, *Social Psychology Quarterly*, 63(1): 16–33.

Cryer, D. and Clifford, R.M. (2003) *Early Childhood Education and Care in the USA*. Baltimore, MD: Paul H. Brookes.

Department for Children, Schools and Families (DCSF) (2009) *Learning, Playing and Interacting: Good Practice in the Early Years Foundation Stage*. Nottingham: DCSF.

Department for Education and Skills (DfES) (2005) *KEEP: Key Elements of Effective Practice*. London: DfES/SureStart.

Dockett, S. and Perry, B. (1999) Starting school: what do the children say? *Early Childhood and Care*, 159(1): 107–19.

Dockett, S. and Perry, B. (2004) Starting school: perspectives of Australian children, parents and educators, *Journal of Early Childhood Research*, 2(2): 171–89.

Dunlop, A.-W. (2002) Perspectives on children as learners in the transition to school, in Fabian, H. and Dunlop, A.-W. (eds) *Transitions in the Early Years*. London: RoutledgeFalmer.

Dunlop, A.-W. and Fabian, H. (2007) (eds) *Informing Transitions in the Early Years*. Maidenhead: Open University Press.

Einarsdottir, J. (2003) When the bell rings we have to go inside: preschool children's views on the primary school, *European Early Childhood Education Research Journal Themed Monograph Series*, 1: 35–50.

Einarsdottir, J. (2006) From pre-school to primary school: when different contexts meet, *Scandinavian Journal of Educational Research*, 50(2): 165–84.

Fabian, H. (2002) *Children Starting School*. London: David Fulton.

Fabian, H. and Dunlop, A-W. (eds) (2002) *Transitions in the Early Years*. Abingdon: RoutledgeFalmer.

File, N. and Gullo, D.F. (2002) A comparison of early childhood and elementary students' beliefs about primary classroom teaching practices, *Early Childhood Research Quarterly*, 1(17): 126–37.

Ghaye, A. and Pascal, C. (1989) *Four-year-old Children in Reception Classrooms: Participant Perceptions and Practice*. Worcester: Worcester College of Higher Education.

Griebel, W. and Niesel, R. (2002) Co-constructing transition into kindergarten and school by children, parents and teachers, in H. Fabian and A-W. Dunlop (eds) *Transitions in the Early Years*. Abingdon: RoutledgeFalmer.

Griebel, W. and Niesel, R. (2005) Transition competence and resiliency in educational institutions, *International Journal of Transitions in Childhood*, 1: 4–11.

Kagan, S.L. (1992) The strategic importance of linkages and the transition between early childhood programs and early elementary school. *Sticking Together: Strengthening Linkages and the Transition between Early Childhood Education and Early Elementary School*. Summary of a National Policy Forum. Washington, DC: US Department of Education.

Ledger, E., Smith, A. and Rich, P. (1998) 'Do I go to school to get a brain?' The transition from kindergarten to school from the child's perspective, *Childrenz Issues*, 2: 7–11.

Margetts, K. (1999) Transition to school: looking forward. Paper presented at the AECA (Early Childhood Australia) National Conference, Darwin 14–17 July.

Martin-Korpi, B. (2005) The foundation for lifelong learning, *Children in Europe*, 9: 10–11.

McLane, J. (2003) *'Does not.' 'Does too.' Thinking About Play in the Early Childhood Classroom*. Chicago: IL Erikson Institute.

Miller, E. and Almon, J. (2009) *Crisis in the Kindergarten: Why Children Need to Play in School*. College Park, MD: Alliance for Childhood.

Mooney, A., Moss, P., Cameron, C., et al. (2003) *Early Years and Childcare International Evidence Project: An Introduction to the Project*. London: DfES.

Moyles, J. (2008) Empowering children and adults: play and child-initiated learning, in S. Feathersone and P. Featherstone (eds) *Like Bees, not Butterflies*. London: A&C Black.

Myers, R. (1997) Removing roadblocks to success: transitions and linkages between home, preschool and primary school. Coordinators' notebook, No.21. Washington, DC: The Consultative Group on Early Childhood Care and Development/World Bank.

Perry, B., Dockett, S. and Howard, P. (2000) Starting school: issues for children, parents and teachers, *Journal of Australian Research in Early Childhood Education*, 74: 41–53.

Peters, S. (2000) Multiple perspectives on continuity in early learning and the transition to school. Paper presented at the Tenth European Early Childhood Education Research Association Conference, London August–September.

Potter, G.K. and Briggs, F. (2003) Children talk about their early experiences at school, *Australian Journal of Early Childhood*, 28: 44–9.

Pramling, I., Klerfelt, A. and Graneld, W. (1995) Forst var der roligt, sen blev det trakigt och sen vande man sig: Barns mote med skolans varld [First it was fun, then it became boring and then you got used to it: *Children's Meeting with the World of School*], Report No. 9. Gothenburg Institute: Institutionen for Methodology, Gothenburg University.

Sanders, D., White, G., Burge, B., et al. (2005) *A Study of the Transition from the Foundation Stage to Key Stage 1*. London: DfES.

Sharpe, P. (2002) School days in Singapore: young children's experiences and opportunities during a typical school day, *Childhood Education*, 79: 9–14.

Stephen, C. (2006) *INSIGHT 28, Early Years Education: Perspectives from a Review of the International Literature*. Edinburgh: Scottish Executive Education Department.

Sutton-Smith, B. (1997) *The Ambiguity of Play*. Cambridge, MA: Harvard University Press.

Sylva, K., Melhuish, E., Sammons, P., et al. (2003) *Effective Provision of Pre-School Education Project (EPPE)* Reports and papers. Available at www.ioe.ac.uk/schools/ecpe/eppe (accessed 15 December 2009).

Waller, T. and Swann, R. (2009) Children's learning, in T. Waller (ed.) *An Introduction to Early Childhood*. London: Sage Publications.

Wood, C. and Caulier-Grice, J. (2006) *Fade or Flourish: How Primary Schools can Build on Children's Progress*. London: Social Market Foundation.

Yeboah, D.A. (2002) Enhancing transition from early childhood phase to primary education: evidence from the research literature, *Early Years: An International Journal of Research and Development*, 22(1): 51–68.

14 Thinking through the uses of observation and documentation

Stephanie Collins, Jane Gibbs, Paulette Luff, Maria Sprawling and Lynsey Thomas

Summary

In this chapter we show that children's playful learning and adults' observation and documentation can be seen as parallel processes. At every age, initial impressions and interests have to be combined with systematic, thoughtful investigation in order to create a pedagogy providing for education and growth. To illustrate how this can be achieved in early childhood education, we begin by seeking inspiration and exemplars from pioneers of early education and contemporary international practice. The *Early Years Foundation Stage* curriculum upholds young children's right to be listened to and valued and emphasizes the importance of documenting and analysing children's interests as a basis for developing play experiences. Four experienced practitioners share and discuss case studies, demonstrating ways in which they are using observation and documentation as a means of thinking through play.

Key questions as you read . . .

1 How do we best record and extend spontaneous play?
2 What is the role of the key person allocated to each child?
3 Can photographic evidence be utilized to support conversations about playful learning?
4 How do processes of thinking through play promote our own professional growth?

. . . and points to consider

- As practitioners we should strive to improve provision and never be complacent about what we do.
- We must remember we are documenting for the children's benefit, while accommodating and considering knowledge and input from parents, reflecting on our pedagogical approaches.
- We should develop continually for the sake of the children in our care.

Introduction

In England, the *Early Years Foundation Stage (EYFS)* framework (DCSF, 2008) requires practitioners to create opportunities for playful learning, based on children's interests, to maintain records of each child's progress and to reflect on their own practice and provision. Importance is also placed on partnership with children's parents and dialogue with other settings and services. Observation and documentation are highlighted as key tools in the implementation of this curriculum. For practitioners who want the best early educational experiences for children and their families, several questions are raised.

The four questions that opened this chapter reveal some challenges of recording and reflecting on children's play. They form the basis for the case studies in this chapter but, first, they are placed in context.

Historical and international context

Dewey ([1933]1998) first highlighted the value of reflective thinking in educational processes. In his view, play offers a means for children to use their natural curiosity to reflect and learn. For young children to benefit from their playful explorations, however, they need support to make sense of their observations and develop their ideas to satisfactory conclusions. Similarly for adults, our curiosity about children's play can be harnessed through systematic observation and careful thinking about what we see. This information can then be used to make balanced judgements about learning that is taking place, and provide possibilities for further development.

The twin processes of adults and children engaging in reflective thinking are vital to early childhood education. Observation and documentation of children's play can be essential tools to support adults' insights about worthwhile provision for play and learning. The work of pioneers of early childhood education is characterized by respect for children's play and careful observation, with the aim of using deeper understandings to create opportunities for learning and growth. Montessori (1919) developed her pedagogical methods using scientific observations as a basis for constructing educational activities and creating environments conducive to learning. She advocated the use of observation to assess children's interests: 'the teacher shall observe whether the child interests himself in the object, how he is interested in it, for how long . . . even noticing the expression of his face' (p. 109). The attentive teacher then used her observations to decide on next steps in learning for the child. In England, Susan Isaacs (1930, 1933) also watched children closely, and reflected on what she saw to promote learning. Her careful analysis of narrative observations is echoed in contemporary research (e.g. Reifel, 2007), which uses different theoretical lenses to explore meanings behind children's play.

Thoughtful, observant pedagogy also characterizes inspirational international curricula, which influence contemporary practice. The Reggio Emilia approach to early childhood education emphasizes reflection, realized through pedagogical documentation (Rinaldi, 2006) as a tool for recalling and discussing learning. The ways in which teachers and atelieristas support the development of children's in-depth projects offer clues to English educators about uses of documentation for planning (Thornton and Brunton, 2009). Basic Development (Janssen-Vos, 2003), a curriculum model from the Netherlands, uses insights from Vygotskian theory to create educational processes in which educators tune in to and extend children's playful learning. Reflective diaries and logbooks are kept and used for planning subsequent activities. Similarly, in New Zealand, practitioners follow the *Te Whāriki* curriculum record and plan for children's play using *Learning Stories* (Carr, 2001). Key features of this approach are the involvement of children and parents as active participants in discussions of activities (Cowie and Carr, 2009) and the use of digital methods of capturing and sharing play experiences (Peters, 2009: see also Chapter 7). In parallel with *Learning Stories*, 'Teaching Stories' record staff reflections on activities, raising questions that prompt teachers to consider to what extent they are providing effectively for children's playful learning (Carr et al., 2002).

In the above examples, observation of children is far more than a means of watching play to judge stages of development; it is a powerful tool for facilitating learning and growth. Importantly, too, observation of children provides a key means for early years practitioners to develop their own professional knowledge. The following case studies, and the accompanying discussions, illustrate ways in which we are seeking to answer key questions in order to use observation and documentation as a basis for thinking through and supporting children's learning. For each of the questions posed, one practitioner describes the answer that her early years setting is currently exploring and colleagues offer responses.

How do early years practitioners best record children's interests, moods and capacities and extend spontaneous play?

Stephanie explains how she responds to this question in the playgroup that she runs:

> Our setting uses a system of home-school liaison books, which travel to and from playgroup with the children every day. When children and families begin attending the setting we offer a home visit. The home visit and induction visits to the setting have become times to share information about the child and important people in their life. At the home visit we take photos of the child at play and leave the camera for the family to take further pictures of special things, people and the home environment. These pictures are added to a home-school book and provide a reference point about the child's life to help settle them into the setting. A picture of the child's key person is added with a brief introduction as to the purpose and use of the book. (An example of the initial pages of the home school liaison book can be found in Figure 14.1.)

Figure 14.1   Initial pages of the home-school liaison book.

The child's key person uses the book to record informal observations of the child while at playgroup. The child's parents are encouraged to write in the books and share information about the child's interests, activities and home events. Observations written by the key person may be supported by photographs or pieces of work the child has done. The information recorded in these books forms the basis of the evidence used to track children's progress in accordance with *Development Matters* (DCSF, 2008).

These narrative observations allow us to capture children engaged in the everyday business of playgroup and they are often of children engrossed in activities of their own making. These observations and accompanying pictures (see Figure 14.2) give parents an insight into what their child is doing at playgroup, allowing them to share in the experiences. The children enjoy looking at pictures we have added to the books and often ask whose book we are writing or sticking pictures into.

Once the home-school book system was established, we considered how we could use information recorded in the books to plan for individual children. Aware that we should include parents' and children's views, we invited parents into the setting for review meetings. The meetings centred on the child's interests and we asked parents to tell us what children liked doing at home so we could add this to our knowledge of what they enjoyed at the setting. We asked children to tell us what they liked doing and recorded the information in a simple speech bubble format shown in Figure 14.3.

From this information we plan activities that we think will capture the child's interests and can be used to support next steps in learning, relative to *Development Matters*. Activities are open to all the children in the setting but have a particular learning focus for the key child. Using this play plan (see Figure 14.4), practitioners make specific observations of the key child engaged in the activity (Photograph 14.1).

Maria responds:

Home visits are a lovely idea and facilitate the building of working relationships between the practitioners and parents, enabling smoother transitions from home to nursery life. Despite being a family-oriented nursery we are unable to offer this service as we accommodate many children (as an 84 place nursery, with approximately 130 children on our register). However we do aim to care for parents, as well as their children. Before children start our nursery we offer settling-in visits, allowing them to experience a new

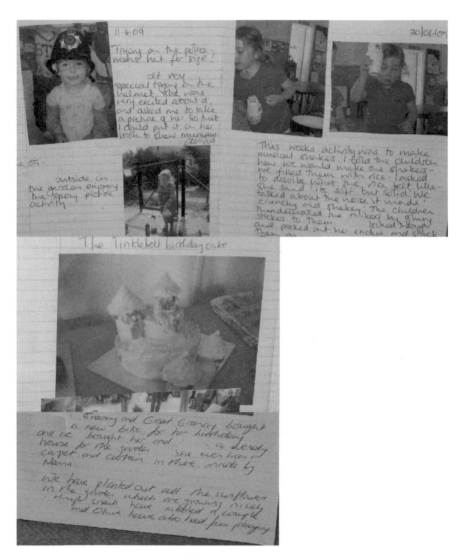

Figure 14.2 Pictures and comments from children's home-school liaison books.

environment, become familiar with new faces and form attachments. This service benefits parents, recognising that their children are the most precious things in their lives and that handing them over to new people can be extremely hard. We want the parent to be happy and confident that their child is well looked after, in a place they trust. During settling-in visits, practitioners and parents fill out an individual care plan for the child, which includes: likes and dislikes,

Key person review for: _____ Date: _____

Present: _____

> B's favourite
> character is
> Sponge Bob

> I enjoyed the
> stick man book

> B enjoys being in the
> garden with Daddy

> B likes going outside.
> He plays with the
> car, seesaw and
> slide

> B likes to dress up

> I like playing with
> the car

> B enjoyed listening to
> the book, Stick Man.
> He looked and pointed
> at the pictures

> B likes to collect
> sticks

> B showed an interest in
> the sorting sticks
> trying them in
> different holes

> B likes to play with
> bricks particularly long
> rectangular ones. He
> also enjoys banging
> them on different
> surfaces

Key:
——— Child's comments
········· Practitioners' comments
- - - - · Parents'/carers' comments
—··—·· Development matter/next steps

Figure 14.3 Collated information from the child's review meeting.

things they enjoy playing with; and favourite toys and activities. This helps ensure each child feels secure and benefits from enjoyable playful experiences.

Lynsey, likewise, responds:

Finding ways of supporting and expanding children's interests is not easy for busy settings. I think that initial home visits are a very good

Activity Plan	w/c 01.06.09

Activity;- Banging Sticks! Equipment;- Basket of different size sticks and wood cardboard rolls, old flower pots and buckets of different sizes.

Instructions Encourage children to explore the collection of sticks. Can they bang them on the pots and buckets like a set of drums? Encourage them to listen for different sounds and make different rhythms.

DMs Maths;- Space Shape and measure PPR 8 Physical;- Using equipment and material PPh 9 Personal;- Making Relationships PP3 Creative;- Creating music and dance CCr5 Communication;- Language for thinking-C3 Knowledge and Understanding of the World;- Exploration and Investigation KK1

Play plan for;- R- Dad says he like to bang on everything with sticks and always has a stick outside. Encourage R to explore his current schema of banging and sticks.

Observation

Reflection

Figure 14.4 Activity plan to meet individual children's interests.

way of getting to know families and enable practitioners to build strong relationships. From reading Stephanie's example, it is something I would definitely consider in the future.

Within my setting we use 'Cheeky Monkey', a knitted toy that the children take home with them. Cheeky Monkey has a digital

Photograph 14.1   R enjoying cardboard rolls while participating.

camera so the children and their parents/carers can document
favourite activities together, such as playing in their gardens or
the park. The children always ensure that *Cheeky Monkey* has a warm
bed and brushes his teeth! *Cheeky Monkey* has recently got his own
passport, has flown in a plane and been on a cruise, the possibilities are endless. Photos are shared with the rest of the group and experiences discussed; we have used cardboard boxes to re-create cruise
ships and made our own flower garden to expand on children's
interests.

Hohmann (2007) describes care relationships as triangular, constructed via
contributions from child, parent and practitioner. This is evident here, where
settings actively involve families in order to share understandings of children's lives so providing relevant, challenging, playful learning opportunities.
Fostering beneficial connections between child, home and early years setting

is often the task of the key person (Elfer et al., 2003) and the next case study considers the significance of this role for thoughtful provision for play.

What is the role of the key person in supporting children through planning personalized play experiences?

Maria answers this by explaining ways of working at the setting where she is the manager:

> Within my day nursery we provide a key person system. Each practitioner takes responsibility for ensuring that children in our care learn and develop at their own pace. We want the best care and education for each child, as do all early years providers, and to achieve this we offer a key person who has a vitally important part to play in providing optimal support. Planning for key children is demonstrated through individual child development profiles, which allow every child to enjoy specific, personalised play experiences. These are provided on the basis of observational recordings of each child by practitioners who take on the role of key person and engage with their key children. Through findings from these observations the key person is able to discover where the needs of the children may be met. Through experience, I am aware that each child is unique, with individual personality traits and interests, and learns in different ways.
>
> Our focus considers the holistic development of each child, as highlighted within the *EYFS* curriculum. This requires use of the practitioners' time to build up child profiles, looking at which stages of development each child is at, how to move them on, and recording and evidencing their progress. Although this method is time-consuming, it does have wonderful results when the individual child is solely the main stimuli and the driving force for a personalised plan.
>
> For the areas of development within the *EYFS*, the key person decides upon a focus for each key child, pinpointing two or three specific areas, the starting point and steps towards further development. To enable each key person to do this, they have good relationships with their key children, forming a basis for planning. This shapes the way we view activities for children. The focus is not necessarily on the activity but on how children benefit from personalised play experiences. I have realised that we, as practitioners, can get fixed on the end result of an activity, rather than the experience the child gains from the process.
>
> Providing an individual development profile allows for playful

learning to occur, tailored to each child's needs, enabling them to feel at ease, open up and enjoy the experiences. For one boy in our care the key person wanted to provide activities to help him with counting, using number names accurately in his play by giving opportunities and reasons to count, having number labels, activities involving counting and providing books with numbers. Many number play activities were planned, providing valuable experiences for the key child. The key person then observed his ability to count and recognise numbers and suggested that the next area to concentrate on could be rhyming, encouraging his communication, language and literacy, listening with enjoyment, responding to rhymes and making his own rhymes up.

His mum responded, '*We are very pleased with his progress, especially with his counting and his ability to read numbers. We agree that development around stories and rhymes would now be beneficial. Many thanks*'.

Through working in partnership with parents the key person builds up a working relationship which allows the best care and education for the child, built from effective communication, bringing nursery and home life together. It is about collaborating with one another and this is one of the vital areas that make the key person approach successful.

The key person carried out rhyming activities with her key child, which were followed up at home through reading poetry books with his parents. He enjoyed repeating rhymes that he heard at home:

> *I saw a farmer eating a banana,*
> *I saw a sailor eating a potato,*
> *I saw a bear eating a pear,*
> *I saw a bear over there.*

During playtimes, activity times and meal times he used language skills to play with words and construct his own rhymes, exploring the use of rhyming words. During tea time he exclaimed that he wanted more ham:

> *I need more ham, on the tram,*
> *Billy bang, on the tram,*
> *I need more ham.*

Aiming to work with each individual can be difficult when there are many children to cater for. We try to have key group activity times especially in the rooms with larger numbers of older children. This allows the key person quality time with their key children, providing opportunities to work closely with them, noting their interests, listening to and valuing each child.

> Our documentation about each child is placed in individual profile books, through the use of observations, photographic evidence and children's work, building up a portfolio, demonstrating their learning journey, developmental progress and personalised play experiences.

Stephanie says:

> Maria's example shows how an effective key person system enables practitioners to sensitively tap into children's needs, build on their individual interest and extend this to other areas. It is lovely to see evidence of their work praised by parents and taken on board by the child, who is then able to apply it independently in a different circumstance. The key person role, originally developed to sustain relationships and enable the child to feel secure (Elfer et al., 2003) increasingly involves responsibility for promoting learning.

In the next section Lynsey describes how information technologies provide tools to support this work.

How can photographic evidence be used to support conversations about playful learning?

Offering an answer to this question, Lynsey describes a current initiative at the nursery she manages:

> At Cheeky Monkeys nursery we have endeavoured to find a solution to simplifying observation and assessment for all stakeholders, ensuring that it is both accessible and productive for everyone. For many years we have used written formats as our main source for discovering a child's developmental progress, some of which have been long, time consuming and confusing for inexperienced staff and parents. Written observations often contained abbreviations and technical language that were placed in the relevant child's folder without explanation or an instruction manual for parents.
>
> Evaluating our provision, we discovered that practitioners had grown to resent observation and assessment, feeling that it reduced their time playing with the children. The formats took too long to complete, often had to be stopped because of various distractions or incidents, and ended up encroaching on their personal time. We gained feedback from a group of parents, whose children had recently left us to go to school. They said they enjoyed the informal open

afternoons, discussing and seeing their child's achievements, but did not always read the observation sheets in the personal folders as they couldn't understand what was being said and didn't feel knowledgeable enough to participate and write further comments on the observation sheets.

Taking all of this on board, at *Cheeky Monkeys* we decided to experiment and trial digital observations, consisting of photos, videos and digital voice recordings – no written work whatsoever. The idea was that children's achievements were evidenced whilst the practitioner could still be a part of play and support every child's needs. This new digital adventure started off well (see Photograph 14.2), parents loved the photos, the pressure of completing X amount of observations stopped and the atmosphere seemed more relaxed. The children were eager to be photographed and become photographer, proudly snapping their own creations. Those children who were often shy wanted to see recordings of themselves singing or dressing-up. Photos and videos were downloaded into individual folders on the pre-school lap top, saving us paper and ink, helping the environment in the process.

The open afternoon was a great success, every parent enjoyed

Photograph 14.2   Capturing evidence for the e-portfolios.

watching the videos and it was easy for the practitioner to discuss where the child was at and what they would like to do in the future to support individual development. One parent emailed the pre-school some photos of their child on holiday and we happily put them in the child's e-folder to support the growing evidence. The children particularly liked the e-folders as some were able to use the mouse to play the videos of themselves over again. If there was a particular activity that the children wanted their parents to see that day we were able to download the evidence and let the child take home their own personal memory stick.

The digital change has not been plain sailing as there have been factors we have had to consider such as parental consent, confidentiality and safeguarding children. It has been important to ensure that the evidence gained still informs future planning and we have had to compromise to resolve this issue, using hand written post-it notes. The idea of saving time by escaping written assessments has not been a realistic one: photos are often enhanced by a short explanation and evaluations and next steps of development are still being written (albeit on the lap top). However, practitioners are spending more time with the children and are less resentful of the observation process and parents are far more responsive and participative in their child's development.

The e-folder can be passed on, by the parent, to other nurseries or pre-schools that the child may attend and in future there is the potential for pre-schools to work together and inform the child's e-folder at the same time, ensuring continuity of care and development. Overall, we are glad to have made the changes within the setting and at the present time we are still learning and developing our ideas further (Photograph 14.3). The key to our success will be to try bold new ideas, allow ourselves to make mistakes but learn from what we have done and from those around us, celebrating and sharing our successes with others.

On reading this, Jane commented:

This sounds a time-saving, workable way forward for observation. Whilst I am keen to move in this direction, the child abuse case in a Plymouth nursery has cast a shadow over the use of digital media. I am concerned this initiative might not be welcome in my setting. Inspired by the use of images within the Reggio Emilia approach, we have been developing the use of photographs in Richmond Pre-school. I realised what a rich resource photographic evidence could be when a child who was new to the setting was beginning to explore the

Photograph 14.3   Reviewing playful learning experiences.

provision. Noticing a display of photographs he singled out one child at a time, asking who they were. I told him the children's names as he pointed. One of the other children who was playing nearby, got up and said the name of his cousin, adding: 'He's at big school now, and that's me' (he pointed himself out). The other child looked at him and at the photograph. The boy then went on to tell the new child about the picture, recalling how we had a snowball fight before the children all made a snowman together. He described how he had to push the snow together to make a ball because 'It drops from your hand if you don't do that'. He told the new child how we had to pat the snowman so that he got that big! This example illustrated to me how observations, captured as photographs, can provoke reflection in children and encourage discussions. The child, describing his experience of making the snowman, revealed the learning that took place as he described the properties of the snow and the need to compact it in order for it to become a mouldable substance. We now have photo albums in the book areas of our provision, which provoke many meaningful conversations.

Maria also responded:

We love using photographic evidence in our child development profiles and on display boards. Photos tell so many stories and stimulate discussions, especially with older children. When practitioners carry out an observation of a child experiencing an activity, they take a photo as extra evidence. From this you can see how a child is engaged within a playful experience showing enjoyment on their faces or delight in experiencing a new activity. Capturing a special moment adds personal evidence to discussions with parents at the end of each day.

The work being done at *Cheeky Monkeys*, and the examples from other settings, show how digital technologies can be a resource to support children to revisit and discuss playful learning experiences (see Chapter 7). This is also a finding of Wang et al. (2004) who demonstrate that the creation of PowerPoint presentations can facilitate young children's reflections. Documentation plays a key role in supporting dialogues, which sustain trust (Rinaldi, 2006) and facilitates adults' understandings of children's learning, which is the area our next question addresses.

How can practitioners' reflections be captured and valued to promote professional growth?

Jane responds to this question, describing how formats for observations at her pre-school setting encourage practitioners to reflect and develop insights:

> During my time at Richmond Pre-school evidencing what and how children learn through observations as well as what and how practitioners learn about themselves and about the children, has often appeared problematic. In continuing my professional development by participating in the Early Years Foundation Degree, I was able to recognise a way to improve paperwork within my setting; enabling experienced qualified and unqualified members of staff to reflect effectively on children's play, whilst aiding their own development.
>
> Initially I reviewed paperwork given to me at an *EYFS* training course (during 2008) and realised terminology such as 'stimuli' and 'foci' could confuse staff members and parents/carers. The paperwork inspired a way forward, in respect of showing intentions for development and planning for the child, whilst also encouraging practitioners to reflect on observations, as a means of taking the child's interests forward on their learning journey. We use these forms to reflect-on-action (Schön, 1983). Sometimes when observations are taken it is too easy to pick only one element out and then put the observation away in the child's file, not utilising it fully. The form provides a basis to list elements taken from the observation so that the practitioner can view the child in a holistic manner, rather than categorising one element of what was witnessed.

This format is simple and easy to follow; it enables the practitioner to contemplate key elements taken from the observation, and to use them in a way they may not have considered at a first glance. Knowing the child as a 'Unique child' (DCSF, 2008) and recognising their preferred areas of play can be utilised in order to support learning within areas of *Development Matters* (DCSF, 2008). Figure 14.5, below, demonstrates how I was able to engage a child in the area of Communication, Language and Literacy (CLL) development of 'Linking Sounds and Letters' (DCSF, 2008). For boys in particular, it seems the literacy requirements of the CLL area of development are often the hardest to meet. Using elements taken from an observation, I was able to determine a way forward for the child within his own preferred area of play.

Asking the children what they feel about the activity can provoke them to specify what part they particularly liked or disliked. In answering my question, the child was pleased to get the letters in the right order, this made me reflect that the acknowledgement I gave was in the right place and the child felt achievement as a consequence. Reviewing the completed 'Reflections for Key Person Planning' form, to recognise the learning I had undertaken, led me to recognise I could have added some letters that weren't in his name as an extension to the activity. As he is not usually eager to participate in activities relating to literacy, I underestimated his ability. The learning I took from this was that I should always have additional resources on standby and give differentiation more consideration, especially when I don't know where the child is, in terms of knowledge on a specific area of development.

In order to reflect-in-action (Schön, 1983), I created a different form below (Figure 14.6) which is how we evidence spontaneous learning that happens as a consequence of unplanned circumstances.

On the 'Spontaneous extended learning form' we use 'look, listen and note' (DCSF, 2008) techniques to document what took place. When the session ends we review this in order to reflect on the situation and assess who learned what or indeed if any learning took place. Reflecting for the benefit of the children and ourselves can only improve provision.

Maria agrees:

I have always been reflective about my practice and have tried to encourage staff to reflect as well, highlighting that reflection is a means to improve practice and should not be a negative exercise. In my experience, practitioners have seen reflection as negative, noting

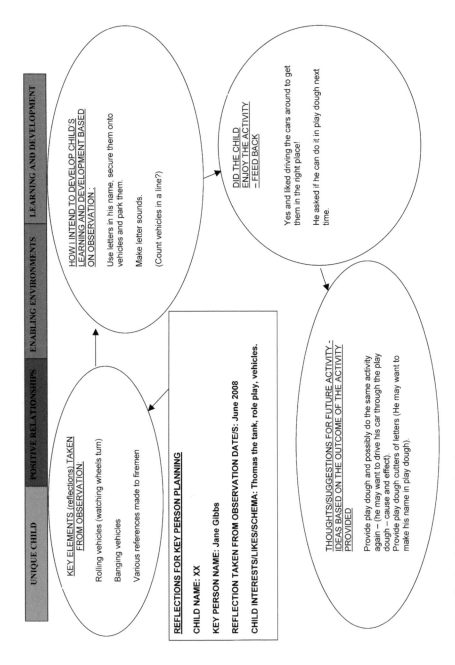

| UNIQUE CHILD | POSITIVE RELATIONSHIPS | ENABLING ENVIRONMENTS | LEARNING AND DEVELOPMENT |

KEY ELEMENTS (reflections) TAKEN FROM OBSERVATION:

Rolling vehicles (watching wheels turn)

Banging vehicles

Various references made to firemen

HOW I INTEND TO DEVELOP CHILD'S LEARNING AND DEVELOPMENT BASED ON OBSERVATION :

Use letters in his name, secure them onto vehicles and park them.

Make letter sounds.

(Count vehicles in a line?)

DID THE CHILD ENJOY THE ACTIVITY – FEED BACK

Yes and liked driving the cars around to get them in the right place!

He asked if he can do it in play dough next time.

REFLECTIONS FOR KEY PERSON PLANNING

CHILD NAME: XX

KEY PERSON NAME: Jane Gibbs

REFLECTION TAKEN FROM OBSERVATION DATE/S: June 2008

CHILD INTERESTS/LIKES/SCHEMA: Thomas the tank, role play, vehicles.

THOUGHTS/SUGGESTIONS FOR FUTURE ACTIVITY - IDEAS BASED ON THE OUTCOME OF THE ACTIVITY PROVIDED

Provide play dough and possibly do the same activity again – (he may want to drive his car through the play dough – cause and effect).
Provide play dough cutters of letters (He may want to make his name in play dough).

Figure 14.5 Reflections for key person planning.

UNIQUE CHILD	POSITIVE RELATIONSHIPS	ENABLING ENVIRONMENTS	LEARNING & DEVELOPMENT

SPONTANEOUS EXTENDED LEARNING FORM (SELF)

CHILD'S NAME :

D.O.B. :

DATE TODAY :

KEYPERSON :

WHAT TOOK PLACE :

WHAT LEARNING TOOK PLACE :

WHAT DID PRACTITIONER LEARN :

Figure 14.6   Spontaneous extended learning form.

problems that occurred. This really is not the case. Reflection helps us look at how things can be extended next time, something positive, helping to inform playful learning for children, whilst also developing our own professional practice, therefore improving outcomes for children. We must not become discouraged when something does not go to plan but reflect and learn from it, seeing it as a learning experience.

Conclusion

These case studies are offered, modestly, as practical examples of work-in-progress which show how observations can form a basis for reflection about children's play and professional learning. We hope that you, the reader, will add your voice to ours in discussing the questions posed here and that the suggestions made will provide food for thought when considering uses of observation and documentation to facilitate playful pedagogy.

What do we, the writers, feel about the contribution of this chapter to supporting critical reflection?

Reflective thinking is challenging and these examples, from early childhood settings in Essex, show how we and our colleagues are using observation and documentation to record and plan for playful learning, to meet the demands and requirements of the *EYFS* curriculum. In providing templates for documentation, we are hopeful that practitioners can identify their own learning as well as that of children in their care.

Implications for pedagogy: What might *you*, the reader, reflect on now?

- From reading this chapter, how do you evaluate your practice, for example, do you have user-friendly, jargon-free documentation?
- Are children's learning journeys shared?
- How do you take ideas from other settings and adapt them for use in your own?
- From reading the chapter, will you note helpful ideas and, after reflection and discussion with peers, action plan with your team?

References and further reading

Carr, M. (2001) *Assessment in Early Childhood Settings: Learning Stories.* London: Paul Chapman.

Carr, M., May, H. and Podmore, V.N. (2002) Learning and teaching stories: action research on evaluation in early childhood in Aotearoa-New Zealand, *European Early Childhood Educational Research Journal,* 10(2): 115–25.

Cowie, B. and Carr, M. (2009) The consequences of socio-cultural assessment, in A. Anning, J. Cullen and M. Fleer (eds) *Early Childhood Education: Society and Culture,* 2nd edn. London, Thousand Oaks and New Delhi: Sage Publications.

Dewey, J. ([1933]1998) *How We Think.* New York: Houghton Mifflin Company.

Department for Children Schools and Families (DCSF) (2008) *Development Matters: Practice Guidance for the Early Years Foundation Stage.* Nottingham: DCSF.

Elfer, P., Goldschmied, E. and Selleck, D. (2003) *Key Persons in the Nursery.* London: David Fulton.

Hohmann, U. (2007) Rights, expertise and negotiation in care and education, *Early Years,* 27(1): 33–46.

Isaacs, S. (1930) *Intellectual Growth in Young Children.* London: Routledge & Kegan Paul.

Isaacs, S. (1933) *Social Development in Young Children.* London: Routledge & Kegan Paul.

Janssen-Vos, F. (2003) Basic development: developmental education for young children, in B. van Oers (ed.) *Narratives of Childhood.* Amsterdam: VU University Press.

Montessori, M. (1919) *The Montessori Method* (trans. by A.E. George). New York: Frederick A, Stokes Company. Available at www.web.archive.org/web/20050207205651/www.moteaco.com/method/method.html (accessed 7 October 2009).

Peters, S. (2009) Responsive, reciprocal relationships: the heart of the Te Whāriki curriculum, in T. Papatheodorou and J. Moyles (eds) *Learning Together in the Early Years: Exploring Relational Pedagogy.* London and New York: Routledge.

Reifel, S. (2007) Hermeneutic text analysis of play, in J. Amos Hatch (ed.) *Early Childhood Qualitative Research.* London and New York: Routledge.

Rinaldi, C. (2006) *In Dialogue with Reggio Emilia.* London and New York: Routledge

Schön, D. (1983) *The Reflective Practitioner: How Professionals Think in Action.* London: Temple Smith.

Thornton, L. and Brunton, P. (2009) *Understanding the Reggio Approach: Early Years Education in Practice,* 2nd edn. London and New York: Routledge.

Wang, X.C., Kedem, Y. and Hertzog, N. (2004) Scaffolding young children's reflections with student-created PowerPoint presentations, *Journal of Research in Early Childhood Education,* 19(2): 159–75.

Afterword

Janet Moyles

We hope that throughout your reading of this book and its different contributions, you will have been reflecting on your own practice and thinking. We can only help to a certain degree by encouraging readers to adopt and follow this path – reflection is about learning from one's own experiences and only *you* know what your experiences are. Like children, we can only work from what we know, can do and understand. We have shared our reflections in the hope of enabling you to relate these to your own practices and playful pedagogies: the two core elements of the book.

We are all committed to the fact that play benefits children's learning and playful pedagogies are the best way of supporting this. Play is crucial in the here and now of children's lives as well as being more likely to prepare children for an unknown but probably more sophisticated future of great technological and communicative developments, increased knowledge about cognitive science and brain studies and differing cultural contexts. Bergen and Fromberg (2006: 417) predict that by 2050, 'Play will become so valued by adults, who will have the leisure, health and technological resources to engage in more play themselves, that the value of play for children will be more widely recognised' – let us hope so! But the writers also warn that 'Play will be taken over by adults . . . [who] . . . will require children to earn the right to play, after they have mastered some authoritatively determined body of knowledge' (p. 418). Oh dear! We can see this happening now unless practitioners begin to reflect more closely on how they are making provision for children's play, learning and development. It emphasizes the importance of thinking about play, playful learning and playful teaching as three separate but interlinked pedagogies.

Smith and Krumsvik (2007: 274) assert that enhanced reflection takes place when the situation that triggers reflection is made accessible to others, and the reflection process becomes enriched by feedback from colleagues and other significant others, thus developing a professional learning community that draws on the practice of the individual members in developing a collective body of knowledge. We have joined together in this book to present our reflections on practice from a range of different angles. We hope it will support your reflection and practice and enhance learning for all the children with whom you play.

Photograph 15.1 Won't you come and play?

References

Bergen, D. and Fromberg, D. (2006) Epilogue, in D. Fromberg and D. Bergen (eds) *Play from Birth to Twelve: Contexts, Perspectives and Meanings*, 2nd edn. New York: Routledge.

Smith, K. and Krumsvik, R. (2007) Video papers – a means for documenting practitioners' reflections on practical experiences, *Research in Comparative and International Education*, 2(4): 272–9.

Author index

Subject index

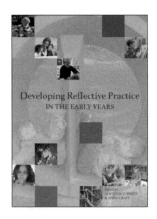

DEVELOPING REFLECTIVE PRACTICE IN THE EARLY YEARS

Alice Paige-Smith and Anna Craft

9780335222773 (Paperback)
2007

eBook also available

Reflective practice is a vital aspect of working with young children and enables a deeper understanding of their learning and development. Whilst there is a long tradition among early childhood practitioners of closely observing children's learning so as to nurture and stimulate their development, they are increasingly expected to reflect on their own practice in a variety of ways, in order to enhance their professional development and improve their practice.

Key features:

- Helps early years practitioners develop their reflective skills
- Supports practitioners in articulating and understanding their own practice in greater depth
- Offers opportunities to reflect on how theory, research and policy relate to distinct understandings of children's development and learning

www.openup.co.uk

OPEN UNIVERSITY PRESS
McGraw · Hill Education